The Sacraments in Religious Education and Liturgy

The Sacraments in Religious Education and Liturgy: An Ecumenical Model

ROBERT L. BROWNING
ROY A. REED

Religious Education Press
Birmingham, Alabama

Library of Congress Cataloging in Publication Data

Browning, Robert L.
  The sacraments in religious education and liturgy.

  Includes bibliographies and index.
  1. Sacraments.   2. Liturgics.   3. Christian education.
I. Reed, Roy A.   II. Title.
BV800.B76   1985   234'.16   84-27536
ISBN 0-89135-044-6

Religious Education Press, Inc.
1531 Wellington Road
Birmingham, Alabama 35209
10 9 8 7 6 5 4 3

Religious Education Press publishes books exclusively in religious education and in areas closely related to religious education. It is committed to enhancing and professionalizing religious education through
the publication of serious, significant, and scholarly works.

PUBLISHER TO THE PROFESSION

DEDICATED:
TO
JACKIE
AND
CECILIA

Contents

Preface

This book is written for pastors, religious educators, theological students, and lay people who are responsible leaders in the worship and educational life of our churches. In many ways the authors enter into dialogue with theologians of liturgy and religious education who are speaking to us today, but this book is not primarily for them. For several years the authors of this volume have together taught a course titled, "Sacraments and the Communication of the Gospel." In this course we have pondered and tried to come to conclusions about the most primary issues of the ministries of learning and worship as these are discovered, particularly in our liturgical "habits" of baptizing, confirming, communing, reconciling, healing, ordaining, marrying, and burying. These activities encompass what our various traditions have sometimes known as sacraments. We have attempted in our teaching and in this book to come to an understanding about the nature of sacrament itself and then to explore sacrament as a means of religious education, of communicating and nurturing faith. Such an enterprise brings us into dialogue with students of human and faith development like Erik Erikson, James Fowler, and others, and into an investigation of the relevance of their work for the exercise of the ministry of sacraments in the church. It also leads us to reflect on the liturgical life of the churches and the patterns of human involvement in worship which both help and hinder our attempts to communicate and nurture through sacraments.

In this enterprise we have searched scripture, examined our history and taken stands concerning many issues which relate to our sacramental life. This does not mean that we have tried to make a definitive statement on each sacrament or arrive at a complete sacramental theology. We have sought to describe what we see as a "quiet revolution" within Christendom, and identify the particular shape of that revolution in the several sacraments. We have sought then to raise the most central issues which present themselves for clarification and dialogue. Finally, we have sought to be helpful to leaders in religious education and liturgy in local churches, by making concrete suggestions about our life together in the Christian community.

This quiet revolution, which is yet to be fully worked out, requires all of us in ministry to consider deeply the foundations of the most hallowed traditions of our life together and to think creatively about the ways in which these traditions are or are not a lively part of what faithful Christians need to do to realize their identity and to be responsible in the world. On the way in this work we continue to be especially grateful to the many students who sat with us in our sacraments course and who both learned and taught; to our colleagues, especially Joanmarie Smith, for their nurture and encouragement; to Larry Hickle and Clark Hyde, pastors respectively of First Presbyterian and St. Peter's Episcopal churches in Delaware, Ohio, who were kind enough to read and critique; and to faculty secretary, Barbara Millisor, and her co-workers, who deciphered, endured, and triumphed with grace.

ROBERT L. BROWNING
ROY A. REED

Part I

Understanding the Nature
of Sacrament

Chapter 1

The Quiet Revolution in Sacramental Understanding and Practice

The breezes of change are blowing in respect to our understanding of the place and power of the sacraments. Leaders in every faith group (Protestant, Catholic, and Orthodox) and in most denominations are discussing a wide range of issues: What is meant by a sacramental view of life? What is the essential meaning of baptism or communion? Should confirmation be a rite or a sacrament, and at what age should it take place? How can we deepen the sacramental meaning of marriage at a time when almost half of all marriages end in divorce? Should ordination be a sacrament? And should there be an ordination or consecration of all persons who are in ministry through their occupations? Should there be other sacraments in addition to the two most Protestants celebrate (baptism and communion) or the seven that the Roman Catholics and Orthodox celebrate?

Many ecumenical study committees on the sacraments have been formed and papers and books written. Fresh liturgical resources for baptism, communion, marriage, penance, and unction have been written and employed in experimental services. Fresh breezes seem to be blowing throughout the churches.[1]

We have discovered after several years of observation and study that a genuine revolution has taken place in the understanding of the essential nature of sacramentality and also in the style of sacramental life in the churches. The revolution is quiet, however. While the assumptions about sacramental life are indeed revolutionary, they have not been communicated clearly to a wide enough audience of clergy and laity to make visible the revolutionary character of the changes. If a wider, deeper analysis and discussion can be accomplished, it is possible that the breezes of change can become the winds of change appropriate to a genuine revolution in the thought and practice in the life of

3

the churches across Protestant, Roman Catholic, and Orthodox communities.

It is our purpose to identify and evaluate some of the changes which are becoming apparent as part of the increasing communication among these three major groupings in Christendom. It is our hope that significant areas of agreement can be described which will become the basis for various ecumenical approaches to sacramental expression. Such fresh paradigms of sacramental life will require creative educational and liturgical designs in order to help clergy and laity alike be better prepared for and participate with more insight and power in the specific sacraments.

We will identify and discuss the following issues and why we believe they are revolutionary in their ramifications for the church in the future:

(1) The movement *from* the battleground of a substantialistic understanding of sacraments *to* the potential consensus of a phenomenological view; (2) the movement *from* seeing the sacraments as religious rites through which God breaks into our otherwise secular and nonreligious everyday lives *to* perceiving them as profound symbols of God's living presence in all of life; (3) the movement *from* a split between word and sacrament (i.e., Protestants have preached the word and Catholics have celebrated the sacraments) *to* a growing unity of word and sacrament as modes through which persons experience and extend God's grace and righteousness in all of life; (4) the movement *from* discerning the sacraments primarily as the means to the privileges of membership *to* discerning them as "rites of passage" or "rites of intensification" with power to help people identify and be open to the Holy at each of the stages of life; (5) the movement *from* the focus of our energy on the theological and liturgical differences to be found in the traditions of various faith groups and denominations *to* a focus on a wide ecumenical dialogue and the quest for a *new model* or understanding of sacramentality around which a growing and unifying consensus can form; and, finally, (6) the movement *from* a split between religious education and liturgy *to* a growing sense of unity between religious education and liturgy without destroying the creative tension needed between these two aspects of ministry.

Now, let us discuss in more detail what the essential characteristics of these "movements" are and why they are potentially revolutionary for the modern church.

I. *The movement* from *the battleground of a substantialistic understanding of sacraments* to *the potential consensus of a phenomenological view*

Much of the confusion concerning the sacraments is related to the different understandings people have about the nature of sacrament. Some see communion, for instance, as a rite in which God pours out grace in a special way by actually changing, through the priest's words and actions, the bread and wine into a new substance, the body and blood of Christ. Others see communion as a memorial.

The early church believed in the reality of Christ's presence in the sharing of the Lord's supper but did not establish a dogma concerning the changing of the substance. While present at different times during the Middle Ages, it was after the Reformation and in reaction to the reforms sought by Zwingli, Luther, and Calvin which denied "transubstantiation" that the Council of Trent took official positions concerning the change of the substance of the bread and wine with which many strongly agreed and many others violently disagreed.

The Catholic church has presented no new doctrine on this subject but it is hearing from its theologians many fresh interpretations. Old terms like *substance* and *species* are being read through other lenses than those of Aristotelian scholasticism. Now, stress is being placed on the real presence of Christ in the communication of the word of God in the eucharist through the relationships of trust and love present in the assembly of believing and caring persons. While there is not consensus as yet, there is a clear trend within the Roman Catholic church away from substantialistic views and toward relational interpretations of Christ's presence.

Another illustration, of significant change in interpretation and practice of course, relates to baptism. Many parents still bring their children for baptism because of their belief that the sacrament is an essential act in which the original sin into which the child is born is washed away and that God's grace is bestowed so that the child can be saved. The assumption is that without infant baptism the child will be outside of God's love. Even though enlightened and educated parents may reject such reasoning they find themselves rushing their child to baptism as if it were true. On the other hand, parents who reject the substantialistic view or who are part of a denomination which sees baptism as only a symbol of God's love may find little motivation for infant baptism and often follow the practice out of convention or for sentimental reasons. In both cases the deeper meaning of baptism is distorted if not lost. More recent understandings of baptism emphasize the incorporation of the child into Christ's body in which the child is surrounded by incarnate love from parents, sponsors, and congregation and is strengthened to participate spontaneously in the ministering community. Infant baptism does not wash original sin from the child in some special way, but it brings the child into relationships and actions which can, in fact, save the child from fear, isolation, and a self-centered rather than a God-centered life.

The fresh breezes which are blowing today were greatly stimulated by the major decisions within the Roman Catholic church at the Second Vatican Council, and the significant theological thinking which has followed the council by Catholic, Protestant, and Orthodox writers.

Some distinguished theologians have done much to move many from substantialistic thinking. One of the most influential is Edward Schillebeeckx.[2] His studies maintain that, while it is true that most Catholics agree with the Aristotelian assumption of the Tridentine position (that the bread and wine are changed into the actual substance of the body and blood of Christ), faithful understanding of Christ's real presence in the eucharist does not depend on such a substantialistic view. He points out that modern physics has left substantialism in serious trouble because what appears to be inert matter is in fact highly interactive atomic life. Moreover, "when it was finally established, long before Merleau-Ponty, that what was perceived by the senses could not be regarded as an objective attribute of reality that was separate from our perception, the Aristotelian doctrine of substance and accidents had to be radically overhauled. The quantum theory in physics made many neo-scholastics realize that the concept *substance* could not be applied to material reality—or at the most that the whole of the cosmos could be seen as only one great substance." Therefore, "more and more theologians came to realize that transubstantiation had no connection with the physical and chemical structures. The general view was the change of the bread and wine was not physical but metaphysical, and the 'physical' approach was thus in principle superseded."[3]

From the metaphysical presence the quest moved in the direction of phenomenology in the study of the nature of persons (anthropology) and the nature of sacramentality.

After analyzing the contribution of many Catholic thinkers, such as Charles Davis, Piet Schoonenberg, and Luchesius Smits, and Protestant interpreters such as F. J. Leenhardt and Max Thurian as they moved toward consensus concerning a phenomenological, non-Aristotelian view, Schillebeeckx outlines his position by describing the way the real presence of Christ is experienced by the believer: The presence, while available in many aspects of life, is experienced within the church as the sacrament of Christ, the visible extension of Christ's life of ministry in our midst today. He asserts, "The real presence of

Christ in the Eucharist can therefore only be approached by allowing the form of bread and wine, experienced phenomenally, to refer to this presence (of Christ and his Church) in a projective act of faith which is an *element of and in* faith in Christ's eucharistic presence."[4] The eucharist, "takes the form of a commemorative meal in which the usual secular significance of the bread and wine is withdrawn and these become bearers of Christ's gift of himself—'take and eat, this is my body.' Christ's gift of himself, however, is not ultimately directed toward bread and wine, but toward the faithful. The real presence is intended for believers, but through the medium of and in this gift of bread and wine. In other words, the Lord who gives himself thus is sacramentally present. In this commemorative meal, bread and wine become the subject of a new *establishment of meaning*, not by man, but by the living Lord *in* the Church, through which they become the *sign* of the real presence of Christ giving himself to us. This establishment of meaning by Christ is accomplished in the Church and thus presupposes the real presence of the Lord in the Church, in the assembled community of believers and in the one who officiates in the Eucharist."[5]

Schillebeeckx, as one can see, is not satisfied to take *only* a phenomenological approach. He does include metaphysical assumptions concerning divine activity which through Christ and the church and also the "re-creating activity of the Holy Spirit . . . acts in the sphere of the actively believing, doing and celebrating church, and the result of this divine saving activity is sacramentally a 'new creation' which perpetuates and deepens our eschatological relationship to the Kingdom of God."[6]

He does affirm, however, the great potential of starting with a phenomenological approach in order to break through the divisions of the past. We have used the issue of the real presence of Christ in the eucharist as a concrete illustration of the radical changes which are taking place in the understanding of the nature of sacramentality.

It may be constructive to look more explicitly at the philosophy of phenomenology and how it has been influential generally and more specifically in respect to the importance of the human perception of the sacramental nature of life. A phenomenological approach to sacramentality focuses on a description of the essences which are being symbolized in the life experiences of those who employ the sacraments—who find them meaningful, illuminating, and genuinely helpful. For instance, the essence of communion is a meal which brings the participants into an awareness of the love of God at the heart of all of life—a love which can be discovered in the breaking of bread between any persons any time and any place, a love which was graphically and powerfully revealed when Jesus gave not only bread and wine but his very body and blood for others that they could believe in the reality of a God of love.

Phenomenology, according to Merleau-Ponty, "is the study of essences; and according to it, all problems amount to finding definitions of essences. . . . But phenomenology is also a philosophy which puts essences back into existence and does not expect to arrive at an understanding of man and the world from any starting point other than that of 'facticity.' . . . All its efforts are concentrated upon reachieving a direct and primitive contact with the world and endowing that contact with a philosophical status. . . . To return to things themselves (as Husserl, the father of modern phenomenology, counseled) is to return to that world which precedes knowledge, of which knowledge always speaks, and in relation to which every scientific schematization is an abstract and derivative sign-language, as is geography in relation to the countryside in which we have learnt beforehand what a forest, a prairie or a river is."[7]

In discussions about sacramentality, a phenomenological approach has to do with trying to get back to the essences of the sacraments in terms of rivers and forests, in terms of what happens in people's lives, descriptively. It is focusing on what people have perceived to be taking place when water is used to baptize an adult or when oil is used to anoint someone who is ill, or a pastor places a hand on the head of another at a moment of decision, or someone breaks bread and gives it to others—actions, noises, colors, tactile sensations, words which combine to speak profoundly to persons about the meaning and purpose of life. As Merleau-Ponty says, "The real has to be described, not constructed or formed."[8]

Of course, when we seek to describe what takes place and how persons perceive some particular experience we realize there are similarities and differences. Moreover, there are mysteries left which no one can quite describe. It is only when we already have theories or doctrines clearly defined and ask people to see their experiences through those lenses that the mystery leaves. Sacraments can reveal profound meanings common to people, but they also point to mysteries which actually exist in varying perceptions and understandings. This does not mean that doctrines or reasons are not important or needed. They are important as we seek to get an overview of the different aspects of life and for making decisions about our actions and directions. But phenomenology emphasizes the truth that mystery is always present when we seek to describe our experiences—and that mystery is left when we do our theological, rational, or scientific explanations! Husserl criticized Kant for being "worldly," for making the world "immanent in the subject instead of being filled with wonder at it and conceiving the subject as a process of transcendence toward the world."[9] Merleau-Ponty maintains that this stance concerning transcendence and the mystery in all experience is rooted in perception itself. "Thus there is a paradox of immanence and transcendence in perception. Immanence, because the perceived object cannot be foreign to him who perceives; transcendence, because it always contains something more than what is actually given."[10]

When we take this descriptive approach we are better able to depict in words, images, signs, actions in what way persons have experienced the ultimate meaning of life or how they have met the creator and sustainer of life in a particular event. Paul Tillich, in his last lecture before his death, said that these descriptions of meeting the transcendent in the present are essential to the religious life. "The universal religious basis is the experience of the Holy within the finite. Universally in everything finite and particular, or in this and that finite, the Holy appears in a special way. I could call this the sacramental basis of all religions—the Holy here and now which can be seen, heard, dealt with, in spite of its mysterious character. We still have remnants of this in the highest religions, in their sacraments, and I believe that without it, a religious group would become an association of moral clubs, as much of Protestantism is, because it has lost the sacramental basis."[11] Tillich recognized the importance of the prophetic in religion because it is a corrective to the tendency to make ultimate any concrete sacramental element—in other words, to take the mystery out of it. He concluded, however, that without the sacramental and mystical element, religion becomes moralistic and finally secular.

Recognizing the mystery which is always present, we can still describe the *essence* implied in the concrete reports of meeting the Holy in particular experiences. Moreover, it is crucial to lift these up and celebrate them because they point to and participate in the transcendent. This is true because people in many cultures have reported that they have experienced the Holy presence through the concrete elements of water, food, birth, death, etc. These reports become interpreted by others in ways the original reporters did not experience or mean. Such distorted interpretations are understandable and inevitable. However, in the process they tend to move from the natural to the supernatural, and sometimes to the magical. The Lord's supper came naturally out of the Jewish meal. This meal was ritualistic in itself. As Tad Guzie reminds us, in most instances no dishes were eaten without a berakah or blessing said by the host. Usually at the beginning of the meal the host took bread, broke it, blessed it and shared it with everyone at the table. Before and after the main course where each dish was also blessed, each person would bless his or her own cup every time it was refilled. At the end of the meal often came a more lengthy prayer of thanksgiving.[12]

This basic ritual meal, with its potential for the loving relationship and thanksgiving to God (the essences), was the reality being celebrated in the passover meal annually. During the last supper Jesus took this already powerful ritualistic meal and asked his followers to remember him in the breaking of the bread and the sharing of the cup. Later interpretations of the meaning of this event have moved from the meal as a experience of love and faith to becoming the central element in Christian worship, to the eucharist with the bread and wine being transformed by the institution of the priest to the actual body and blood of Christ, to the belief that the meal is primarily a remembrance, etc.

These interpretations are important and worthy of study, discussion, and efforts to find consensus, but they are unhelpful when they get too far from the description of the essentials of the experience itself as first reported, with clear reference to the physical and cultural setting, the personal expressions of meaning reported by the participants, the quality of relationships evident in words and acts, the transcendent meanings reported, and honest reference to the various interpretations present *after* the event (in oral or written forms). When we look more carefully at what was going on at the last supper, for instance, we see that "what Jesus did, then, was to attach a new meaning to the most ordinary ritual in Jewish life—indeed, to the only ritual or corporate act he could be sure his disciples would do together regularly in any case."[13] Jesus established the sacrament by taking the profoundly meaningful, life-giving elements of bread and wine and giving them an even deeper meaning: In breaking the bread and sharing the cup his disciples would recognize the gift of his body and his blood so that the transcendent love of God for all would not die with him but live and engender faithful, loving, thankful relationships with God's human family and with the divine presence in their midst—the *essences* being celebrated in the common meal and in the eucharist in ultimate terms.

By taking a phenomenological approach to the study of the power and limitations of sacraments we will be seeking to be descriptive, to find the essences having been experienced in various ritual experiences within culture in general, within the Christian community more particularly, within the life span of persons in their faith pilgrimages throughout life, within our corporate, social, and political life. Finally, we shall suggest what sacramental acts may be fruitfully celebrated within our churches and how we may seek to interpret the power of these experiences educationally and liturgically.

II. *The movement* from *seeing the sacraments as religious rites through which God breaks into our otherwise secular lives* to *perceiving the sacraments as profound symbols of God's living presence in all of life.*

A common distortion or caricature of the sacraments by many Christian people is well described by Karl Rahner, another Roman Catholic thinker who has developed a phenomenological model of sacramentality. The commonly held view is that the sacraments are rites which the church uses to bring God's grace to persons who otherwise are living a secular life without ongoing communion with the eternal. Rahner decries this tendency. He sees God's active presence in all of life and the sacraments as revelatory events illuminating the sacredness of every aspect of life.

At first, the statement that all of life is sacramental sounds innocent enough. However, a deeper look at this concept moves us to a revolutionary understanding of the nature of the relationship between God and the world and changes our view of the essential nature of the sacramental.

Rahner starts by assuming that sacraments point not just to *things* through which the Holy can be revealed. Rather, all of nature and history reveal the cosmic grace of God to which the individual sacraments are witnesses and expressions. God's grace is bringing wholeness and salvation at the roots of human existence. Sanctifying grace and divine life are present everywhere. Grace permeates the world. The sacraments are symbolic manifestations of the liturgy of the world. "The world is constantly and ceaselessly possessed by grace from its innermost roots, from the innermost personal center of the spiritual subject. It is constantly and ceaselessly sustained and moved by God's self-bestowal even prior to the question (admittedly always crucial) of how creaturely freedom reacts to this 'engracing.' "[14]

God's cosmic, essential grace is visible in many ways, but supremely in Jesus Christ, the primordial sacrament, and in the church, the presently *visible*, ministering, caring, serving body of Christ. Because God is active in all of life and reveals the sacredness of life in many ways, Roman Catholics in the decisions of Vatican II, for instance, radically departed from their previous position that all persons must come to faith in God only through Christ, the church, and the sacraments.

Rahner believes that the church is the visible symbol of God's active grace toward all people of whatever cultural or religious background. It is the sacrament of the world, "sign and instrument of unity" among people, as the Dogmatic Constitution on the Church of Vatican II stated. Moreover, "Even those who, through no fault of their own remain ignorant of the gospel of Christ and the Church, but who are nonetheless honestly seeking God and under the influence of grace, are really trying to do his will, which they recognize in the voice of their consciences, are able to achieve eternal blessedness."[15]

The Pastoral Constitution on The Church in the Modern World is even more explicit! The new life in Christ is present "not only in Christian believers but also in all men of Good Will, in whose hearts grace is active in an invisible manner."[16]

The church is the sacrament of salvation for all. The crucial understanding is that the church recognizes that God's grace, while fully revealed in Christ and present in the life of the body of Christ, the church, also transcends the church.

Schillebeeckx clarifies this concept when he says, "What God's grace, his absolute, gratuitous and forgiving proximity has already begun to do in the lives of all men becomes an *epiphany* in the Church, in other words, completely visible. . . . The Church is the 'primordial sacrament of the salvation which is' prepared for all men . . . the salvation which is, moreover, not a monopoly of the Church, but which, on the basis of redemption by the Lord who died and rose again 'for the sake of the salvation of the whole world' is already in fact actively present in the whole world. The Church is therefore both the sacrament of herself, in other words, the visible appearance of the Salvation that is present in her, and, at the same time, the *sacramentum mundi;* what is present 'outside the Church' everywhere whenever men of good will in fact give their consent personally to God's offer of grace and make this gift their own."[17]

The particular sacraments, however, are very greatly needed because they are clear symbols (deep-running, essential, life-giving and renewing, when received in faith) of the grace of God in all of life—symbols which point to and participate in the cosmic grace revealed in life itself but fully in Christ and in the church which communicates this love, grace, and justice through both word and sacrament.

This fact calls us to celebrate the sacraments with abandon and openness to all people, to move out vigorously to the world and to all persons and groups in the pilgrimages of life. We can do this, however, without being exclusive or judgmental of other avenues of grace. Rahner says it well. "Now it is a lasting and tragic misunderstanding for us to turn these sacramental signs once more into a circumscribed enclave, such that it is in this alone that God is present, and that the event of his grace takes place."[18]

Rahner believes that persons in the human family deeply need the sacraments to help them become conscious of the sacredness of all arenas of life. Participation in the sacraments should not take Christians out of the everyday world of commerce, government, politics, etc. The sacraments symbolize that God "erects a landmark, a sign of the fact that this entire world belongs to God, a sign precisely of the fact that God is adored, experienced and accepted everywhere as he who, through his 'grace,' has himself set all things free to attain to himself, and a sign that this adoration of him takes place not in Jerusalem alone but everywhere in spirit and in truth."[19]

This wider stance, articulated well by contemporary Roman Catholics, can be found in Orthodox and Protestant circles in equal eloquence.

Alexander Schmemann, an imaginative Orthodox theologian, dedicates his important book, *Sacraments and Orthodoxy*, to the creative Roman Catholic scholars such as Odo Casel, Lambert Beauduin, A. J. Jungmann, Louis Bouyer, Romano Guardini, and H. A. Reinhold who helped to develop a truly Catholic language "without which no fruitful ecumenical conversation is possible." Published in 1965, Schmemann's book reflects many of the same themes which Schillebeeckx, Rahner, and others have developed, but in beautiful imagery.

Schmemann lifts up the sacramental nature of life through his interpretation of the nature of God and humankind. The biblical picture is one in which God created and blessed the world by filling all that exists with divine love and goodness. So, the only "natural" reaction for us as human beings to whom God gave this blessed and sanctified world, is to bless God in return, to thank God, to see the world as God sees it—and, in this act of gratitude and adoration, to know, name, and possess the world.

Our essential nature, then, is "homo adorans." We are persons who by our nature adore God and are priests standing in the center of the world and unifying it in acts of blessing God, of both receiving the world from God and offering it to God. Here again we see the emphasis on God's activity and grace in the whole cosmos. As we celebrate God's gifts we transform life into eucharist, into communion with

God. Schmemann sees matter, the material, then, as a part of an all-embracing eucharist and all persons as priests of "this cosmic sacrament."[20] Believing that there can be no ultimate sacred-secular split, Schmemann says that as human beings we instinctively recognize these realities. For instance, we recognize that food is the natural sacrament of family, friendship, and of life that is more than eating and drinking. Food, then, is given to us as communion with God and each other. It is not material which is opposed to spiritual. All that exists is God's gift to us and it all exists to make God known to us. Therefore, particular sacraments are important celebrations which we lift up as priests before God; and these sacraments are related naturally to the normal experiences of life—from birth to death, from baptism to unction—and are related profoundly to the natural elements—bread, water, oil—found among God's gifts to us.

This more universal view of sacramentality can also be found in Protestant thinkers. One of the most stimulating has been Max Thurian of the Taizé Community in France. His ideas are representative of many Protestant leaders who are in communication with Catholic and Orthodox thinkers. Thurian agrees with Schillebeeckx and Rahner that the work of God is in each of us and in the world and cannot be confined to his word and sacraments. He says, "although it is beyond question that God is acting invisibly and secretly in people and in the world by his providence and his mercy, we know the means of grace through which he acts visibly and explicitly; they are his word and the sacraments of his presence and his working. . . . Although the activity of God is universal, far exceeding the reach of his word and sacrament, it is in them that we can be sure of hearing him and meeting him."[21]

This more universal assumption can be seen in the ecumenical movement, of course, but more explicitly within Protestantism. James White's analysis is descriptive of the various historical phases through which Protestants have gone, one of which was a linking of sacramentality to social concern. He underscores the renewed interest in the sacraments among Protestants and indicates that for many "the Christian sacraments became a strong incentive to fight for justice. . . . New seriousness about the sacraments confronted us with how human, worldly, and materialistic the Christian God is. I remember first being propelled into politics by the realization that, 'This is my body' means 'This is my precinct.' And baptism jumped out at us as the ultimate condemnation of racism and sexism."[22] Here we have less of an emphasis upon the universal sacramental nature of life as a base for the particular sacraments and more of an emphasis upon the universal, revolutionary, and liberating ramifications of the Christian sacraments themselves. The latter is an emphasis with which we heartily agree!

III. *The movement* from *a split between word and sacrament* to *a growing unity of word and sacrament as modes through which persons experience and extend God's grace and righteousness in all life.*

For too long the image which prevailed was: The Protestants are the church of the word and the Catholics are the church of the sacraments. To be sure Protestants did emphasize the centrality of preaching the word of God and Catholics did develop and practice a sacramental life in which preaching of the word held a secondary position. Actually, however, the split was never as rigid as it appeared. Sacraments have been important to Protestants, with baptism and communion becoming the occasions for defining unique aspects of various denominational approaches; moreover, Roman Catholics generally used homilies to interpret not only the scriptures but also the sacraments themselves. Today Protestants are rediscovering the power of the sacraments and Catholics are immersing themselves in biblical study and lifting up again the central importance of preaching, of proclamation of the word. While these tendencies are constructive they do not actually represent the quiet revolution which is at hand.

That revolution is symbolized by the fact that Catholics, Protestants, and Orthodox are saying that the word of God is deeply involved in the sacraments and the specific sacraments are indeed means of communicating the word. This means that there is no split between word and sacraments; or more positively, word and sacrament are a unity. They are more than audible and visual means of communication of God's good news in Jesus Christ, even though they do reflect the uniqueness of those two means of communication. The word of God came primarily to us through the incarnate word in Jesus Christ who then became the visibile arch-sacrament of God's love and justice among all people. Christ is the primary representative of the unity of word and sacrament. Likewise, the church as the visible extension of the body of Christ becomes the community in which the word is preached, taught, experienced, lived, and shared and also the community which makes visible the love of God in Christ and thus becomes the sacrament of Christ in the world.

Rahner argues for this unity and believes Protestants and Catholics can agree that word and sacrament are measured in terms of whether or not the good news of God's new life in Christ is really exhibited, is experienced by persons as wholeness, and experienced by the total faith community as salvation in terms of loving, trusting, just relationships! He says, "The word of God in the strictest and truest sense . . . can exist at all only as an event of grace. Hence it must have an exhibitive character. It must be a saving event."[23]

The question in respect to judging the validity of the sacraments in communicating the word is whether they make visible the saving relationship between people and God as revealed and made visible in Christ. Jesus may be said to have instituted communion and baptism more explicitly (although baptism is less clear). He also instituted foot washing as a symbol of the *essence* of a faithful response to God's love of all people: namely, humble servanthood. (So, by the standard of institution we have omitted a central and essential sacrament and its meaning.) In Jesus' whole ministry he certainly was deeply involved in ministries of healing and wholeness in life and death (unction), with ministries dealing with guilt, failure, conflict, between persons and groups, forgiveness and reconciliation (penance), with calling and commissioning followers to concrete ministries (ordination and consecration), with blessing persons for life together (marriage) and with helping people find and seal their faith in relation to the body of believers (confirmation). Today, most Protestants are at least open to the definition of a sacrament in this more experiential way. Such openness is promising for finding symbols and rituals of meaning wherein the good news of God's love and justice can be communicated concretely in relation to the actual experiences we have throughout the stages of life from birth to death.

While there is openness within Protestantism to the wider, more phenomenological approach to word and sacrament, there are many differences of opinion, of course. For instance, one of the most respected Protestant theologians, John Macquarrie, agrees with the intent of many Roman Catholic thinkers but not with their conclusions. As an example, Macquarrie sees how Advent as the incarnation of God's love could be understood as a sacramental sign and a highly effectual one. "But it is better to think of Christ as the author of the sacraments rather than himself a sacrament, even a primary one." Also, he understands why some see the church as a sacrament (because the church points to the vision she seeks to embody). "But, it is better to speak of the church as the bearer of signs and sacraments, than as itself a sacrament."[24] Macquarrie agrees, however, that word and sacrament should be together. Also, while he discerns that the other five rites are "sacraments" of a sort he reserves that designation for baptism and communion. While he understands the sacramental nature of all of life, he believes that the world has an ambiguous character, and if we come to view it sacramentally it is "because we have had the experience of some quite specific and concrete sacraments and have extended the sacramental outlook to the world as a whole."[25] Macquarrie's views are reported here to point to the nature of the issues under study and dialogue. Consensus is not with us, nor need it be in order for there to be communication and communion between groups. It can be said that in the midst of this dialogue between Roman Catholics, Protestants, and the Orthodox there is general agreement with Macquarrie that "word and sacrament are not opposed to each other; they complement each other and have regard to the complex and many sided being of men and women."[26]

IV. *The movement* from *discerning the sacraments primarily as the means to the privileges of membership* to *discerning them as "rites of passage" or "rites of intensification" with power to help people identify and be open to the Holy at each of the stages of life.*

This beginning movement finds quite different forms in Protestantism, Roman Catholicism, and Orthodoxy. Protestants reacted against the sacramental system especially in relation to penance, baptism, and communion. In doing so most Protestant denominations desacralized such life stages rites as confirmation, marriage, ordination, confession, and services having to do with healing or death. The result of this desacralization was, in some cases, not only the devaluation of the rites but more important the deemphasis on the resources of faith at *each* of the stages of life. Since most Protestants have only two sacraments, baptism and communion, and see them as means of membership in the church they, until quite recently, have been less aware of the constructive power of ritual in relation to the struggles of life. Protestants have often rejected rituals as boring, magical, or legalistic. They have not discerned the ritualistic elements in their own patterns, e.g., the rituals of silence in Quakerism to the rituals of singing, witnessing, praying, or visiting each other during the service in free church worship.

While Roman Catholics and the Orthodox have kept the sacramental system very much at the heart of their self-understanding and practice, they, until recently, have been much less aware of the profound issues of human development. Likewise, often they have been less sensitive to the human elements of doubt, fear, psychological illness, and distortions in perception through which people sometimes view the sacraments. Moreover, both groups have often been less conscious of the positive drives towards self-fulfillment, responsibility, creativity, wonder, and awe which persons at the various stages of development bring to the reception of the sacraments.

Recent research in social anthropology and history of religions has opened up the exceptional power of the rituals of life in personal identity and social vision. At the same time very important psychological studies of the stages of human development have recognized the need of persons for meaningful rituals in life which reveal the visions which society has for its members and also the destructive aspects of rituals which are not in touch with deep human needs, and become wooden, lifeless, and legalistic (see chapter 6). Moreover, these studies are interested in the constructive nature of *faith* in human growth and human stability and how faith is related to ethical and moral behavior. Interest is also high in the description of the religious qualities of the numinous and the transcendent at each of the stages of human development. Such studies will be reviewed and correlated with the existing ritualizations in family life and culture as well as the sacraments which have emerged undoubtedly with reference to many of these human needs, problems, and potentialities. We shall also discuss the nature of symbol, sign, rituals, and myth and how these are related to sacramentality. The issue is: Can persons discover the power of faith and perceive the self to be in communication with the ultimate when decisions are being made regarding interpersonal relationships, philosophy of life, vocation and occupation, marriage or the single life, children and family, contributions to social and political life, conflict, failure, forgiveness, reconciliation at personal and societal levels, illness and health, the experience and meaning of death?

It is our thesis that persons, in fact, do have *faith* in something or someone. The question is: What is the nature of the faith and is it adequate and related to reality? People do need and do develop rituals which reflect the visions of reality of those around them. The question here is: Are these rituals constructive, open, life-giving, and related profoundly to the issues merging at each of the stages of life from birth to death or are they empty, dead, and legalistic? Also, are the rituals perceived to be sacramental or not? It is our conviction that the church in its education and liturgy has a great opportunity to relate persons to the profound resources of the Christian faith through sacramental life at each of the stages of human development and to the major social issues of our time (e.g., sexual and racial justice, civil rights, equal opportunity for all, better destribution of food, shelter, and material wealth, medical care and education). If all of life is sacramental and related essentially to God, it follows that a sacramental approach to life must be capable of helping us deal with the full range of political and cultural matters before us in a fast-moving, technological world.

V. *The movement* from *the focus on theological and liturgical differences to a focus on a wide ecumenical dialogue and the quest for a new model of sacramentality around which a growing and unifying consensus may form.*

We are all aware of the long years spent on defining our differences. These distinctions have been evident throughout the history of Christendom, of course, but they became quite pronounced during and after the Reformation. Each denomination broke off from other bodies over some difference of opinion which was seen to be essential to the integrity of faith. The nature of the sacraments was often at the center of these debates.

Today, the opposite is true. Not only are some denominations seeking to merge, many are seeking to transcend organic merger to find genuine unity in their beliefs and practices. The many dialogues which have taken place point in this direction.

James White has sought to analyze this history and to characterize the major groupings which are present today. He does this with strong support for the attempt to find an ecumenical consensus which will go beyond the two major groupings he identifies. Seeking to characterize the way American Protestantism is currently viewing the sacraments he discusses the two trends in terms which include Roman Catholics and the Orthodox as well. The two views he distills out of our past and present responses to the sacraments are those of "enlightenment" and "traditional."

The *enlightenment view* regards the sacraments as "human actions to help us remember God's actions." White believes this is a prevalent interpretation even for denominations which originated prior to the Enlightenment of the eighteenth century. Communion, then, becomes the Lord's supper which is an event to remember what Christ has done for us, stimulating our reflection on the death and resurrection of Jesus and calling us to moral earnestness. It is seen as a remembrance of God's past action and as a "strong incentive for leading a better life in the future and for helping others do likewise."[27] Because the sacrament focused upon intentionality and honest response of the individual and not upon God's present action, self-examination and introspection are often emphasized. White believes this is a reason why communion is seldom practiced and is often resisted, being one of the least well-attended services in churches which have come out of the enlight-

enment mentality. White believes that Ulrich Zwingli was most responsible for this trend with his views on baptism, written in 1525. Zwingli
says in his *Of Baptism* that baptism is a dedication and a pledge. With
the acceptance of this view baptism then became a service of dedication in which parents pledged to bring up the child in the Christian
faith. Adult baptism was seen as an initiatory sign or pledge with
which we bind ourselves to God. The water, the bread and wine were
seen as external elements which had only the power to evoke and
represent. Zwingli believed that the external elements had no power
to purify the internal soul of persons.

The second pattern White calls *the traditional.* This approach to the
sacraments asserts that "God is the chief actor in the sacraments and
that humans are the recipients of what God does through the sacraments for us and our salvation."[28] God changes our beings through
the operation of divine grace through the sacraments. This view sees
persons as those in need of sign-acts as well as words in order to
become recipients of God's love. It also assumes that God can use
physical objects and actions in order to accomplish divine purpose.
This is a liberating view, he believes, because "it is not our ability to
imagine the Savior in the upper room or on the cross that ultimately
matters, not our staunch resolution to lead a holier life that finally
counts, not the fervor of our devotion that is crucial, but simply the
trust that God works here to accomplish his purposes in his way."[29]
White likes the traditional approach, though in some nontraditional
ways. The traditional approach preserves the biblical image of a God
who acts in history and who uses objects and actions to reveal divine
will. This approach also brings together many Protestant groups,
stemming from Luther, Calvin, Wesley, etc., with Roman Catholics
and the Orthodox.

While White's analysis is thoughtful, it is not helpful to use "traditional" to describe the quiet revolution which we perceive going on in
respect to sacramentality. Genuinely new elements are present.

We, in fact, have been indicating those new realities in the discussion of the six major movements which we perceive to be taking place
in sacramental thinking. Therefore, we have problems with both of
White's categories. We do agree, however, with his assessment of the
ecumenical potential of the current emphasis on a biblical image of a
God who acts in history and also uses objects and actions as well as
persons to reveal divine will.[30]

More issues remain, such as: (a) the problems of substantialistic
interpretations which emerged in the history of the "traditional" approach and which are still present in the minds of many laity and some

clergy, (b) the problem of the nature of persons—whether or not they are involved in original sin, an assumption which several historic and present-day leaders believed to be a major motivation for baptism, the eucharist and penance, for instance, (c) the issue of how to get to the *essences* of the sacraments when a phenomenological approach to sacramentality is taken, etc. Karl Rahner and others call for (and project) *new models of sacramentality* which will attempt to deal with these issues in relation to what we know today about human nature, human perception, and the power and limitations of ritualization. While we will dialogue with the recommendations for a new consensus which are coming from others, we will seek to build a fresh approach of our own. (See chapters 2, 3, 4, and 7.)

It is our belief that a new model of sacramentality is increasingly possible and can become the basis for much creative educational and liturgical life in an ecumenical church. It is our intent to explore the dimensions of such a new model of sacramentality and to outline some possible ways to relate sacramental life to persons and groups throughout the stages of life from birth to death and in relation to the major social and moral issues before us as a people moving rapidly toward the twenty-first century.

VI. *The movement* from *a split between religious education and liturgy* to *a growing sense of unity between the educational and liturgical life of the congregation—without destroying the creative tension needed between these two aspects of ministry.*

The tension between religious education and liturgy has not always been creative. In Protestantism, liturgy (or worship) has often been seen as the province of clergy who "held" services. On the other hand, religious education has been seen as the primary responsibility of laity. Lay leaders "ran" the Sunday school or church school. Not only was there a split in the primary leadership of these two facets of church life there was little relationship in the perceptions of laity who often expressed the split in such graphic terms as, "Shall we stay for church?" or "We only attend worship." Of course, some Protestants did participate in *both* worship and study; but, the matter of seeing worship as profoundly educative or seeing religious education as profoundly significant for worship has only more recently broken through in Protestantism. There is now an attempt to relate the liturgical celebrations within the Christian year and the sacramental celebrations from birth to death to the educational experiences which prepare persons not only to understand and to participate in them but also to critique and renew these liturgical events so that they are genuinely humanizing and life-giving rather than deadening or life-denying. Probably the work of John Westerhoff III and colleagues is most representative of this trend within Protestantism.[31]

In Catholicism and to some degree in Orthodoxy, religious education too quickly became catechetics with a view to indoctrinating learners into the correct beliefs and the correct liturgical expressions of those beliefs. The tension between religious education and liturgy again was too easily lost. Liturgy was much more important. Sacramental life was crucial to the reception and strengthening of grace for the person. An ethos developed which was, in fact, very powerful in the education of believers. The focus was more on liturgy as the obligation and joy of the believer. Education, with its liberating, experiential, critiquing, analyzing functions fully alive, was not affirmed widely on the part of the clergy or laity. So, in a sense there was a unity of catechesis and liturgy but a split between religious education and liturgy. Today there is beginning to be a movement toward a unity of religious education and liturgy, seeing how both are needed to help persons grow *honestly* in faith while also preserving the creative tension. Religious education is needed, not only to introduce persons experientially to the basic elements in the good news of the faith, but also to free them to critique and relate the faith to all the elements in their lives personally and corporately. The liturgy can be seen as powerfully educative of the whole person. Still, educational life, in relation to the liturgy, is being designed also to critique the life-giving or life-denying elements of the liturgy. Religious education which is genuine, not only introduces persons into the great cultural wealth from the past and helps them to experience the power of that wealth, but also invites persons to critique, analyze, appreciate, and reconstruct the manifestations of meaning which are outgrowths of a life-giving community.[32] In this sense religious education should employ the total life of the faith community—the relationships, the celebrations, the master faith stories, the sacramental acts in worship and in service in the world, the unique language of the faith community found in liturgical life. But religious education which is worthy of the term *education* must lead persons to experience and discern the absolute and unmerited love of God in Christ while at the same time seeing the relativity of all our attempts to capture this great truth in language, creeds, or rites. Religious education should express a sense of unity with the wider liturgical and action life of the community while, at the same time, preserving the needed critical and constructive roles, to keep the vision of God's love for all creation strong and to seek to renew the liturgical life of the community so that it is indeed open and growing in harmony with the vision.

We shall indicate that religious education is powerful and in harmony with the experiential nature of the sacraments themselves when it balances concern for changes in understandings, attitudes, and actions. While leaders in religious education have emphasized for many years the importance of attitudes and actions, there is still a tendency to focus upon understandings and information. We know that persons learn existentially through participation in relationships of trust and love as they share their lives with one another, create their own stories of faith, symbolize their own joys and struggles in music, art, drama, dance, create their own liturgical celebrations, and reflect upon their attempts to minister in society. These experiences of participation in educational and liturgical life which touch the emotions and the behavior of persons are especially crucial in our approach to sacramental life. They will be highlighted in our discussion but in a way which does not rob the critical and constructive functions of religious education or the prophetic role in liturgy of their power. The drama of creation and redemption can be experienced powerfully in the direct contact with the symbolic elements of water, bread, wine, oil, and touch in the context of an affirming community. Such communication and communion can be deepened and refined, however, by reflection and evaluation in the light of the gospel and in comparison to insights from other communities of faith. Our discussion of the relationship of religious education and liturgy will be deepened and related to our basic model of sacramentality in chapter 7.

More specifically, we shall discuss the educational and liturgical aspects of sacramental life throughout the life span in Part III. This will be done as we analyze each of the sacraments in relation to the stages of the ritualization of life (Erik Erikson's views) and the stages of faith development (James Fowler's views). Finally, we shall illustrate how religious education and liturgy can function cooperatively (while maintaining a necessary creative tension) in respect to each of the sacraments presented.

Notes

1. Such study committees include the many sponsored by the Faith and Order Commission of the World Council of Churches (from paper no. 29, *One Lord, One Baptism*, 1960, to paper no. 107, *Forum on Bilateral Conversations*, to the most recent paper no. 111, *Baptism, Eucharist and Ministry* [Geneva: World Council of Churches, 1982]), the Consultation on Church Union (reported in *Principles of Church Union*, A Forward Movement Miniature Book, 1966, and

other documents including *In Quest of a Church of Christ Uniting: An Emerging Theological Consensus* [Princeton, N.J.: Consultation on Church Union, 1980]), and countless bilateral and multilateral study groups of Roman Catholics, Protestants, and Eastern Orthodox (many of these meetings are reported and analyzed by Hans Küng in "Vatican III: Problems and Opportunities for the Future," in *Toward Vatican III: The Work That Needs To Be Done*, ed., David Tracy, Hans Küng, and Johann B. Metz (New York: Seabury Press, 1978).

2. His significant early study is *Christ, the Sacrament of the Encounter with God* (New York: Sheed and Ward, 1963).

3. Edward Schillebeeckx, *The Eucharist* (New York: Sheed and Ward, 1968).

4. Ibid., p. 150.

5. Ibid., pp. 137-138,

6. Ibid., p. 151.

7. Maurice Merleau-Ponty, *Phenomenology of Perception* (London: Routledge and Kegan Paul, 1962), pp. vii-ix.

8. Ibid., p. x.

9. Ibid., p. xiv.

10. Maurice Merleau-Ponty, *The Primacy of Perception and Other Essays*, ed. James M. Edie (Evanston, Ill.: Northwestern University Press, 1964), p. 3.

11. Paul Tillich, in *The Future of Religions*, ed. Jerald C. Brauer (New York: Harper & Row, 1966), p. 87.

12. Tad Guzie, *Jesus and the Eucharist* (New York: Paulist Press, 1974), p. 44.

13. Ibid., p. 46.

14. Karl Rahner, *Theological Investigations*, XIV (London: Darton, Longman & Todd, 1976), p. 166.

15. Dogmatic Constitution on the Church, in *The Documents of Vatican II* (New York: The America Press, 1966), p. 35.

16. "The Pastoral Constitution on the Church in the Modern World," in *The Documents of Vatican II* (New York: Herder and Herder, 1966), p. 221.

17. Edward Schillebeeckx, *The Mission of the Church* (New York: Seabury Press, 1973), p. 48.

18. Rahner, *Theological Investigations*, XIV, p. 169.

19. Ibid., p. 169.

20. Alexander Schmemann, *Sacraments and Orthodoxy* (New York: Herder and Herder, 1965), pp. 8-16.

21. Max Thurian, *Our Faith: Basic Christian Belief* (Taizé, France: Les Primes de Taizé, 1978), pp. 111-112.

22. James White, *Christian Worship in Transition* (Nashville: Abingdon Press, 1976), p. 141.

23. Rahner, *Theological Investigations*, XIV, p. 141.

24. John Macquarrie, *The Faith of the People of God* (New York: Scribner, 1972), p. 76.

25. Ibid., p. 76.

26. Ibid., p. 76.

27. White, *Christian Worship in Transition*, p. 32.

28. Ibid., p. 38.

29. Ibid., p. 39.

30. See James White, *Sacraments as God's Self-Giving* (Nashville: Abingdon Press, 1983).

31. See John Westerhoff III and Gwen R. Neville, *Learning Through Liturgy* (New York: Seabury Press, 1979); John H. Westerhoff III and William Willimon, *Liturgy and Learning Throughout the Life Cycle* (New York: Seabury Press, 1980).

32. See the interview of Dwayne E. Heubner by William B. Kennedy in "Theory to Practice: Curriculum," *Religious Education* 77, No. 4 (July-August, 1982), pp. 363-374.

Chapter 2

A New Vision

Threat and Promise

The quiet revolution in the understanding of sacrament is experienced as both threat and promise. The threat is given in the fact of the revolution: Models of sacrament cherished in the past seem impotent in the present. Some cannot make the journey to a fresh perception. The promise is that new insight into scripture, tradition, and human behavior will provide a sound basis for sacramental renewal in the church. The promise is also that a new synthesis will transcend the psychological-theological "trenches" of reform and counterreform dug in the sixteenth century.

The reality is, of course, that threat and promise belong to one another because there is no way to seize the promise of the future without facing the threat of the challenge to traditional understandings. It is our contention, for instance, that a primary reason for perfunctory and legalistic sacramental life consists of faulty definition of what we are talking about and doing. The answers we all—Catholics, Orthodox, and Protestants—have accepted to the question, "What is a sacrament?" have been forced from us by mighty conflicts of the past and consequently they are in no small measure sophistries concocted to legitimate historical practice.

Questioning a "Classic"

Consider, for instance, the assault upon the medieval synthesis by Martin Luther. Luther sought a biblical understanding of sacrament and limited the sense of the term to what had been instituted by Jesus with certain *signs* connected to specific *promises.* This classic Protestant definition has some serious difficulties as a "biblical" definition of sacrament. As a technicality one should point out that it omits footwashing, which qualifies according to the definition. The more serious problem is that the definition fails to have a subject. Since the term *sacrament* nowhere appears in the New Testament the definition really begs the question. Luther sought in the Bible a freeing, evangelical understanding of sacrament; what he found owes more to Augustine and the Middle Ages than it does to the New Testament. Consequently, failing a biblical definition, we Protestants have a biblicistic one which tends to operate as a new law. "Go baptize" (Mt. 28:19). "Do this in remembrance" (Lk. 22:19). Sacraments are practices authoritatively commanded. They are, as some denominations designate them, "ordinances," which we obey, but usually relegate to special and narrow confines. We will baptize, as required, but the liturgy is usually an awkward intrusion into, or addendum onto "normal" worship, and it is usually unprepared or poorly prepared by counseling or instruction, and not followed by any consequential program of incorporation or training. Yet such activity would seem to be an indispensable part of what baptism means, for adults or infants. We will commune, in response to the order to "do this," but ordinarily four times a year, when we observe a "memory"—as opposed to our usual work of dealing with what is present, real, and necessary. And people generally understand this difference betwen memorial and what is current, for they often stay away in significant numbers when they know the service will be communion.

Toward a New Vision

This situation will certainly not be helped by a new *definition*. A new *idea* probably will not help us. A new *vision* might, if it can disclose to us a picture of sacrament as God at work in our lives, in our world, and of our relatedness to one another in faith.

It is our conviction that we need to seek this vision in the New Testament, which surely must provide our primary discernment because our faith has one truth, Jesus the Christ, and one witness to this truth in the accounts of scripture. All questions of the faith of the Christian family are appropriately questions put to Jesus as author of this faith. We will need to seek this vision also in Christian traditions in history where sacrament has identity as ways of faithfulness. And we will need, furthermore, to seek a vision of sacrament in the observance of ordinary human behavior because part of the strategy of sacrament in the history of its practice has been attention to significant moments in the evolution of human life.

Mysterion and Sacramentum

What we find searching for sacrament in the New Testament is "mystery." *Sacramentum* is the Latin word chosen by the Fathers of the early church and New Testament translators to render the Greek *mysterion*. Tertullian (c. 160-c. 225) makes the first application of this term to liturgical rites.[1]

This translation of *mysterion* with *sacramentum* is something of a puzzle and certainly a significant transition. *Mysterion* is a word about the ineffable, used in the New Testament to refer to the secret purposes of God revealed and worked out in the world through the mission of Jesus as the Christ. *Sacramentum* was not at all an exact equivalent of *mysterion*. It was a more definite term. *Sacramentum* comes from the root *sacrare*, to consecrate. By the first century it had come to refer to a particular thing or particular event. The *sacramentum* was a sum of money put in a sacred place as a guarantee by a litigant in a legal case. The *sacramentum* of the person who lost went to the gods (i.e., the priests). A *sacramentum* was also a consecratory act, or something consecrated. Its most popular use was to designate the military oath of allegiance to the emperor. A *sacramentum* bound or obligated a person.

Exactly why this term was used to translate *mysterion* is a matter of conjecture. The word *mysterium*, a latinization of *mysterion*, was available and sometimes used. *Mysterium* was, however, commonly used to refer to the rites of the so-called mystery religions. By careful choice of terms, refusing to translate *mysterion* with *mysterium*, and never referring to pagan ritual as *sacramenta* the early Latin Christians were apparently safeguarding the identity of their own worship. Translating *mysterion* as *sacramentum*, conjoining Christ-mystery with pledge-consecration, they were also establishing a kind of "genetic" code which would determine much about the form and content of Christian worship in the future.

A Gospel Word

The crucial things we need to know about *sacramentum* lie within what the New Testament reveals to us about *mysterion*. *Mysterion* is a word prominent in the New Testament only in the letters of Paul. It appears only once in the synoptic gospels, in a logion in Mark 4:10-12 and parallels (Mt. 13:10-13, Lk. 8:9-10). Strangely, its isolated usage here seems decisive for our conception of sacrament. The passage reads:

> And when he was alone, those who were about him with the twelve asked him concerning the parables. And he said to them. "To you

has been given the *mysterion* of the kingdom of God, but for those outside everything is in parables; so that they may indeed see but not perceive, and may indeed hear but not understand; lest they should turn again and be forgiven."

This enigmatic saying presents serious difficulties of interpretation,[2] but for our purpose it is unambiguous and illuminating. In the gospel the "*mysterion* of the kingdom of God" cannot remain hidden; it is revealed as "dynamic presence in the person of Jesus."[3] Jesus is not only the messenger of the rule of God, he is its agent and in him God's own time, the time of the kingdom of God, is beginning to take place. Any doubt about this is erased in Jesus' acknowledgement of Peter's declaration at Caesarea Philippi: "You are the Christ" (Mk. 8:29).

Mysterion→Christ

To say "to you has been given the *mysterion* of the kingdom of God," is to say that *mysterion*, because God's mystery is the Christ, is more than an idea or even a message; it is a presence. To share a sacrament is to share a presence. The sacramental sign, a symbol, is always the sign of a presence and this presence is the abiding reality. We are tempted to forget this as we arrange and manage our ceremonies. But sacrament means, "to you have been given the *mysterion* of the kingdom of God," and this *mysterion* is no abstraction, but the Christ of God revealed to us in Jesus of Nazareth. Sacrament is a gift, and the gift is not a scheme, a plan of salvation; it is not even a right word, not even the parabolic speech (which is the point of Mk. 4:10-12); it is a presence. It is an embodied and an enacted word.

Mysterion→"You"

Something else is said clearly in this logion: God's *mysterion* is neither abstract nor remote; it is a relationship within a human community— "to *you* has been given." This "you" is "those who were about him with the twelve" (4:10). At the end of chapter 3 Mark used similar language to describe the company attracted by Jesus: "Those who sat about him" (3:34). Refusing to see his mother and brother, Jesus looks on those "about him" and says, "Here are my mother and brother" (3:34). What we have here is not a repudiation of his blood-relations, but rather, reading 3:34 in the light of 4:10-12, the strongest kind of affirmation of the communal nature of the kingdom of God. Those who are drawn to Jesus are a family, a unique gathering, belonging together as sharers in the divine mystery which is Jesus and fellowship with Jesus.[4]

The word of Mark 4:10-12 is from a pre-Easter source, but it is written to a post-Easter context.[5] It declares to the church its own character as a particular people alive in the intimacy[6] of Jesus as the Christ. To be "one of those about him" was to receive the gift of the *mysterion*, which is none other than what God is manifesting on earth in the mission of Jesus of Nazareth. And this gift, this *mysterion*, this perception and relatedness, is exactly what a sacrament is. It is not a thing; it is an event; it is personal; it is radically social. It is human bondedness in the family of Jesus. It is, as a reality of experience, the mystery of divine participation in our nature.

Mysterion→World

These conclusions out of Mark 4:10-12, that sacrament is Christ as the *mysterion* of God, and this Christ present to us in intimate human relationship, form an essential conception which is unfortunately open to serious misunderstanding. The temptation of misunderstanding is toward exclusivity. If Christ and our communion in him is sacrament, does it not follow then that the *mysterion* of God is the possession—a monopoly—of the church? This conclusion has been made often enough in Christian history. Jesus' warning that "many that are first will be last, and the last first" (Mk. 10:31) should deter any of us from defining ourselves as "first" in the fold of the Good Shepherd. And his reply to James and John, who sought to be first in the kingdom, that "whoever would be first among you must be slave of all" (Mk. 10:44), should teach us all that the attempt to understand ourselves as "first" in the kingdom, or as the exclusive "friends" of Jesus, is automatically self-defeating.

St. Paul provides the corrective that is necessary to a false reading of Mark 4:10-12. He understands God's *mysterion* as wisdom "decreed before the ages" (1 Cor. 2:7; Eph. 3:9; Col. 1:26) and certainly not captive to the Christians, who rather than its possessors are its servants and stewards. "This is how one should regard us, as servants of Christ and stewards of the mysteries of God" (1 Cor. 4:1). God's *mysterion*, which is God's self-giving, and what we call loving grace, has been hidden; this does not mean that it has been absent. It is revealed in Jesus as the Christ, and those who receive and grasp this revealing of the kingdom of God are indeed blest, not as those who can rest secure in divine favor, but as agents of God in the world. The Matthean parallel to Mark 4:10-12 makes this clear, that the gift of *mysterion* is both blessing and obligation:

Then the disciple came and said to him, "Why do you speak to them in parables?" And he answered them, "To you it has been given to know the secrets *(mysterion)* of the kingdom of heaven, but to them it has not been given. For to him who has will more be given and he will have abundance; but from him who has not, even what he has will be taken away. This is why I speak to them in parables, because seeing they do not see, and hearing they do not hear, nor do they understand. . . . But blessed are your eyes, for they see, and your ears, for they hear. Truly, I say to you, many prophets and righteous men longed to see what you see, and did not see it, and to hear what you hear and did not hear it (Mt. 13:10-13; 16-17).

Because we are the witnesses, servants, and stewards of what God has created in the world, we dare not behave as if the sacraments, God's *mysteria,* are really ours to order or bestow. They are God's, and they do not create God's grace in the world—the divine self-giving— they are rather occasions when grace is proclaimed, dramatized, recognized, and enjoyed. We need to begin with Karl Rahner's recognition that "the world is constantly and ceaselessly possessed by grace from its innermost roots, from the innermost personal center of the spiritual subject. It is constantly and ceaselessly sustained and moved by God's self-bestowal even prior to the questions (admittedly always crucial) of how creatively freedom reacts to this engracing."[7] Sacraments are metaphors in the church of what the grace of God in Christ can do, will do, and is doing in the world.

From such a perspective, Theodore Runyon, in a provocative monograph[8] argues that since the world is the object of God's redeeming and transforming activity, church and sacraments must be seen in the context of that overarching purpose.[9] Because this is so, he maintains, we should always look from kingdom to creation, understanding first things out of last things. This means that "in the hands of its Creator the world was itself the first sacrament, the first use of the material to communicate and facilitate the divine-human relation."[10] He thus concludes that "the original sacrament is not the church, therefore and not even Christ, important as the sacramental nature of Christ and of the Church are for Christian faith and practice. But the original, visible sign of God's grace is the world he entrusts to our care. Moreover, in giving us this gift God gives not just something. In, with, and through it he gives us himself."[11] Runyon is well aware that the world is not an unambiguous sign of God's grace:

If the world as we experience it is unrecognizable as the creation of a loving God; if it has become more a threat than a promise, a tragic destiny in which we are embroiled but over which we feel we have little control; if it is the domain of principalities and powers rather than the creature of God, how can the sacrament represent both the world and Christ? Are they not antithetical? Yet precisely here the redemptive work of Christ is made evident in the sacrament. In the hands of Christ, the sacrament is presented to us as *the world in its original eschatological form.* He takes the bread and wine, which are products of our ordinary world—and therefore related to the complexities of international grain cartels, embargoes, starvation, alcoholism, and all the other ways in which God's good gifts have gone awry—and turns them into signs of his kingdom of justice and love. He does this by identifying them with himself and his mission, just as he did the paschal bread and wine at the last supper. Having joined them with his life for the kingdom, he hands the bread and wine back to us to make us participants in that kingdom by sharing its first fruits which nourish us along the way. . . . As overwhelming as the task of stewardship of the world may seem, it is not meaningless and without ultimate purpose because it joins us to Christ's own redemptive work of bringing order out of chaos. In the end he will prevail.[12]

Runyon makes a compelling case for understanding the world as the original sacrament. His emphasis is much needed, even if his conclusion is an overstatement. Christ remains *the* primordial sacrament because we do not recognize the world as sacrament until and unless we have recognized Christ as sacrament. Bread and wine are signs to us of the world's redemption because they are signs to us of Christ. And when we see Christ as the sacrament of God and the world as the sacrament of God then we understand the role of the church in relation to *mysterion*. We are not its repository, its possessors; we are its witnesses, servants, and stewards. All of this is clear in what the New Testament tells us about God's *mysterion*, that it is Christ, that it is the intimate life of Christ with his people, and that it is in the world for the world's transformation.

Our attempts to understand sacrament should begin with these simple principles because *mysterion* is the root from which the tree of sacrament grows. Being faithful to these principles, our roots, is not a matter of ideology; it is a matter of identity.

A Common and Unhelpful Definition

Most of our definitions send us astray into historical and theological distortions. Consider the famous definition of sacrament as "an outward and visible sign of an inward and spiritual grace."[13] The definition could be said to be antisacramental in that it sets "spiritual" against "outward," and it is exactly the "outward" in gestures, symbols, and events that constitutes sacrament. What is operating primarily in this definition is the platonic tradition which sees the heavenly world distinct from the earthly and views the whole world of sensible realities as image and shadow and the *real* world as that of the invisible, heavenly realities. A scriptural definition will see the world as pregnant with God's presence and purposes and generative of revealing signs of this divine vitality.

Sacrament as Mysterion-Sacramentum

If we begin with a scriptural definition, considering sacrament from its roots in *mysterion,* we must move forward incorporating *sacramentum* and sacrament's historical evolution. Let us observe, therefore, that a sacrament in the church is a *mysterion* and a *sacramentum.* That is, it is created out of biblical substance *(mysterion)* and ecclesial strategy *(sacramentum).* The Reformers were correct in their insistence that sacrament must be understood out of scripture. Our forebears in the church were also right when they understood that the *mysterion* of God is not completed in the New Testament nor captive to it; it is expressed and takes logical forms in the unfolding traditions of Christian people and in the world. As *mysterion* sacrament is personal and dynamic and finally eludes definition. But *mysterion* is translated into the life of the church as *sacramentum.*[14] The ineffable mystery remains mystery; it never ceases to be mystery, but its celebration, articulation, and realization become in the life of the church occasions of affirmation and experience: *sacramenta.* God's *mysterion* is spoken in story and preaching, but if the faith will become our faith it will be not just proclaimed: "A living faith is one which comes to expression in a gesture of commitment; in the baptismal immersion, and in the gesture of anointing; in the breaking of bread and in the taking of the cup; in prostration and prayer, in the lifting of hands and the bending of the knee, in singing, reading, and processing . . . by all of which we commit ourselves."[15]

While taking many forms, sacrament is one reality. The number and character of "gestures of commitment" probably ought never to be a fixed system; the church as a living organism should be free to discover the sacraments which can communicate and celebrate the *mysterion* of God.

Temptation

The translation-transition which takes place when *mysterion* becomes *sacramentum* is natural and inevitable and bears with it natural and inevitable temptation. The most dangerous of the seductions has been well described by William Bausch: "The mystery was stripped to what some thought were the bare essentials. Then these essentials were put in the concrete of laws and rubrics. Now there was a quick and easy measurement of their validity. It was easier for everyone to say, '*This* is a sacrament. *That* is not.' It was easier to figure out precisely where grace resided and what to do to get it. Every person with rubrical savvy could call it forth. The step to magic was a short one."[16]

Bausch notes how, in this reduction, *mysterion* ceases to be gift and becomes instead possession. As possessions, structures of word and action could themselves be seen as causes of God's self-giving, of grace, which could be activated and manipulated by correct ritual.[17] When *sacramentum* loses a lively and clear grounding in *mysterion*, we become possessors of what we should be possessed by and our liturgical word and deed become either the praxis of magic or the dead hand of the past upon us as "ordinance," ceremonies we do because they are *regulation,* even though we have, in fact, forgotten why. If we are not to be thus "absent minded" in what we are about in liturgy, we shall have to set to work at three primary tasks: to understand the ways in which *mysterion,* or let us say Mystery Present, is revealed to us in particular sacraments, to gather together in the sacramental event in styles which make evident to us that we are brothers and sisters in the family of Jesus, and to shape signs of commitment which do not end as empty gestures in the sanctuary but as witness and stewardship in the world.

Notes

1. Unless one considers the use of the term in the letter of Pliny the Younger to Trajan (c. 112) a reference to an act of worship.

2. The problems focus primarily on the implication in the passage that the purpose of Jesus' parables is to conceal the truth. That this is not the purpose of parables is made clear in this same chapter of Mark:

> For there is nothing hid except to be made manifest; nor is anything secret except to come to light (Mk 4:22).

> With many such parables he spoke the word to them, as they were able to hear it (Mk. 4:33).

And, that this is not the purpose of the parables is clear to anyone who has read them thoughtfully.

The most usual explanation of the contradiction posed here is that the word of Jesus has been distorted by dogma. (Günther Bornkamm, *Jesus of Nazareth* [New York: Harper & Row, 1973], p. 71.) "One imagines a certain in-group who alone understands the parables which are hidden from the comprehension of outsiders." (John Dominic Crossan, *The Parables* [New York: Harper & Row, 1973], p. xiv.) Some suppose that the word of Jesus was garbled in transmission. (T. W. Manson, *The Teaching of Jesus* [Cambridge: University Press, 1951], pp. 75-78.) Others contend that the contradictory language could be a result of Mark's method. The word of Jesus he had at hand did not reconcile with the whole text, but it could not be altered as the word of Jesus. This assumption is bolstered by textual critics' reference to the "foreign" character of the passage in its context in Mark 4 and its origin in an Aramaic-speaking environment. (Aloysius M. Ambrosic, *The Hidden Kingdom* [Washington, D.C.: The Catholic Biblical Association of America, 1972], p. 45.)

While there is no glossing over the contradiction in Mark 4 concerning the purpose of parables, there is an aptness in thinking about them as presenting a secret. The Evangelist presents Jesus' whole ministry as a kind of secret. The disciples continually fail to see the truth before them (8:18), and then they are told to keep it to themselves (8:29-30). And Jesus' way of teaching in parables does indeed contain an element of hiddenness. The parable of the sower, which is the context of the passage in question, makes this point. It is a parable about parables and the key to them all. Its message is about a kingdom, present now in a hidden manner, but waiting to be manifested with power. Now is the time of sowing, but the harvest will come; the sowing will bear fruit (4:20). The parable is about Jesus' ministry as a whole and its character *en parabolis*—as a kind of secret. The evidence does not support the notion that Jesus taught in parables so that people would not "perceive" or "understand," but there is about them a hiddenness, whereby God and the way of God in the world are cloaked in simple stories about life and nature.

3. Ambrosic, *The Hidden Kingdom*, p. 92.

4. Juan Luis Segundo, *The Sacraments Today* (New York: Orbis, 1974), p. 91.

5. Some scholars have maintained that this post-Easter context is the source of the distinction between those who were about him "and those outside." This is possible, but seems unlikely. Nothing is clearer in the gospels than the unique "authority" of Jesus in his call: "Follow me." The witness is that a particular group did follow, more than twelve, and that they were with him as a special object of his teaching and extension of his mission.

6. Tad Guzie, *The Book of Sacramental Basics* (New York: Paulist Press, 1981), p. 132; G. S. Worgul, *From Magic to Metaphor* (New York: Paulist Press, 1980), p. 81ff.

7. Karl Rahner, *Theological Investigations*, XIV (London: Darton, Longman & Todd, 1976), p. 166.

8. Theodore Runyon, "The World as the Original Sacrament," *Worship* 54 (1980), pp. 495-511.

9. Ibid., p. 500.

10. Ibid.

11. Ibid., p. 501.

12. Ibid., p. 504.

13. Based on St. Augustine, *City of God*, Book 10, Chapter 5.

14. Cf. Jürgen Moltmann, *The Church in the Power of the Spirit* (New York: Harper & Row, 1977), p. 27.

15. Mark Searle, "The Journey of Conversion," *Worship* 54 (1980), p. 49.

16. William J. Bausch, *A New Look at the Sacraments* (Notre Dame, Ind.: Fides/Claretian, 1977), p. 7.

17. Ibid., p. 8.

Chapter 3

The Sacraments as Mystery: Freedom from Idolatry and Freedom to Create

It is not self-evident that *mystery* is a useful word for contemporary theological-liturgical language. The term enjoys a certain vogue today[1] and has always been at least a tangential referent to sacraments, but its use raises several problems.

In the first place, it could be said that using *mystery* to refer to sacrament is an archaism. It is an ancient liturgy-word which, in part because it is archaic, is also arcane, too obscure; instead of explaining it opens the door to greater misunderstanding.

A second consideration which could lead us to avoid *mystery* as a useful word for theology today is its notorious use as a substitute for rigorous theological thinking. To say that this or that is a mystery is sometimes an excuse to avoid thought. When Captain Fitzroy told Charles Darwin not to inquire how shell fossils found their way up into mountains, but rather to accept God's mysteries, he was not being helpful either to geology or theology; he was indulging in obfuscation. Maybe the term *mystery* is too convenient a hiding place and should be abandoned—left as a refuge for obscurantism.

As a third objection, it could be pointed out that *mystery* is not a very prominent word in the New Testament. It is used, as we have seen, but once in the synoptic gospels, nowhere in the Gospel of John; it is primarily a Pauline word. Why use a term of such limited biblical reference to define something so comprehensive as the idea of sacrament?

A fourth argument concerns the use made of *mystery* by various cults in the early Christian era to designate their sacred rites. This has led to debate and confusion over the origins of Christian sacraments. Would we not be better off to drop the term and put as much distance as possible between our sacrament and the "mystery religions" of antiquity?

36

Too Archaic and Arcane?

These considerations are important and need to be addressed. It is true, in the first place, that *mystery* is archaic, and it is certainly the very property of the word to be obscure.

Strange to say, this may be a value. Thinking of sacrament as mystery keeps us in touch with the real roots of the idea of sacrament. This does, indeed, prevent a simple, tidy definition. This is good. Our definitions have mostly been reductions which have tended to "narrow down the mystery to certain words and actions."[2] The "mystery of the kingdom of God" is too vast and too free for these definitions.

In a fundamental sense, the idea of sacrament is open and embraces everything which serves to reveal Mystery Present to us. While all created agents and actions may have sacramental properties, not all are sacrament in *mysterion-sacramentum*. It is our celebration in the family of Jesus of the Mystery of the Kingdom of God, as our affirmation and experience with one another, for one another, and for the world. Such occasions need to be more than encounters with Mystery Present; in order for the family to share in them they must be *paradigms*, that is, models and patterns of the gift to the family of Jesus of "the *mysterion* of the Kingdom of God." We will have more to say about this in chapters 4 and 16.

Is "Mystery" Too Much Mystery?

Our second demur about *mystery* was that the theme is sometimes an excuse for undisciplined or crude thinking. Indeed, the appearance of "mystery" in theological discourse is sometimes a signal of the avoidance of rationality. On the other hand, its thematic appearance may be a sign of something else: not irrationality, but the everlasting limits of our rationality. Suppose Maurice Merleau-Ponty is right when he writes:

> The world and reason are not problematical. We may say, if we wish, that they are mysteries, but their mystery defines them: there can be no question of dispelling it by some "solution," it is on the hither side of all solutions.[3]

The human mind is restlessly at work pushing back the boundaries of the mysterious; this is inevitable and good. But mystery is not simply a limitation to be overcome; it is an abiding quality of our existence with which we have to come to terms. Paul Tillich puts this matter best, perhaps, when he evokes "mystery" to name "the infinity of questions with which every answer confronts the human mind."[4] Our difficulty with the word "mystery" comes from our association of it with the "questions" of life which we always push toward solution. Some other word, we suppose, is appropriate for solutions. The truth is, as Tillich points out, that "questions" and "answers" participate together in a mystery which embraces both. "Reality, every bit of reality, is inexhaustible and points to the ultimate mystery of being itself which transcends the endless series of scientific questions and answers."[5]

The theologians in our own time who have dealt most positively with "mystery" as a quality of theology are probably Karl Rahner and Abraham Heschel. Rahner sees it as the primary function of theology not to explain but to show that it is impossible to explain everything: "The theologian reduces everything to God and explains God as unexplainable."[6] Such a conclusion is not obscurantism; Rahner does not see "mystery" as indicating the spooky or the problem-oriented, as the point where reasons run out and contradictions appear, as the "stumbling block" of faith. He sees, like Tillich, that there is no place in existence where there is not mystery.

Heschel understood faith to begin with wonder, which he characterized as radical amazement. What corresponded objectively to wonder he saw as mystery—the wonder of the world which could be apprehended but not comprehended. "The religious question is what to do with the feeling of mystery and wonder."[7]

Such positive affirmation of mystery is not a refusal to seek truth clearly and diligently; it is rather an expression of truth about transcendence. Its acknowledgment is crucial, for it is a restriction upon us which keeps us from falling into idolatrous crystalizations of our own partial understandings.

Use in the New Testament

Our third reservation concerning the use of the term mystery as a designation for sacrament concerned its limited significance in the New Testament. It is mostly an aspect of the theology of St. Paul. The use which the apostles makes of the term connects exactly with the qualities of mystery we have just discussed. The mystery he proclaims is exactly the unexplainable "depth of the riches and wisdom and knowledge of God." *Mysterion* for him denotes the ineffable way or pattern of God (Rom. 11:25; 16:25; Eph. 3:3; Col. 1:26) or the means or medium by which the hidden intentionality of God is revealed in specific intentions, as made known in Christ (Eph. 1:9, 3:4; Col. 2:2; 4:3), in the gospel (Eph. 6:19), through the church (Eph. 3:9), or in individual believers (Col. 1:27).

Paul is the first and the greatest of the theologians of the church;

mysterion-theology is part of what we inherited from him. We ought to nourish and develop it because it is an expression of truth about reality and our faith. It is true that the concept of mystery he articulates is not developed in the New Testament outside his writings (or those attributed to him) and certainly not in the synoptic gospels whose singular image of the term we have discussed above. But his expression of Christ as a *mysterion* disclosed from the heart of the inexpressible reality of God is a profound and consistent development of the word of Jesus, "To you has been given the *mystery* of the Kingdom of God."

Mystery and Faith

From this conclusion concerning *mysterion* in the New Testament it does not necessarily follow that mystery and sacrament should be conjoined. Karl Barth, for instance has made an absolute distinction between *mysterion* and sacrament.[8] He points out that *mysterion*, whenever used in the New Testament, always refers to the revealing work of God in history and never to corresponding human responses. Faith is not referred to as *mysterion* in the Bible,[9] nor is hope, love, baptism, or the Lord's Supper. *Mysterion* refers only to what can be freighted with the "divine Word and act," as the bearer of "grace and salvation." Faith and the sacraments are not the bearers of the divine *mysterion*, they are human responses to it.[10] Barth concludes that the use of *mysterion* to refer to the sacraments owes nothing at all to a biblical usage.

> In the vocabulary of Christian theology "sacrament" came to have irresistibly the sense of *mysterion* derived not from the New Testament but from the Greek and Hellenistic mystery religions.[11]

Two issues are joined in Barth's argument. What can be the bearer of the divine word and act? Are the sacraments, as mysteries, simply an inheritance to us from the mystery religions?

Concerning the first question, one must admit that Barth is right when he points out that *mysterion* in the New Testament refers to God's disclosure. It does not necessarily follow that sacrament is devoid of that same disclosure and is simply human response. Differences of opinion in this matter are long standing. Zwingli and Luther are probably the most famous theologians to debate this issue. Barth represents Zwingli's point of view. Zwingli valued sacraments but saw them as pictorializations of the faith having no capacity to communicate or create faith itself.

> The sacraments not only set them (the things of Christ's sacrifice) before our eyes, but even enable them to penetrate to the mind. But what leads the way? The Spirit . . . which must first give faith.[12]

Luther, on the other hand, trusted sacrament to convey the reality of God's grace. He saw sacrament and word as different forms of one reality, both "God-given means of knowing God."[13] He doesn't argue that salvation without the sacraments is impossible and sees sacraments as means and occasions whereby the testament is set forth. The distinction, so clear to Zwingli and Barth, between God's grace proclaimed and a human response in sacrament is not understood by Luther. He sees God's gift in both the spoken and the enacted word.

Zwingli feared idolatry. One of his favorite phrases in his debates with Luther was, "The flesh profits nothing." He saw in bread and wine opportunities for idolatry. His attitude about sacrament, and in particular the Lord's Supper, was a correlate of his Christology, where he made a clear distinction between the human and divine natures of Christ. He did not believe that what was worldly was interpenetrated by what was Godly. Luther, on the other hand, saw the reality of God in nature and the creatures. In Christology he emphasized not the two natures but the fact of incarnation.

> I am determined to know nothing of a son of God who is not Mary's Son who suffered, the God enveloped in humanity who is one person. I dare not separate the one from the other and say that the humanity is of no use, but only the divinity.[14]

To his mind, *the God who was love in Jesus Christ is also restlessly active in all creation.* So when Zwingli insisted that Christ could not possibly be present in the eucharist, because, as the creed affirms, he is "seated at the right hand of God," Luther commented that, "the right hand of God is everywhere."

Zwingli's conclusion may be the more logical. To us, Luther's seems the more profound.[15] If Luther is correct, Barth is wrong. *Mysterion,* God's self-disclosure, can meet us and address us in the word expressed in earthly symbol and human event.[16]

Basic issues of anthropology as well as Christology were involved in the Zwingli-Luther debates over sacrament. When Zwingli says that "the flesh profits nothing" he means to say that what profits is Spirit, with a capital "S," as the enlivening reality of God communicating with spirit, with a small "s," as the vital center of an individual. What results from this assertion, given the strong mind (spirit)-body (flesh) dualism of Zwingli's theology, is a severe intellectualism.[17] What Zwingli achieves is a definition of the person as intellect, as conscious awareness. The conclusion of Paul Tillich about such an anthropology, as it relates to the possibility of sacraments, is, we think, decisive:

> If the nature of man is conceived simply in terms of conscious awareness, of intellect and will, then only words, doctrinal and moral words, can bear the Spiritual Presence. No Spirit-bearing objects or acts, nothing sensuous which affects the unconscious, can be accepted.[18]

Tillich understands very well what happens to the sacramental life of the church in the situation where this anthropology prevails. "Sacraments, if retained, become obsolete rudiments of the past."[19]

Signs of Renewal of Sacramental Life

This judgment may capture the Protestant situation more accurately than we would like to think. Nevertheless, we doubt the permanency of this conclusion and see signs of a positive future for sacramental life in the churches.

One should perhaps note first the discovery that since Freud we know that Zwingli and Descartes were wrong about us. We are not to be defined as conscious awareness-rational creatures reached simply by words. We are more complex, what Tillich called "multi-dimensional unities,"[20] and affected as deeply by what is sensuous as by what is rational. This discovery means that sacrament may be as effective in communication as word. New anthropologies create openness for reconsideration of the modes of human celebration and communication.

Second, we should recognize that we live in a new world of communication where the electronic media, in affecting what we receive and how we receive it, have significantly changed us as receptors of ideas, feelings, and images. The balance of the senses has been altered in the way we receive information. In the new communication of simultaneity, our eyes now function as our ears do, picking up stimuli from all directions. We are being freed from the tyranny of the written and spoken word and opened up inevitably to disclosures in forms where our senses function in a new balance with one another. Like our medieval ancestors we are open for vision and action, no longer captive to description and argument.[21] This means a new confidence in the sensual. This is without doubt threatening to some of the faithful. It ought not to be feared unduly. It is a retreat from intellectualism, but not into the irrational or into unknowing. The senses are means of *knowing,* as Thomas Aquinas pointed out:

> The senses delight in things duly proportioned as something akin to them; for the sense too is a kind of reason—as is every cognitive power.[22]

For purposes of abstraction we may refer to ourselves as having reason, or will, or emotion, but these are qualities which have no real separate existence in the human multidimensional unity. Sacraments, the ancient sign-acts of our faith should have a new viability in this new age of communication.

A third reason to believe in the renewal of sacramental life in the churches is the evidence of this renewal around us. In some situations this portent is a cloud, the size of a man's hand (1 Kgs. 18:44), but like Elijah's cloud, it can be expected to grow. The most obvious hallmark, in our own time, of liturgical research and creativity in the building of forms of worship is ecumenism. The "traditions" are beginning to be transcended. This phenomenon is created, paradoxically, by emphases on both the present and the past. The new "post-Christian" cultural situation, where Christendom is no longer the basic presupposition, forces us to attend to ritual and its values for socialization in the *present.* But the models in our tradition for a liturgical life without Christendom are those of the pre-Constantinian era, the first four centuries. This fact has created a new interest in the *past,* in the worship of the early church. What is diminished in this situation is interest in the sixteenth century, the epoch of divisions; the new interest in common *present* and common *past* creates our current epoch of ecumenical liturgical endeavor.[23]

This endeavor has been fruitful, not only of dialogue but of new denominational liturgical structures and many commentaries and guides which accompany them. The extent of ecumenical conversation involved, and the high quality of practical, liturgical work accomplished are encouraging signs. The primary danger facing this development lies in the possiblity that we will fail to integrate strictly liturgical concerns with the wider pastoral concerns of the church. This danger is in part the peril of overspecialization in the tasks of ministry. The renewal of sacramental life in the churches is not a narrow concern for worship; it is a matter of vision, communication, and participation which should absorb the interest of the whole church struggling to perceive and embrace the Lordship of Christ, to proclaim and demonstrate the gospel and nurture it in the faithful, and to gather us all together into a people of love and mission.

Mystery and the Mystery Religions

The fourth difficulty we encountered concerning the use of mystery is the problematic relation between sacrament and the rites of the so-called mystery religions of antiquity. Karl Barth, as we saw, believed that the sacraments, as mysteries, were simply an inheritance from these cults. What Barth sees is a picture of hellenistic piety intruding into the church, transforming biblical simplicity into mystical-sacramental forms.

It should be admitted that there is truth in this view. Despite protestations to the contrary by the Fathers of the church and many subsequent scholars, it is true that the mystery rites of the ancient world left an imprint upon Christian worship.[24] The points of similarity are too many to be simply coincidental. Popular characteristics of both are: initiation, with purification and self-offering; separation between the initiated and the uninitiated; vows of silence laid on the initiate; participation of worshipers in the "destiny" of God; the promise of salvation and regeneration; the suffering of God enacted in the cultic rite; a sacred meal; feasts and celebrations connected with the change of seasons; patterns of worship as dramatization of the relation between God and the faithful.[25]

When you take into account the fact that many scholars of the history of religion vastly overestimated the influence of the mysteries on Christianity, building false bridges and ignoring vital distinctions, you are still left with a powerful portrait of the influence of hellenistic religion upon Christian worship. The question one has to ask is whether this is a matter of simple apostasy or of brilliant and effective apologetic theology and evangelical missionary strategy. Barth claimed the former; there are many who have argued the latter.

Christian apologists and missionaries in the first centuries of the faith faced the task of making Christianity rational in terms of the hellenistic world. In this labor they helped Christianity absorb elements from the mysteries.[26] The third century, a little understood but crucial time in the formation of the liturgical life of the church, has been called an age of "mysterization," when the hellenistic mysteries provided the principle ethos of the spiritual life of the Mediterranean world.[27] The culture and people of the Graeco-Roman world were decisive *media* available to the Christian church for its articulation and dissemination of the faith. Without doubt, this sometimes meant that gnostic ideas, mystery concepts, scriptures, neo-platonism, and more, became mixed up in what Harnack referred to as "a promiscuous confusion."[28] The Alexandrian school is an example of this in theology. Its syncretism was doubtless promiscuous, but it did provide a basis for educated and thoughtful people to encounter and accept Christian faith. Clement of Alexandria articulated just this intention: "I will give you understanding of the mysteries of the Logos by means of images with which you are familiar."[29] The mystery cults were sensible images at hand in the culture which Christianity to some extent pirated to express and dramatize its faith and involve men and women as actors in its own *mysterion*.[30]

It is important for us to understand that before Christians took over words, images, and gestures from the mysteries, they were a people of their own *mysterion*.[31] Christians boldly made use of what served their purpose in the ancient world, secure in their own revelation and tradition. *Mysterion* was not an exclusively hellenistic term. It had for St. Paul, and other Christians, a semitic history and an anchor in their biblical inheritance.[32] Any comparison of the Christian mystery—as scriptural expression or sacramental reality—with the mystery concept and rites of antiquity demonstrates the vivid difference between doctrinally amorphous nature religions and the *mysterion* of Christian faith—the revelation of the hidden God in human witness, who makes ethical demands and whose purpose is the redemption of the lost and least in a future where love rules. The mystery cults served for the Fathers of the church the same function that Greek religion served for Paul. They are an altar bearing the inscription: "To an unknown God."[33]

Mystery: A Boundary and a Freedom

In our time it is important for us to recognize that sacraments are not "ordinances" of Christ, but are means—culturally conditioned means—whereby we may communicate and participate in the good news of our faith. In order to understand this we need to know that sacrament is a translation of *mysterion*. This realization has limiting and freeing significance. As limitation it means that sacrament is perennially in need of reform. Its words, forms, styles, need to be critiqued, pruned and redone to guard against the reductions and acculturations that threaten the authenticity of the *mysterion* of God. As freedom it means that we are free to adopt and adapt the media and symbol-structures of our own time, so that our life in sacrament will not be lived out as perfunctory ritualization, but as our meeting with the mystery of time and space, in our world, in our human community, and in our Lord Jesus Christ.

Notes

1. One thinks, for instance, of the work of Karl Rahner, cf. *Theological Investigations*, Vol. 4 (Baltimore: Helicon, 1966), and work influenced by this theologian: Cf. James H. Ebner, *God Present as Mystery* (Winona, Minn.: St. Mary's Press, 1976).

2. William J. Bausch, *A New Look at the Sacraments* (Notre Dame, Ind.: Fides/Claretian, 1977), p. 5f.

3. Maurice Merleau-Ponty, *Phenomenology of Perception* (New York: Humanities Press, 1962), p. xx.

4. Paul Tillich, *Systematic Theology*, Vol. III (Chicago: University of Chicago Press, 1963), p. 88.

5. Ibid.

6. *New York Times Magazine*, 23 September 1979, p. 69.

7. Perry LeFevre, *Understandings of Prayer* (Philadelphia: Westminster Press, 1981), p. 174. See Abraham Heschel, *Man's Quest for God* (New York: Charles Scribner's Sons, 1954); *God in Search of Man* (New York: The Jewish Publication Society of America, 1955); *Man Is Not Alone* (New York: Farrar, Straus & Young, 1951).

8. Karl Barth, *Systematic Theology* IV, 4 (Edinburgh: T. & T. Clark, 1969), p. 198ff.

9. The references in 1 Timothy 3:9 and 16 do not really contradict this conclusion for Barth, because they refer to the *fides quae*, faith as creed.

10. Ibid., p. 108f.

11. Ibid., p. 109.

12. "Letter of H. Zwingli to the Most Honorable Princes of Germany," *Selected Works of Zwingli* (New York: Longmans Green, 1901), p. 110.

13. Heinrich Bornkamm, *Luther's World of Thought* (New York: Concordia, 1915), p. 98.

14. *Luther's Works*, Vol. 23 (St. Louis: Concordia, 1955), p. 102.

15. One of the tragedies of the Marburg Colloquy (1529) was the clash of right versus right. Zwingli against Luther's literalism insisted that "*is* equals *signifies*" in the phrase "This is my body," and Luther against Zwingli's literalism insisted that "seated at the right hand of God" means "everywhere." Biblicism is hard to overcome in polemical situations.

16. Hugo Rahner, in *Greek Myths and Christian Mystery* (New York: Harper & Row, 1963) expresses this conclusion compellingly: "Christianity is never only the religion of the naked word, of pure reason and of moral imperatives. It is at the same time the religion of the veiled word, of loving wisdom, of grace hidden in sacramental symbols." P. 42.

17. It might be contended that what Zwingli says is not more than what St. Paul says concerning spirit and flesh. The sense of the language, however, is not the same; Zwingli lays more stress on spirit-flesh dualism. Paul is a master psychologist. Zwingli's source for this opposition is much less St. Paul than is his thorough Renaissance education in the categories of Greek philosophy.

18. Paul Tillich, *Systematic Theology*, Vol. III (Chicago: University of Chicago Press, 1963), p. 88.

19. Ibid.

20. Ibid., p. 11.

21. Marshal McLuhan, "The Medieval Environment: Yesterday as Today," *Listening*, Vol. 9 (1974), pp. 9-27.

22. Quoted in Erwin Panofsky, *Gothic Architecture and Scholasticism* (New York: Meridian Books, 1957), p. 38.

23. So it is that those whose primary work is in the liturgical fields are today generally the most ecumenically minded of Christians. Even a glance at the work of Societies or the content of journals will bear this out.

24. It is now clear that the reverse is also true. By the time Christian writers were most strenuously attacking the mysteries, Christian thinking and practices, now popular, had found their way into some of the mysteries.

25. Cf. Günther Bornkamm, "Mysterion," in *Theological Dictionary of the New Testament* (Grand Rapids, Mich.: Eerdmans, 1967), pp. 802-827.

26. Adolf Harnack, *The Mission and Expansion of Christianity* (New York: Harper Torchbook, 1961 [1908]), p. 234ff.

27. H. Rahner, *Greek Myths and Christian Mystery*, p. 25.

28. Harnack, *The Mission and Expansion of Christianity*, p. 237.

29. Quoted in H. Rahner, *Greek Myths and Christian Mystery*, p. 12.

30. Harnack, *The Mission and Expansion of Christianity*, p. 237. "Christianity gained special weight from the fact that in the first place it had mysterious secrets of its own, which it sought to fathom only to adore them once again in silence, and secondly, that it preached to the perfect in another and a deeper sense than it did to simple folk."

31. H. Rahner, *Greek Myths and Christian Mystery*, p. 11f.

32. Raymond E. Brown, *The Semitic Background of the Term "Mystery" in the New Testament* (Philadelphia: Fortress, 1968).

33. H. Rahner, *Greek Myths and Christian Mystery*, p. 38.

Chapter 4

The Sacraments: Action Parables of the Kingdom of God

Kingdom Signs

Alexander Schmemann, the Orthodox liturgist, calls the eucharist "the journey of the church into the dimension of the kingdom."[1] This is a true and beautiful way to put the matter. The eucharist is indeed a visible symbol of the new age if it is "the bread of God which comes down from heaven; and gives life to the world" (Jn. 6:33). It is the purpose of every sacrament to draw us into the dimensions of the kingdom of God. It exists to dramatize our commitment to the *mysterion* of the kingdom and the human situation to which it is related.[2] And, as Jürgen Moltmann puts it, since "Jesus as the Messiah is the mystery of the rule of God, the signs of the messianic era are also a part of his mystery."[3]

If sacraments are indeed signs of God's time,[4] it must be demonstrated that they are expressions of significant themes of the kingdom of God as this is discoverable in the words of Jesus in the gospels. The sacraments are not generally analyzed in this way. In times past they were compared with scripture and, so to say, "proof-texted" to demonstrate that they were all inaugurated by Christ, a specious bit of scholarly quackery. More recently they have been compared to critical episodes in the human life cycle and their natural relevance argued.[5] How relevant are sacraments to the themes of the kingdom of God?

Gospel Stories: Parable and Sacrament

God's new time is the message of Jesus; it is the ultimate referent of Jesus' parables[6] and the eventuality his actions intend. What it is, exactly, is difficult to say, because Jesus in the gospels nowhere tells us what the kingdom of God *is*. What he tells us is what the kingdom of God is *like*.[7] In simple stories he offers dramatizations and pictures.

47

Because these images, as Paul Ricoeur puts it, "don't allow a translation into conceptual language," we can never create a simple definition of the kingdom of God. What we can do, and many have done, is create patterns of the imagery of Jesus' stories to help us to a more comprehensive understanding of what Jesus meant by "kingdom of God." Paul Ricoeur analyzes a typical thematic of the parables as "first, encountering the Event, then changing one's heart, then doing accordingly."[8] He does not see these movements (Event, Reversal, Decision), necessarily, in every parable, but observes that "each of them develops and, so to say, dramatizes one or the other of these three critical themes."[9] Another New Testament scholar, John Dominic Crossan, speaks of essentially the same three themes in his exposition of parables, only he calls them, *Advent, Reversal,* and *Action.*[10] By advent he means exactly the event of the kingdom encountered, the finding of the treasure, or the sowing of the seed. Reversal is the change of heart, the bold new direction, or the completely changed situation; it is the good Samaritan, the prodigal son; it is the publican praying while the Pharisee boasts. Action is behaving, out of the insight of event-advent and the changed heart of reversal; it is risking with the talents you have; it is the Samaritan's real help for the wounded traveler; it is finishing the tower you set out to build.

It is possible to relate sacraments to this kind of analysis. Consider, for instance, the perspective of Tad Guzie who invites us into a new vision, where, instead of enumerating the sacraments, we think of them in certain categories. He understands the eucharist, or what he calls "The Breaking," as the vital center of the church's sacramental life. Around this the sacramental categories of initiation, healing, and ministry are arranged:

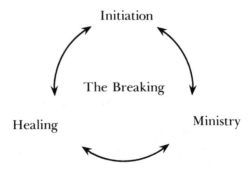

There is, of course, a clear correlation between Guzie's categories of sacrament and Ricoeur's or Crossan's categories of parables—the themes of the kingdom of God:

Advent—Initiation
Reversal—Healing
Action—Ministry

It does not strain credulity to understand the historic sacraments through the Crossan-Ricoeur categories of advent, reversal, and action. Sacraments of initiation, baptism, and renewal in confirmation are particularly about the "kingdom-event encountered" which Ricoeur calls event and Crossan calls advent. One might say that all of the sacraments in one way or another have this quality, and this is right; but baptism and confirmation intend "encounter" in a primary way. Reconciliation and healing (unction) are especially about reversal, the change of heart and the change of life. Decision-action can be related to all the sacraments, but are obviously a particular theme of sacraments of initiation, marriage, and order.

Limitations

The limitations of this comparison need quickly to be pointed out. The "meaning-schemes"[11] proposed by Crossan-Ricoeur or Guzie to understand parables and sacraments bear a more or less crude relationship to the realities they want to comprehend. Advent-reversal-action does not comprehend parable, or initiation-healing-ministry comprehend sacrament much better than id-ego-superego comprehends person. Meaning-schemes can be helpful, but they are imperfect. When we try to compare them with one another we compound the imperfection. So, understand that we are not saying that the historical sacraments are an exact expression of the kingdom of God, as one finds the kingdom described in the parables of Jesus. And, as helpful as we find the schematizations of Crossan-Ricoeur and Guzie, we are not saying these are necessarily the best way to understand parables and sacraments. One might, for instance, construct other patterns for comparing kingdom-parable and sacraments out of alternate schematizations of parable, such as those of Joachim Jeremias, Madeleine Boucher, Neal Fisher, or Norman Perrin, etc.[12]

Not every student of the parables has used a schematization of themes as a way of understanding. Some simply enumerate the particular themes, such as joy, faith (decision), hope (eschatology), judgment, forgiveness, repentance, reversal of values, etc. One does not, of course, find a sacrament for every possible subject of parable. What we do find are qualities of the kingdom of God—the intentions of Jesus' parables—explicit and implicit in the liturgies of sacrament. The parable of the hidden treasure and pearl (Mt. 13:44-46), and the parable of the marriage feast (Mt. 22:1-10) are part of the content of the eucharist, not because Jesus evokes them in the upper room or because they are somehow hidden proof-texts which validate our liturgies, but because in the nature of the case, *eucharist* is joy in the receiving of a great gift and a foretaste of the banquet of the kingdom to which Jesus invites humanity of all sorts and conditions. *Baptism* is an embodiment of the imagery of the parables of the fig tree (Mt. 24:32-33: Mk. 13:28-29; Lk. 21:29-31), new wine and wineskins (Mt. 9:16-17, Mk. 2:21-22; Lk. 5:36-39), and the lost sheep (Mt. 18:12-14; Lk. 15:3-7), because it is about a budding, effervesant new life which is born in us in response to the seeking, gracious God. The parables of tower builder and king going to war (Lk. 14:28-32) and of the two sons (Mt. 21:28-32) are naturally integral to the substance of *confirmation* or *baptismal renewal* because they are about the character of service in God's kingdom. The sacrament of *reconciliation* can only exist in the church because of what parables like the Pharisee and the publican (Lk. 18:9-14), the rich man and Lazarus (Lk. 16:19-31), the rich fool (Lk. 12:13-21), and the good Samaritan (Lk. 18:25-37) tell us about human nature and the judgment and forgiveness of God. *Healing*, as a sacrament, is not dependent upon teaching in parables. It is rather based upon the healing work of Jesus and the understanding that his healing is a sign of God's new time.

Marriage and *orders* as traditional sacraments we may think are arbitrarily based upon Jesus teaching about the kingdom until we reflect upon them as events and symbols of decision and commitment. Marriage, St. Paul pointed out, is a paradigm of the basic human relationship in faith. He called it a *mysterion* as a profound expression of the central meaning of "Christ and the church" (Eph. 5:32). The Christian couple and their marriage, the simplest unit of love, is, as Alexander Schmemann points out, never simply a matter of a relation between a man and a woman. Because this little family is a family of the family of God, the sacrament of matrimony is always something bigger than two people.

> It is the sacrament of divine love, as the all-embracing mystery of being itself, and it is for this reason that it concerns the whole church and—through the church—the whole world.[13]

Ordination is a sacrament of vocation and an appropriate symbol of decision for the kingdom. It does seem an anachronism, in the light of current understandings, that a sacrament of vocation as ministry is something exclusively reserved for "professional" Christians. The need for a broader sacrament of vocation has been noticed by many.[14]

In the fifth century, Leo the Great in a famous sermon said that "what our Redeemer did visibly has passed over into the sacraments."[15] Considered legalistically-fundamentalistically, this has been and is a mischievous idea. Considered symbolically-dynamically, this is an idea which understands exactly the character and purpose of sacrament. Sacraments are expressions of the Jesus story and the Jesus stories which describe for us the kingdom of God. Unhappily the connections we make between sacrament and story are usually too narrow and literalistic. In the great thanksgiving of eucharist we recall, usually, the scene of the upper room. In the thanksgiving over the water of baptism we recite a holy history of faith and water. Those connections are vital but they are not exclusive. Room needs to be made in place of these stories and around them for other narratives, particularly for the parables of Jesus and the drama of the kingdom of God they present to us. The story of eucharist, for instance, is much too narrowly conceived as the story of the upper room. It is the story of the Emmaus road, of the feedings of the multitudes, of breakfast by the sea, of the finding of a pearl, of a great banquet. It is notable that in the early church there were eucharistic prayers which made no reference to the upper room.[16] There should be again, not that we should forget the meal of Passover, but that we should extend the meanings we have of eucharist into greater dimensions of what we understand as God's time.

When ritual loses its root in story it goes astray and loses its power. How this may happen and what the result is, is humorously described by William J. Bausch in a parable of his own making:

Suppose someone of prosaic mind tried to get at the meaning of our national Thanksgiving Day. He worked at it until at last he declared that the whole "essence" of this holiday could be captured in the turkey wing. That told it all. But, of course, what a fantastic reductionism! What a poor substitute for the whole turkey itself, the whole range of long-term preparations, family gatherings, reunions, old friendships, familial visitations, renewed emotions, old joys and meaningful spirit of what families and individuals had to be thankful for. It is conceivable that the reduced turkey wing might mean all of this, but surely it is a terribly reduced symbol of all that the ritual of Thanksgiving has come to mean for the American family. If fact, to carry the example one step further, it is conceivable that in due time the turkey wing might become the only symbol of the interlacing celebrating patterns of Thanksgiving Day. Future generations might well be perplexed as to what it was all about. Worse, a future generation might be content to go through some brief motion with the turkey wing in order to get on with the "real" business of life.[17]

We need a strong and cogent alliance between the gesture of sacrament and the story-word about the kingdom of God. What this requires of most of us is a richer understanding of how the gospels speak to us about God's time and the wit to connect this story with the sacramental symbol. (The feeding of the multitude is a kingdom sign. And it is about eucharist; it is the basis of our thanks for the Lord who breaks bread and blesses and gives and satisfies.)

The seven historic sacraments Christians now celebrate are not an inheritance passed down to us by clever theologians who wanted to make sure that our worship conformed to Jesus' word. The forces which generated, formed, and decided these liturgies were of every kind, sublime and ridiculous. The sacraments are very different and they are not of equal "weight," but they, in their unique ways, are the bearers of major themes of the kingdom of God as described by Jesus in the parables and kingdom sayings. They are action-parables.

Mysterion and Parable

At the point of this conclusion we need to clarify a potential misunderstanding. In defining sacrament, we made a distinction between *mysterion*-sacrament and parables, listening to Mark's report of Jesus' words (Mk. 4:10-12). This distinction contrasted sacrament as encounter-participation and parable as teaching-hearing. This discrimination is important; it recognizes the difference between the community around Jesus, the people of intimacy and commitment, and those who just hear Jesus. While significant, this distinction is nothing like absolute.

The most obvious problem with this distinction is the false impetus it can provide, and clearly has provided the community of the followers of Jesus, for a kind of tribal self-righteousness. In its milder forms this is a kind of pious isolationism; in its worst forms it is inquisition, with persecution and sometimes death for people identified as outside the circle of "those who were about him" (Mk. 4:10). Such a sad eventuality ignores the simple way Jesus identifies his own family. He does not set up anything like the "tribal" criteria familiar to us for identifying a people. He says simply, "Whoever does the will of God is my brother, and sister, and mother" (Mk. 3:35).

When we arrive at this issue, the problem of the identity of "brother, sister, and mother," we are at one of the most difficult issues of Christian life. If we are to take discipleship to Jesus seriously we have to risk judgments about faithfulness and unfaithfulness to the kingdom of God, indeed the parables of the kingdom invite us to this judgment. But the making of this judgment tempts us to tribalisms where the identification of members and nonmembers proceeds according to certain quantitative norms which mock the qualitative values of the kingdom of God. There seems to be no way for Christians to escape this dilemma. By its very nature the kingdom of God bids us to join one another in discipleship. Our human efforts to do this succeed imperfectly; they bind us too often with petty loyalties and blind us to God's graciousness and the hurt of the world. Probably the best we can hope for is that, aware of our dilemma, we will be bold in our identification and participation in the family of Jesus, all the while understanding the idolatrous possibilities in this identification-participation and willing to hear Jesus and seek first the kingdom of God. The church after all, as we are reminded by bolder and better theologies, ought not to be a creation which exists primarily for the benefit of those who are within it.[18] If we are faithful to the time of God (kingdom of God), the people of God will be a community transformed into sacrament. That is, we will be a parable of the kingdom of God to the world. Alas, this consummation comes to pass partially and periodically, and we need always to remind ourselves, as Juan Luis Segundo put it, that

> the Church is not the ideal image of the world. It is not the world as it ought to be. It is the community—just as human as any other—which possesses and is obliged to transmit elements of a solution that were revealed by God and that are addressed to the historical problems of mankind as a whole.[19]

It is a frustration and yet a glory to be the human bearer of the good news. It is, of course, the human and very imperfect nature of this enterprise that is the possibility of sacrament.

The second problem with the distinction between *mysterion* and parable is the possibility that in making the distinction we shall forget what they have in common which binds them inseparably to one another: the kingdom of God. *Mysterion* and parable in sacrament belong to one another for they both live to draw us into the kingdom of God. What they have in common is far more important than any distinction we can make between them. <u>Sacrament is a participative form of parable.</u> We have noted that Jesus does not tell us in parables what the kingdom of God is. He tells us what it is like in dramatizations and picturalizations. It is the power of sacrament that it can transport us into the realm of image and drama. In sacraments we join together in Christ's name sharing his presence. We wash, eat and drink, apologize and hear words of pardon, make vows—not simply to hear and understand but to role-play our commitment of life to the startling new time Jesus called the kingdom of God.

Animating the Metaphor

In order for a sacrament to function as parable and be a moving and truly human experience, worshipers, the ministers of the church, and the church itself must present the sacraments as truly human events which set us into Christ's new time and invite and animate our participation. Our difficulty at this point, as ministers and as an institution, is that we prefer and trust concepts more than we do images.[20] So in our realization of sacrament we tend to substitute words and concepts for the dramatic and imaginal elements of sacraments.

Nothing illustrates this better than the way in which a great many Christians celebrate baptism. One cannot read accounts of baptizing in the early church without being impressed with the dramatic character of the celebrations.[21] It was *absolutely* personally involving and employed every human sense. Contrast this rich ceremony with a few drops of water and an ocean of text and concept and you may have some idea of what apostasy really is. Perhaps the absurd ultimate of what we are getting at was described by one of our colleagues who reported a eucharist at which the minister, just before the people's communion, elevated the chalice and solemnly declared, "This wine is grape juice!" This poor pastor was destroying the metaphor and mocking the symbol, but this was not, of course, his intent; he wanted to get the concept straight. Wanting to get the concepts straight, we convert sacrament into text and subvert its parabolic character.

We need to be honest and admit that there is clear reason for our preference for text and concept and our mistrust of image-symbol-dramatic event. The latter, even if clearly a part of Jesus' kingdom announcement, has a certain rational ambiguity. It has been asked,

What would happen if we defended the faith ritologically instead of theologically?—if we said, for instance, that my Christian brother *is* whoever breaks bread with me instead of my Christian brother is one who *ought* to assent to this creed and when he does, he may eat with me? What would be gained and lost if we valued symbolic actions more than symbolic words, and thus defined "Christian" descriptively and gesturally rather than confessionally and theologically?[22]

This kind of talk will threaten many Christians. Concept, and its articulation in text, protects the territories of our several "tribalisms." This element will not disappear from sacraments and their celebration. All of us, to one degree or another, have a stake in it. It is possible, however, to recognize the limitations of this rational-textual dimension of sacrament and reform our sacramental life, giving new emphasis to its dramatic and imaginal dimensions.

Such a reform will not begin with new liturgical structures of sacrament. Indeed, while we need liturgies which are as well constructed "ritologically" as they are theologically, which realize the potential of sacrament as parable, we dare not wait for these better instruments; they will come in their own time if they are needed. For many Christians there has been more than enough liturgical change in their lifetimes. Adjustments to recent and current changes will occupy us for some time. Complaining about the liturgies holy mother church provides us becomes a major cop-out. There is usually plenty to complain about, but also, usually the liturgy has some adequate presentation of the basic metaphor; the imaginative minister has plenty of room in and around the liturgy to make some improvisations; in spite of problems in the form, our basic problem is not form but spiritual dullness.

Overcoming or escaping this dullness is a matter of vision and participation. Vision and concept are not the same thing; they are not unalike, but vision involves more exercise of the imagination. This is appropriate in the understanding of sacrament, where we are dealing with image and drama. The exercise of imagination is not really the use of a rare gift, given to some persons and withheld from others. It is rather a kind of primitive curiosity, which we all have, or had, and with some effort can recover.

Essentials

To celebrate—truly to animate—a sacrament among a people we have first of all to grasp its essence. This will not be given to us as a concept, even if we can express it in a few words—"unto you is given the mystery of the kingdom of God" but as a vision. This discernment is sometimes hard for us to come to because the sacrament appears to us as a text. Hidden from us often in the text are both the *nature* of the sacrament itself and the *parable*, the involving dramatic action which can allow the sacrament to transcend text and become life. So, grasping the essence of the sacrament means understanding it not only theologically but dramatically. This is not hard to do, but it is easy to avoid doing it. In 1972, the United Methodist Church published a contemporary text of the sacrament of the Lord's Supper as an official alternative to its traditional Elizabethan language text. It has gone through minor revisions, and been widely accepted, as anyone can observe, noting the many copies of the liturgy sold by The United Methodist Publishing House. In 1976, the United Methodists published a small volume, called *Word and Table*. It is not an order, or orders of worship; it is, as its subtitle indicates, "a basic pattern of Sunday worship." What this book does is to unfold the basic nature of the eucharist, its idea and its drama, some possibilities of text, and invites ministers and leaders to choose or create the specific elements of the eucharist. *Word and Table* has sold reasonably well to pastors, but it is not widely used. Its use requires "essential" understandings. Most of us do not have these, although they are not difficult. We may think that we have these but usually we do not and the proof of this is that we just do not function as if we did. We now know how to read the text. We know some ways to get the bread and wine distributed. But could it be the lifeless charade it often is if we in fact comprehended what we were doing? Robert Hovda in *Strong, Loving and Wise* contrasted his experience of Leonard Bernstein's *Mass* with eucharist in church the following Sunday:

> The contrast between the two experiences was striking. If one had not got the true word from the TV interviewees, one would have been tempted to say that Bernstein's theater piece grasped what Catholic liturgy is about, while those who were actually doing it in a parish didn't seem to have the faintest idea. In the theater piece, everything that was done was done in earnest, with respect and care that were visible and tangible in gestures and in movements and in the quality of all the materials employed. The audience there could not help but become involved, because everyone the audience could see on the stage was totally *into* this thing. In the actual mass, everyone seemed to be absent.[23]

This quality of absence is the failure of essential understanding. We can become automatons working our way through a text. If we have essential understanding, if we know the inner dynamism of a sacrament—its accent of the time of God, its basic metaphor, its dramatic action—we are not likely to be absent when it happens.

What sometimes substitutes for essential understanding and the primitive curiosity that can lead us to it, is a kind of theatricality. This is created usually out of something like panic. We sense that things are not working well; people seem bored and uninvolved; they aren't coming in the numbers we expect. What to do? The answer which comes in many forms usually gets down to this: "Jazz up the act!" "Quick—the guitars, the slides, the colored lights, the coke and potato chips, anything!" We may interest some people with these gimmicks; we may also obscure or destroy the meaning of the sacrament itself as its own "story" disappears in the multiplication of illustrative material, or substitute stories. The things we do to interest people may interest them only in the "entertainment" and in ourselves (a certain kind of personal exhibitionism often substitutes for essential understanding, especially in Protestantism) but not in the sacrament itself. To say this is not to denegrate music or dance or any of the arts nor the lively, earnest participation of the minister, but simply to say that all of these have high potential to capture our attention and lead us astray from the sacrament itself. When these serve an essential understanding of the sacrament they neither obscure nor detract, but shed an incandescence around this understanding which illuminates it and clarifies it and helps us to become part of it.

What we must attend to first is an essential understanding of sacrament. Our discussion this far has attempted to move us toward this understanding. It may be helpful at this point to summarize, extend and conclude our discussion of sacrament itself and proceed then to reflect on the particular motifs of the seven historical sacraments. We will conclude our consideration of sacrament itself under five headings: Christ, church, world, symbol, and commitment.

1. Christ

"To you have been given the *mysterion* of the kingdom of God." Sacrament is *mysterion*, and *mysterion* is Christ manifested in the world. This is a very primitive and essential comprehension. It is a formulation out of a naive and simple etymology, but it would not be made apart from the pioneering theological work of Edward Schillebeeckx, especially, *Christ, the Sacrament of the Encounter with God* (1963).[24] The work of several theologians leads up to this; one especially needs to credit Odo Casel (1886-1948) who adopted the patristic practice of referring to the sacraments as mysteries and who understood the sacraments as the saving activity of the risen Christ.[25] The work of these and other Roman Catholic scholars who have moved thinking about sacrament beyond text and ritual legalisms has been influential for many Protestants, who in their own way have had to overcome similar difficulties in the way of a discernment of sacrament as personal encounter. Protestants have their own heroes in this cause. P. T. Forsyth (1848-1921) in *The Church and the Sacraments*[26] called sacrament "Christ's personal act met by his Church's."[27] He understood that sacrament was essentially "holy personality" and like Luther he perceived that the apposition of word and sacrament was false.[28] His pathfinding work has inspired many contemporary scholars.[29]

It should be underscored that the development we are indicating is not a matter of novelty. It is very much a movement of rediscovery—a direction forward which is also a kind of theological and liturgical archaeology. This dimension of rediscovery may lead some to say, "So what's new? Its all a return to Aquinas, Luther, Wesley, the early church, et al. There is nothing new here." There is, in fact, nothing new here, but what is achieved is something new even so. The disclosure particularly of the Bible and the liturgical life of the first four centuries as newly relevant for our understanding and life of sacrament produces a new situation, overcoming nonhistorical and dogmatic approaches. it introduces a dynamism which frees Christ to be the living subject of sacrament and us to be its object.

Sacrament is *mysterion* and *mysterion* is Christ manifested in the world. We celebrate this *mysterion* again and again, because, praise God, it does not cease to be manifested in the world. It continues to be present in the world. As Robert Jenson puts it: "Jesus is always beyond the body that arrived at the cross, and beyond what on any occasion happens with the bread and cup and water."[30] He is beyond any fixed point in time in his voice—a word which recurs freshly on our ears; he is beyond an immovable history in his compassion—a love which often seems defeated and submerged, but which is resurrected, even in unlikely places and among perverse people. This *beyond* is what Christians have traditionally called a *presence*. The presence of Christ in the world is not a possession of the Christians; but the church, when it is the people of its Lord, is the milieu which celebrates and is obedient to the presence of Christ in the world.[31] Sacraments are primary ways in which Christians experience the intimacy of the presence of Christ, listening to his voice and discovering the patterns of the kingdom of God. As actors in its dramatization we invite its formation in our lives.

In order for this formation to take place there needs to be a clear realism in the event of sacrament. It needs to be clear, for instance that what is happening is a meeting of the presence of Christ. One can appropriately say "meeting of" because among the people of the *agape* it is simply inadequate to say "meeting with." It is the nature of this happening, when it is authentic, that it has the quality of participation rather than simply meeting; this is the particular intimacy of our relation to Christ. So we speak of a *real presence*. This term cannot apply simply to certain "elements" and be set before us as a kind of abstraction. Real presence is nothing abstract. It is a living reality; it is a word we hear and a love we know and feel, and this is why St. Paul called "the cup of blessing" and "the bread which we break," a participation (1 Cor. 10:16).

The comprehension of this realism is necessary to the sacramental event. Knowing this, and fearful that the liturgy will not be the kingdom scene it is meant to be, the presiding ministers sometimes interpose themselves with running commentary, hoping thereby to keep the service lively, or they add the kinds of "interpretive" actions to interest us and let us know what is supposed to be going on. Some of this can be helpful; mostly it just gets in the way. Nothing substitutes for a simple liturgy where the kingdom parable is central and clear, which is understood and carefully prepared by presiding ministers and lay leaders, who *know* that what is happening is an event of the real presence of Christ, and whose convincing invitation and leadership is prepared by an inner life of faith and prayer. Real means *real*.

2. Church

We only interrupt ourselves, and redundantly, to bring "church" into the discussion of what is essential. It is obviously already in the discussion. (The fact is that none of the four summary categories we are lifting up has any separate existence. They are only points of emphasis.)

St. Paul tells us that a sacrament can do more harm than good, that it can be even a profanity (1 Cor. 11:17, 27).[32] Many Christians obviously believe this; they will come to the Lord's Supper, for instance, and not participate because they believe, for one reason or another, that they are not worthy to receive the holy food. The reasons usually given are highly personal. The reasons St. Paul gives are highly social. They are about divisions in the church. The profanity he sees is eating and drinking "without discerning the body" (1 Cor. 11:29). When you read further in First Corinthians, you know that "body" refers not only to the bread of eucharist but also to the people of eucharist. It is a metaphor that unites the subject and the object of the sacrament. When subject and object fall apart it is never only a personal matter it is always a *communal* matter. It is a situation where we cannot see one another because we have not discerned the real presence. When we can discern the real presence, we can see one another because we cannot be abstracted from this presence. Our communion is in this real presence. This is the whole burden of St. Paul's argument (1 Cor. 11-13).

We need to approach this matter exactly as St. Paul did, with realism. If he speaks of an ideal, it is not to theorize but to be thoroughly realistic. He knows the problems of the Corinthian church; he is very clear about them; he accepts their human differences; but he calls them into a kind of unity, without which there can be no church. Their "liturgical" problem, he tells them in effect, is that they have no real communion. It comes down in his mind to a matter of love. If they will be in love in Christ, they will be in love with one another.

We should not say about this conclusion, "Impossible ideal!" That stifles everything. We should say, rather, "This is what it is *really* all about," and then set to work. Juan Segundo makes the crucial point when he writes, "The signification of the church does not depend on some sort of impersonal unanimity . . . but it does depend on a communitarian activity that points toward unity."[33] This means that, like St. Paul we accept, even glory in, the different gifts and graces— yes, foibles—of our brothers and sisters, but refuse to accept the blindness in "church" "which allows people to call themselves Christians even when nothing unites them with each other."[34] The primary item on the liturgical agenda of any congregation should be *mutuality.*

An essential understanding of sacrament knows that it is its nature to be "activity that points toward unity." Such knowledge colors entirely the way we go about every sacrament, and each must be carefully thought through toward this end. We know, for instance, that the eucharist is, at heart, a meal and that a meal wants to be convivial. But mostly we manage eucharist in styles where few are apt to meet one another in the solemn and stylized event. Indeed, the eucharist may not be a jolly dinner party, but it does not have to be doleful and lonesome either. Its origins as kingdom-meal can dictate the character of the event. And this need not be a small and intimate occasion. A large crowd can be a truly human meeting, as we have all witnessed on television, seeing the eucharist celebrated amid the throng before St. Peter's Basilica in Rome. Every sacrament has its own unique potential as a human meeting in the real presence. When we say "To you is given the *mysterion* of the kingdom of God," we need to know the "you" is *you-plural.*

3. World

The world was created as the "matter," the material of one all-embracing eucharist, and man was created as the priest of this cosmic sacrament.[35]

This "vision" of sacrament articulated by Alexander Schmemann ought to be before us as a prolegomenon to every sacramental event. We should be brash enough to believe that every isolated "time" of *mysterion-sacramentum* is part of the transformation of the world. Our perennial temptation is to the kind of timidity which keeps the "sense" and practice of sacrament within the axis of Christ-church. It is then a rhythm of family ceremonies and a kind of rescue operation which provides the respite of the sacred as deliverance from the secular. This is *not* what the whole business is really about. The signs of sacrament, like bread, wine, and water, and the human actions of sacrament, like the loving pledge of a man and a woman, or the "touch" of healing words—these *things* speak loudly to us about the conversion of what is *nature* and what is *human* by the mystery of the God who comes to us to change us and our world. The very fact of the sacraments and their *mundane* focus on what is essential in life is eloquent testimony about the *mysterion* of God alive in the world as transforming power.

In the essay by Theodore Runyon, which we quoted on this topic in chapter 2, he arrives at a point which he admits it is surprising for a Protestant to make, namely, that in the doctrine of transubstantiation there is one element "that is well worth retaining, the emphasis upon transformation and change."[36] Runyon is not interested in the medieval theories, of course. He is concerned to underline that "where the kingdom breaks through, even provisionally, it brings change in this world."[37] This means that "a sacrament that mediates the power of the new age in Christ must be affected at its very core by the kingdom reality of which it is a part."[38] This is the heart of the matter and brings us exactly to the point of this chapter. Every sacrament is at its core exactly a kingdom-enactment. It is the job of the ministers of sacrament to let this fact be eloquent in the assembly of Christians. This means that we must have the wit to connect the signs of sacrament with their correspondences in our sacred kingdom-story and with their correspondences in our human lives *and* in the world which is the context of our living.

All of the sacramental signs are indicators of transformation, of the holy redeeming the mundane: ordinary water is means for the washing away of evil and the appearance of God's newness; bread is life; oil is balm of Spirit; the love of a man and a woman becomes covenant; work becomes vocation. These are wonder-working signs, like the miracles of the gospels. But like those "wonders," they are, as Runyon puts it, "never ends in themselves but parables of the kingdom. The focus is not upon change for its own sake but for the kingdom's sake.

This change is at one and the same time the transformation of the world and the empowering of the sanctified world to be the bearer of Christ to as many as will receive him; it is the proleptic renewal of the order of creation and the reconciliation of humankind through his body."[39] This is not a matter of theory. It is a matter of speaking, hearing, singing, standing, bowing, kneeling, processing, signing, dancing, praying, pledging; it is a matter of sacrament in multiple gestures of commitment which shape, as action parables, God's kingdom in the world where God's entrance is transforming power.

This *eschatological* interpretation, Runyon maintains, "seeks to follow the arrow of God's intention through to its ultimate goal as Jesus enunciated it, that kingdom where God's will is done as it was intended to be in creation."[40] Sacraments "rethought in terms such as these . . . can speak more directly to our contemporaries who are at a loss to know how worship illumines the larger world in which they live, and who seek for their own lives a more ultimate context within which to understand and practice the responsibility for the world which they feel."[41]

4. Symbol

> Grace has countless signs, countless efficacious signs. But a community recognizes its unity and commitment in those signs that turn it back to its origins.[42]

The sign-acts which are sacraments, the water, the bread and wine, the healing touch, the approving touch, the reconciling word and sign, the vows and commitments are parabolic dramas of the most basic meanings of Christian faith. They are, we have tried to say, primary kingdom of God involvements. With this in mind we need to realize that we do not perform the sacraments; they, so to speak, *perform us.* Again, it is Juan Segundo who makes this point best: "What the church does, her labors, are not sacraments; rather, it is the sacraments that fashion human beings into a church."[43]

Knowing this makes every difference in the way in which sacraments happen. It means, for instance, that the minister of sacrament will plan carefully to allow the sign-act of each sacrament to be clear, to be involving, and to dominate the liturgy. We have all been a part of sacramental occasions where the actual event of sacrament was inconsequential and where a "side-show" of one kind or another became the main event. This can happen in a grandiose way where one event swallows another, or it can happen in a simple and subtle way, such as baptizing using a rose to christen. The rose as symbol obscures and confuses water as symbol. The result is a profound sentimentalizing of the event of baptism.

An essential understanding of sacrament knows that its sign-acts well up from primary creative moments in the manifesting of *mysterion* and trusts these symbols to communicate and include.

5. Commitment

Jesus tells us that we live in relation to the kingdom of God in an emergency requiring decision. He tells a story of a man who gave a great supper and invited guests (Mt. 22:1-14; Lk. 14:16-24, Thomas 64). He sent his servant to these guests who were invited and they made excuses. He invited instead "the poor and maimed and blind and lame" (Lk. 14:21) and announced, "none of those men who were invited shall taste my banquet" (Lk. 14:24). The message is clear: "decide *now.*" The strange story of the wretched unjust steward, who, faced with disaster had the wit to *decide now* (Lk. 16:1-13), makes the same point. Luke climaxes the story with these words of Jesus: "No servant can serve two masters; for either he will hate the one and love the other, or he will be devoted to the one and despise the other. You cannot serve God and mammon." It is a primary quality of the kingdom: "Decide now."

It is a primary quality of sacraments that they are small dramas of decision.

> Every Christian sacrament . . . offers opportunity for us to identify the meaning of our experience in terms of the Gospel of death and resurrection and to commit ourselves to God in faith. It is the inherent quality of sacrament as a sign-act that it is a human gesture of commitment—the affirmation, or reaffirmation of an intention.[44]

To say that sacrament is an event of the family of Jesus does not mean that it is a role-play of the righteous who can go through their family ceremonies secure in the abundance of the house. It is ever the nature of the kingdom's advent in real presence that it can undermine our security, our comfortable truce with the world, and present us suddenly, brusquely, before our loving, yet demanding Lord, who sets before us an unavoidable requirement: "Decide now."

An essential understanding of sacrament knows that it is commitment and will not let its presentment and enactment proceed without the careful underlining of this "evangelical" dimension.[45] An essential understanding does not guarantee a lively and redemptive sacramental life in any gathering of Christians. It is but a prelude to careful preparation, and much human interaction in planning and enacting. But it is the *sine qua non* of these things. Our cleverness is legendary; it frequently gets way ahead of our basic understandings.

Notes

1. Alexander Schmemann, *For the Life of the World* (Crestwood, N.Y.: St. Vladimir's Seminary Press, 1973), p. 26.
2. Raymond Vaillancourt, *Toward a Renewal of Sacramental Theology* (Collegeville, Minn.: The Liturgical Press, 1979), p. 72.
3. Jürgen Moltmann, *The Church in the Power of the Spirit* (New York: Harper & Row, 1977), p. 204.
4. Gerhard Ebeling, *On Prayer* (Philadelphia: Fortress, 1966), pp. 61-70.
5. Aidan Kavanagh, "Life Cycle Events, Civil Ritual and the Christian"; David Power, "The Odyssey of Man in Christ," *Concilium 112: Liturgy and Human Passage* (New York: Seabury Press, 1979).
6. Norman Perrin, *Jesus and the Language of the Kingdom* (Philadelphia: Fortress, 1976), p. 55.
7. Paul Ricoeur, "Listening to the Parables: Once More Astonished," *Christianity and Crisis* 34, (1975) p. 306.
8. Ibid., p. 305.
9. Ibid.
10. John Dominic Crossan, *In Parables* (New York: Harper & Row, 1973).
11. Herbert Fingarette, *The Self in Transformation* (New York: Basic Books, 1963), p. 22.
12. Joachim Jeremias, *The Parables of Jesus* (New York: Charles Scribners and Sons, 1963); Madeleine Boucher, *The Parables* (Wilmington, Del.: Michael Glazier, 1981); Neal Fisher, *The Parables of Jesus: Glimpses of the New Age* (Nashville: Womens' Division, Board of Global Ministries, United Methodist Church, 1979); Norman Perrin, *Rediscovering the Teaching of Jesus* (New York: Harper & Row, 1967), p. 83.
13. Schmemann, *For the Life of the World*, p. 82.
14. Cf. James F. White, *Christian Worship in Transition* (Nashville: Abingdon Press, 1976), p. 35.
15. Quad Redemptoris nostri conspicuum fuit in sacramenta transivit. Quoted in Geoffrey Wainwright, *Doxology* (New York: Oxford University Press, 1980), p. 71. Serm. 74, 2, PL 54,398.
16. This is a matter of considerable debate. Cf. Dennis C. Smolarski, *Eucharistia: A Study of the Eucharistic Prayer* (New York: Paulist Press, 1982), p. 25ff. & p. 99ff.
17. William J. Bausch, *A New Look at the Sacraments* (Notre Dame, Ind.: Fides/Claretian, 1977), p. 6f.
18. Juan Luis Segundo, *The Sacraments Today* (New York: Orbis, 1974), p. 7; Jürgen Moltmann, *The Church in the Power of the Spirit* (New York: Harper & Row, 1977), p. 205. Moltmann makes his point in these words: "Even if the church is termed the fundamental 'sacrament,' the thing that makes it so

points beyond itself. 'The eschatologically victorious grace of God' leads the church beyond its own present existence into the world and drives it toward the perfected kingdom of God." P. 205. Moltmann's contention in his innovative trinitarian hypothesis is for a primacy of *Spirit*.

19. Segundo, *The Sacraments Today*, p. 82.

20. Ricoeur, "Listening to the Parables: Once More Astonished," p. 306.

21. Edward Yarnold, *The Awe-Inspiring Rites of Initiation* (London: St. Paul Publications, 1972).

22. Ronald L. Grimes, "Modes of Ritual Necessity," *Worship* 53 (1979), p. 141.

23. Robert Hovda, *Strong, Loving and Wise* (Washington, D.C., The Liturgical Conference, 1976), p. 73.

24. Edward Schillebeeckx, *Christ, the Sacrament of the Encounter with God* (New York: Sheed and Ward, 1963).

25. Odo Casel, *The Mystery of Christian Worship* (Westminster, Md.: Newman, 1962).

26. P. T. Forsyth, *The Church and the Sacraments* (London: Independent Press, 1917).

27. Ibid., p. 141.

28. Ibid.

29. Cf. Laurence H. Stookey, *Baptism: Christ's Act in the Church* (Nashville: Abingdon, 1982), p. 178, p. 72ff.

30. Robert Jenson, *Visible Words* (Philadelphia: Fortress, 1978), p. 47.

31. One of the best statements of the central importance of this idea is the book, *Memory and Hope* (New York: Macmillan, 1967), by Dietrich Ritschl. It is an essay in the history of this idea; criticizes the Augustinian heritage and applauds Greek patristic thought. His definition of *Christus Praesens:* "He is that 'power' or 'interest' (formally speaking) which makes the church see that it is taken into possession, used in service, invited to hope; and this 'power' is called Christ because the church recognizes it in no one else than the one whom it remembers as the earthly priest Jesus of Nazareth and whom it expects in the future, though in no other terms than those of the promises of the past." P. 218.

32. Cf. Segundo, *The Sacraments Today*, p. 99.

33. Ibid., p. 10.

34. Ibid.

35. Schmemann, *For the Life of the World*, p. 15.

36. Theodore Runyon, "The World as the Original Sacrament," *Worship* 54 (1980), p. 505.

37. Ibid., p. 506.

38. Ibid.

39. Ibid.

40. Ibid., p. 511.

41. Ibid.

42. Segundo, *The Sacraments Today*, p. 99.

43. Ibid., p. 44.

44. Mark Searle, "Journey of Conversion," *Worship* 54 (1980), p. 49.

45. Cf. Segundo, *The Sacraments Today*, p. 96. A volume on sacrament by Regis Duffy is entirely devoted to this dimension of commitment. *Real Presence* (New York: Harper & Row, 1982).

Part II

Sign, Symbol, and Ritual in Human and Faith Development

Chapter 5

Communication, Communion, and Community: Sign and Symbol in Sacramentality

The sacraments have to do with communication, communion, and community. God has chosen to create us as free persons. God, then, enters into communication with us and invites us into the community of love, trust, and justice which we have come to call the kingdom of God. In this estate we are called to have communion with God and with others in spontaneous, joyous, and profound ways. There are many ways God communicates with us. In a sense all of these ways are "sacraments." They are signs or symbols of God's presence. Yet, we usually and properly reserve the word sacrament for certain acts which have come to have deep meaning within our Christian community and through which we have found that our communion with God and others has been clearly extended. Still, as we seek to communicate concerning what these sacraments really are and how we use them in our life together we find that we have many "communication problems" within the Christian community. We like or dislike certain liturgical forms. We fear or affirm various leaders who are seeking to help the wider Christian community to come to common understandings of the sacraments or to find interpretations and practices that will unify approaches to religious education and worship across Protestant, Roman Catholic, and Orthodox communions. Let us seek to sort out some of the communication problems we may be having, discern the varying ways we are using the symbols coming out of our different traditions, seek to discern how the sacraments can be powerful means of extending God's communication with us, and help identify the nature of the community we so much wish to find.

Problems of Communication from the Perspective of Communications Theory

You will note that we used the word *communion* in several different ways in the paragraph above. The word was used to refer to the most profound level of communication with God and others; it was used to refer to the eucharist or the Lord's supper, the particular sacramental act which has become central to our understanding of the depth of God's love for us; it was used to refer to the three major faith groups within Christendom, the Protestant, Roman Catholic, and Orthodox communions.

From the perspective of communications theory, it could be said that the word communion is a symbol which points to something not physically present and allows us to communicate with others employing some common language (in this case, English). If another language is involved we immediately have a new problem of communication and must find some word, action, or sign which will reveal that we are talking about the word communion.

Part of our difficulty in our education and worship life within and between denominations and faith groups can be found in our being insensitive to the different ways we are using the same words or actions. In communication theory, as distinct from theological reflection, it is recognized that all words, actions, facial expressions, sounds, silences, physical arrangements, smells, clothing, hair length, etc., are *symbols* which must be *decoded* by others. All of us use words, actions, physical arrangements to *encode* messages we wish to communicate to others. For instance, suppose you are a Roman Catholic who is used to receiving communion at the altar from a priest who gives you a wafer which has become the body of Christ through the consecration of the priest. If you are invited by a friend to a Disciples of Christ service, and see lay persons giving the communion prayers and serving the grape juice and bread to each person in the pews, conceivably the differences between the two modes of the sacrament will be large enough to prohibit communion with one another and perhaps a sense of communion with God from taking place. These differences in understanding of communion take place because of the communication which has occurred. Theoretically, communication can be defined as what happens when a receiver of a message assigns meaning to it. In other words, persons have to interpret the messages sent to them. When they interpret the words or actions used to send the messages, communication has taken place. It may not be the communication *intended* by the sender, but a level of communication has taken place.[1]

In order for accurate communication to take place, persons need to have two-way communication about the meaning of the symbols used. If this dialogue is held in an atmosphere of trust and openness the two persons may check out how they are perceiving the various symbols (grape juice instead of wine, laity giving the prayers instead of the priest, serving the elements in the pew instead of going to the altar). In the dialogue the two persons come to recognize that the different outward forms are pointing to and helping them participate in the same quality of communication with God, and helping each to receive God's forgiveness, love, and continuing sense of presence and to feel renewed and strengthened for ministries of love and care within and beyond the immediate faith community. The larger and deeper the communication about the meanings of the different symbols the greater the sense of community may become. On the other hand, communication which is honest may well identify deep-running differences in interpretations concerning the nature of God, the church, Christ, and the meaning of life itself.

Part of the risk of communication, whether in informal ways between two friends, or in deliberate educational efforts, or in experimental ecumenical worship, is the identification of conflicting views and feelings about which we may need to enter into a new level of communication. For instance, within the same denomination but in different congregations we find very different *inferences* coming from the use of the same sacramental rituals. Congregations develop unique patterns which lead people to say, "We have always done it this way!" These patterns become *codes* by which the people involved communicate. Those within the congregation are reared to understand the *code words* and *actions*. Those on the outside of that congregation do not *decode* the words or actions in the same way. Also, many pastors discover quickly that they must become aware of these unique codes in order to communicate with persons within a particular congregation.

In seminars we have conducted concerning baptism and confirmation we have found many illustrations of local church patterns which were in conflict with the interpretations and teachings of the denomination or faith group as a whole. For instance, infant baptism is normative within the United Methodist Church. Several pastors, nevertheless, have shared that they were baptized as many as two or even three times prior to their decision to prepare for ordained ministry. When these stories were analyzed it became clear that these persons had been in congregations with varying practices at different points in their spiritual pilgrimages. These patterns were serially supportive of baptism as infants by sprinkling, a second baptism as an adolescent at the time of confirmation (again by sprinkling), and then a third baptism by immersion as a young adult after a conversion experience during an evangelistic crusade. All of these baptisms were seen as meaningful in the spiritual development of such persons. Each was viewed as a sacrament in which the person experienced communion with God and others. Yet, theologically, baptism in the United Methodist Church is seen as a one-time engrafting of the persons into the body of Christ and not as a repeatable sacrament. Here again, we see communication problems for those involved in education concerning the teachings of the church as well as for those making decisions concerning liturgical services appropriate in the various stages of development throughout life.

Very often the communication problems have to do with encoding and decoding through music, location of elements, garb of clergy and laity, degree of emotion, style of leadership (formal or informal, personal or impersonal, intimate or distant) of the ministering person. These matters may seem to be secondary, but are very important aspects of the communication of the gospel through the sacraments.

The Importance of Learning More Adequate Interpretive Codes: Lessons from Semiotics

One of the major needs in our communication concerning the sacraments is the recognition that everyone understands and internalizes the experience of a particular sacrament through the lense of an interpretive code. We have just illustrated how we learn these ways of interpreting our experience through participation in a particular family, a particular church, and through reflection on our experiences. Certain primary and secondary symbols of our faith are decoded in a somewhat predictable way (i.e., an interpretive code—certain meanings and feelings we have come to have for certain words and actions in baptism or communion, for instance). Semiotics, usually understood as the study of signs, has in fact become the study of codes, according to Robert Scholes. Semiotics, coming out of the work of Ferdinand de Saussare in linguistics and Charles S. Peirce in philosophy, has helped us see that we are never dealing with reality in a final way but always with systems of signs which become codes through which we capture the meaning of our lives and communicate our understandings and feelings about ourselves, others, and ultimate reality.

The study of semiotics is important for our approach to the sacraments and their significance for us as persons. One of our tasks in religious education and in liturgy is to help older children, youth, and adults not only acquire the interpretive codes of their particular faith community but increasingly be able to see them as codes. We need to help persons see the liturgical text (and actions which go with it) as "the product of a person or persons, at a given point in human history, in a given form of discourse, taking its meaning from the interpretive gestures of individual readers, using the grammatical, semantic, and cultural codes available to them. A text always echoes other texts, and it is the result of choices that have displaced still other possibilities."[2] In other words, persons should be taught, not only more adequate and engaging codes, but also that these codes are, in fact, *interpretive codes* (signs and symbols which have come out of particular past experiences of the faithful along with several layers of interpretation by creators of the liturgical forms of the sacraments, by teachers of the meaning of the sacraments, and countless previous interpretations of participants). Such a recognition should not rob us of the power of the sacraments. Rather, such effort should help protect us from the tendency to idolatrize the *form* of the sacrament or the persons celebrating the sacrament. In this way we can break through to a lively response to the living God.

Semiotics as a field of study alerts us to the importance of the clarity of the words, actions, music, style of communication of the sender, the truth and relevance of the messages we send, the importance of the preparation of the receiver to decode accurately, and the freeing of the receiver to interpret and become an active creator of meanings and attitudes, the crucial nature of the feedback of the receiver to the sender, the essential nature of the meanings already present in the context (a particular local church), and the quality of the contact between senders and receivers (liturgical leaders and participants). There is an implied broadening of the integrity of interpretations while, at the same time, a recognition of the authenticity of the history of past practices and beliefs. Persons cannot interpret particular sacraments just any way they please without reference to past valued interpretations and without sensitivity to current feelings and views of participants. Our religious education concerning the sacraments should help persons become exposed to varying interpretive codes (alternative understandings and experiences of the sacraments) and to increase their awareness of the codes by which they are living, with the goal of helping them experience the richness of varying codes and also to test and refine their own codes of interpretation. This can be done in a way which illumines the understandings, deepens the commitment, and stimulates the participation in creative and fresh forms of expression in an atmosphere of reverent experimentation or playfulness. (See chapter 6.) Such openness can keep us sensitive to the mystery which is present after our best efforts to refine an interpretive code which relates our personal and corporate lives to the great liturgical celebrations of the faith community.

Distinctions Concerning Symbols and Signs and their Significance for Sacramental Life

When we teach images concerning how God communicates with us we must be very careful to be honest about what we are doing. We are not teaching others, or showing others in some definite way, what God is like. We may say with conviction what we believe God has revealed to us, but God is a mystery at the deepest level. Schillebeeckx's description is helpful. God is an "identified mystery which still remains a mystery."[3] Schillebeeckx rejoices that Christ has revealed the heart of the mystery which is God and that Christ in this sense has made visible the nature of God's character and will as the primordial sacrament. In this rejoicing Schillebeeckx recognizes our finite limitations and God's infinite life which always transcends our ability to comprehend.

In seeking to communicate about God's actions among us we use both signs and symbols, but at the deepest level we employ symbols. God transcends all of our efforts to conceptualize divine nature; the object of theology is never God but religious symbols which we use to point to and help us participate in the life of faith which relates us to God. This distinction helps us remember that when we talk about the "identified mystery" which is God there is still mystery left. Such an attitude can greatly enhance our communication about the sacraments or other religious symbols which we use in our different traditions. As Tad Guzie says so well, we need to learn how to befriend our symbols.

While "sign" and "symbol" are often used interchangeably it is important to identify that they have more precise definitions. *Signs*, according to Susanne Langer, indicate meanings which we want to convey. The red light indicates that we should stop. Signs, curiously enough, need to be precise so that we will not make mistakes. However, from culture to culture signs can change their meaning. For instance black clothing can be worn for mourning in some cultures and white clothing in others. The sign of mourning changes. The reality of mourning does not. There are *natural* signs such as wet streets which indicate that it has rained (pointing to a wider state of affairs) and there are *artificial* signs such as a blowing of a whistle or the waving of a flag to indicate that a train is about to leave. In discussing sacraments we sometimes use the language of sign. We say that communion is a sign of Christ's death and resurrection or that sacraments are "outward and visible *signs* of an inward and spiritual grace." While this language is understandable it is more helpful to think of sacraments in symbolic terms.

Symbols, according to Langer in her classic study, "are not proxy for their objects, but are vehicles for the conception of objects. To conceive a thing or a situation is not the same thing as to 'react toward it' overtly, or to be aware of its presence. In talking about things we have conceptions of them, not the things themselves; and it is the conceptions not the things that symbols directly 'mean.' "[4] A symbol leads us to conceive or imagine an object or event. It is not concerned necessarily with direct action in the way that the sign must always be. Rather it stimulates us to imagination and thought. Langer believed that there was "no one to one correspondence between symbol and conception, but there are patterns of correspondence which govern the relation between the two and prevent the connection being purely arbitrary and ephemeral."[5] In respect to the sacrament of communion there are those who wish to adjust to the realities of cultures where the common drink does not include the fruit of the grape (either in its natural state or as wine). People in such cultures sometimes select other elements to symbolize the giving of the body and blood of Christ and our thanksgiving as a community of believers. At one level the common elements of any culture which are employed at a simple meal are precisely what Jesus was employing in the last supper. At another level, the elements of bread and wine have identified with them many conceptualizations which have come out of the Christian tradition. It is the possible loss of those understandings and meanings which is being protected by those who resist making the bread and wine into mere *signs*. This question is raised in the World Council of Churches' study of the sacraments by African and Asian Christians when they wish to substitute other elements for the bread and wine.[6] In Langer's categories, the issue is whether or not the deeper meanings of communion can be captured by *presentational symbols* (which evoke new experiences and may break certain recognized rules in order that new forms may be created) or must remain in line with *discursive symbols* (which bear a recognized meaning and obey well-established rules).

One well-known student of symbol, Paul Tillich, maintained that it is the essence of a religious symbol that it actually *participates in the power it symbolizes*. According to Tillich, "the symbol is not a mere convention as is a sign. It grows organically. . . . The symbol opens up a stratum of reality, of meaning and Being which otherwise we could not reach; and in doing so, it participates in that which it opens. And it does not only open up a stratum of reality, it also opens up the corresponding stratum of the mind. Symbols open us, so to speak, in two directions—in the direction of reality and in the direction of the mind." This means that symbols grow out of the life of any community of faith in which meanings are deepening as they are shared. In this sense, Tillich stated, symbols of religious power cannot be invented. "They are always the result of 'a creative encounter with reality.' They are born out of such an encounter; they die if this encounter ceases. They are not invented and they cannot be abolished."[7] Tillich kept the mystery in his view of religious symbols when he said that such symbols point to and participate in ultimate reality but that

> the ultimate transcends all levels of reality, it is the ground of reality itself. It transcends all levels of meaning itself. But in order to express it, we must use the material of our daily encounter. . . . Therefore, religious symbols take their material from all realms of life, from all experiences—natural, personal, historical.[8]

Tillich was forceful in his call to Protestants to balance their passion for symbol breaking (which has been a dominant concern in order to reform Christian faith) with a deepening of their understanding of the healing and creative power of religious symbols in the pilgrimage of faith. He guarded against making symbol into an idol when he observed that religious symbols come from the world of finite things but they point to the ground of being and meaning, to "being itself and meaning itself. . . . The religious symbol participates in the holiness of that to which it points, that is, to the holy itself. . . . A holy book, a holy building, a holy rite, a holy person. They are not themselves the holy; they are not the ultimate concern," but they are more than signs. "They not only point beyond themselves to something else, they also participate in the power of that to which they point."[9]

Any renewal of sacramental life in the church will take place in relation to the profound meanings which have grown organically within the community of faith. In sacramental experiences the meaning appears through participation in the symbol. It is, of course, absolutely crucial that the symbol be perceived *as symbol* positively for the sacrament to work and negatively that the sacrament not fall into the danger that "in sacramental holiness . . . the holy is identified with that which is the hearer of the holy. When this happens religion relapses into magic."[10]

There is indeed a quiet revolution within the church concerning the power of the symbolic to meet the deeper spiritual hunger present in the lives of people. One of the reasons for this is the recognition that persons in a technological society are under great threat to their mental security. As Susanne Langer saw in the 1950s, the new way of living "has made the old nature-symbols alien to our minds, and the new modes of working have made our personal activity often meaningless and unacceptable to the imagination."[11] Since this was written we have seen a movement to recover the natural, to emphasize ecological stewardship. She suggests that we are hungry for new symbols of depth and meaning which transcend the scientific symbols being used (which are often barren of ultimate meaning).

Many of these "new" symbols may be able to come from our oldest, most unconscious ones. This is the hope of many who are working on the deeper issues in communication.

F. W. Dillistone, for instance, wrestled with the implication of Carl Jung's depth psychological studies and specifically his view of the power of symbols to reach the unconscious levels of human life. Jung found universal symbols which transcended all cultures and times, symbols repeatedly present in our dreams, myths, and practices. He found in culture after culture the hero figures, the child wonder, the virgin, the witch, the temptress, the evil force, the saving element. Jung chastized Protestants for throwing away or rationalizing many of these powerful symbols. Dillistone agrees, saying that "the power of the archetypal images is too great to be rendered null and void by any process of deliberate exclusion. If they are not sanctified with the Christian context they will almost certainly present themselves in demonic forms." Speaking of the deep-running archetypal power of water, in all cultures (with its life giving and taking powers), Dillistone maintains, for instance, that "to find a way of allowing baptism to exercise its power within the Christian community at the deepest levels of the human psyche is one of the most urgent tasks of our day."[12] Indicating correctly that the machine model of reality is not acceptable for modern men and women, he calls for a deepening of the communications model from interpersonal and intercultural to communication and communion with God and others, employing the natural symbols coming out of every culture but also employing the religious symbols of our Christian community which speak universally to the human condition of every person. This must be done while recognizing the normal problems of communication. This means we must increase our ability to encode our messages of love, trust, and justice, communicating the Christian gospel in ways which recognize differing perceptions of persons from different backgrounds and experiences. We need to stop from time to time and ask people to say what is happening to them in our liturgies, how they are understanding what is going on, how they feel about what they are experiencing, what differences our sacramental expressions are making in their lives. Our communication is enhanced as we provide many opportunities for feedback and perception checks between persons, recognizing the differing contexts and code systems, the different feelings and attitudes we bring so that the decoding of meaning will help us get to core meanings with which we may all identify. Hopefully, we may do this while still maintaining an openness to new meanings, an awe before the mystery which always transcends our efforts to communicate, commune, and to discover community.

Moving to Primary and Core Meanings Through Sacramental Life

Symbols are dangerous as well as inspiring. They can lead us into emotional highs or into depression. We tend to accept or reject them with feeling. In short, we always bring ourselves (our feelings about ourselves, our personal self-affirmations or our self-doubts, our likes and dislikes from the past concerning various forms or expressions, our positive and negative feelings concerning the people in the congregation or the pastoral leadership) to the symbolism present in the sacramental experience. We often get "turned off," as we say, by seemingly unimportant factors so that the essential or core meanings of faith, love, forgiveness, thanksgiving, or renewal are not experienced. Then we tend to complain about the presence or absence of certain symbols which have always disturbed us or which we come expecting to find. Again, our feelings about participation in communion, baptism, or other sacraments are reflective of complications of communications at one level or another. Tad Guzie has made an additional distinction concerning symbolism and sacramental life which may provide a way for us to keep our focus on the core or essential meanings while, at the same time, free us to improve or reform our sacramental liturgies and our educational interpretations.

He speaks about *primary* and *secondary* symbolism present in the sacraments. For instance, examples of primary symbolism, in respect to the eucharist or communion, are the actions of eating and drinking and the accompanying words and gestures which help us participate in the supper with the Lord. Examples of secondary symbolism, in respect to the eucharist, are the symbols which have built up over the years around the primary symbols which various people have thought would enhance the core meaning. These secondary symbols are altar location, candles, crosses, prayers, readings, processions, gestures, music, color, dress, the arrangement and design of the church building itself. Most of us are helped or hurt in our response to the sacrament itself by our positive or negative identification with secondary symbolism. It is Guzie's opinion that, especially within Roman Catholicism, "most of the liturgical changes over the last decade or so have had to do with eliminating secondary symbolism which detracted from the primary, and replacing it with ritual activity which would once again focus on the core. Most of the symbolism of the old Roman rite was calculated to call attention to the *objects* of bread and wine; the new rite stresses the *action* of a faith community which is celebrating its redemption."[13]

What is the core meaning of communion, for instance? We have asked this question of persons in various workshops we have conducted with Protestant, Roman Catholic, and Orthodox backgrounds, and they have answered the question with words or phrases such as: "a feeling of thanksgiving for God's love to me in Christ," "forgiveness," "a remembering of what Christ has done for me," "knowing the depth of God's love for the human family," "renewal of my faith," "being strengthened to participate in Christ's ongoing ministries of love and care," and many others. We have found it to be constructive to ask persons what their expectations are concerning the sacrament. Such communication among the pastoral and lay leadership often results in a "focusing in" on the core meanings and feelings in ways which encourage participants to change secondary symbols or eliminate some in order to enhance the primary symbols and the essential meanings. The communication itself creates wider and deeper trust and a richer sense of community. In so doing, participants can study the scriptures, their denominational or faith stances, the more recent history of their own practices. This process itself helps to create the elements of trust, love, honest confrontation of differences, forgiveness, and resolution which become the seedbed for genuine communion with God and others. Such a process is rich religious education as well as preparation for liturgical renewal.

When we push back to the core meaning of communion we find the natural sacrament of the meal and all of the everyday communication which takes place, the sharing of our common lives with one another, and our raising of the deepest questions of the meaning of existence. It is at the meal that we recognize our dependence upon persons and forces other and greater than ourselves from whom the bread and wine of life have come. Families in every culture have sensed the eternal in the midst of this basic experience of preparing and sharing a meal. Jesus did not "institute" a new ritual or call us to a new sacrament. Rather, he recognized the sacramental nature of the meal which his Jewish friends knew so well that they could never forget it. As we have observed, the Jewish meal was always a ritual meal with blessings of bread and wine and thanksgiving prayers at various times during the meal. The meal was a common occasion for deepening relationships, conversation, and mutual discussion of family concerns or work. When Jesus said, "Do this in memory of me," he was pointing to the qualities of communication and communion with God and others which his disciples already knew, and he was reminding them of the communion with God, one another, and all creation which he had brought alive for them and all the world.

It is for this reason that our interpretation of communion keeps returning to the core meaning which is God's presence in our lives through creation (bread and wine) and through our redemption (Christ's giving of his life—body and blood—for all of God's family). Various attempts to capture and preserve this essential reality have focused on the secondary symbols—for instance, whether or not the faithful receive only the bread or both the bread and wine, whether or not lay persons can participate in serving the elements, whether or not communion is served to persons in the pews or only at the altar, whether or not lay persons may serve one another in intimate family-like groups.

Communication at its core focuses on essentials of our relationship with Christ (really allowing him to be present in our lives) or being present to one another (really allowing other persons to share their burdens and their joys with us), and on the discovery that through Christ's gift to us we have experienced God's presence and are in touch with God's will and way as well as in touch with the selves God created us to be.

Today, many Christians would agree with Guzie when he says that "Christ's eucharistic presence is a personal presence, a type of presence which is humanly much more 'real' than mere physical presence. I can be physically present in a room with you; indeed I can be personally present to someone I love even when I am physically absent. . . . People can even make love without being present to each other. At the level of primary symbolism, the kind of presence of which the eucharist speaks cannot be laid out on a table, any more than you or I nail down and take hold of what makes another personally present to us, least of all in intimacies like the act of love. We can say a great deal about what personal presence is *not*, but we can never objectify everything it is."[14]

Guzie moves us beyond the attempt to capture God in our sacramental symbols. He moves us to look at the essential relationships with God and others which the gospel calls us to reenact and personally commit ourselves to extend to all of the human family. We are talking about the real creation of a community of trusting, loving, caring, righteous, honest, confirming, serving, and accepting people throughout our earth and even throughout the universe. Christ came to us because "God so loved the world." The purpose of sharing in any of the sacraments is to strengthen us to be present to God and to one another so that God's life of justice, love, and trust will be born in our midst. When we are clear about the core meanings and experiences we can be more open to changes in the way we communicate or the symbols we accept or reject.

When the gospel, as communicated to us through sacramental symbols, really "hits home" in our lives, we are led into a process "of conflict and change because God calls us to reexamine the purpose of our lives and the use of our time. Religious symbols are God's practical way of inviting us to assess the current position of our lives and the new commitments that may be needed."[15] Regis Duffy reminds us to look critically at our praxis, at what we are actually doing in the liturgical experiences we plan. If we are going through the rites perfunctorily or in a distorted way, we are revealing in the process the real nature of our commitments. For instance, our educational and liturgical praxis will reveal whether or not we really believe in the equality of members of the body of Christ—whether or not women, racial and ethnic minorities, persons of all ages, ordained and lay ministers are all included in the *way* we celebrate the sacraments.

The task of religious education in our churches is to help us look behind the symbols we use to the realities of faith and the life of love and justice which the gospel proclaims. Likewise, liturgical renewal is aimed at helping persons participate (in and through such symbols) in active communication and communion with God and others so that the community of faithful persons will widen and deepen its life.

At the practical level with people in a fast-moving technological world, Guzie notes, "religious educators have found that if they can talk people into making one meal a week a real family meal, a ritual meal with a blessing and a sharing of thanks and a cup of wine passed around the table, catechesis on the eucharist becomes easy sailing."[16] Well, perhaps not "easy" but certainly easier and more in terms of normal communication with one another, communion with God through Christ, and the kind of presence to others and God which creates a divine community.

Notes

1. Robert Hopper and Jack L. Whitehead, Jr., *Communications Concepts and Skills* (San Francisco: Harper & Row, 1979), p. 5.

2. Robert Scholes, *Semiotics and Interpretation* (New Haven, Conn: Yale University Press, 1982), p. 16.

3. Edward Schillebeeckx, *The Understanding of Faith* (New York: Seabury Press, 1974), p. 16.

4. Susanne K. Langer, *Philosophy in a New Key* (Cambridge, Mass.: Harvard University Press, 1942), p. 25.

5. Ibid.

6. This problem is identified but not resolved in the World Council of Churches' study, *Baptism, Eucharist and Ministry*, Faith and Order Paper No. 111 (Geneva: World Council of Churches, 1982), p. 7 and 17. Baptism is also an issue. Some African churches, for instance, practice baptism of the Holy Spirit without water, through the laying on of hands, while also recognizing the baptism by water of other churches.

7. Paul Tillich, "Theology and Symbolism," in *Religious Symbolism*, ed. F. Earnest Johnson (Port Washington, N.Y.: Kennikat Press, 1955), p. 109.

8. Ibid.

9. Ibid., p. 110.

10. Ibid.

11. Langer, *Philosophy in a New Key*, p. 171f.

12. F. W. Dillistone, *Christianity and Symbolism* (London: Collins, 1955), p. 187.

13. Tad Guzie, *Jesus and the Eucharist* (New York: Paulist Press, 1974), p. 110.

14. Ibid., p. 113.

15. Regis Duffy, *Real Presence: Worship, Sacraments and Commitment* (San Francisco: Harper & Row, 1982), pp. 3-6.

16. Guzie, *Jesus and the Eucharist*, p. 58.

Chapter 6

The Importance of Religious Rites and Sacraments in the Stages of Human and Faith Development

To be human is to find rites and ceremonies which celebrate our perception of the meaning and purpose of life. Our rituals start at birth with the rituals around feeding and elimination and continue throughout the stages of our lives to the rituals which celebrate the pains and joys of life and the ultimate meaning we proclaim our lives have had and will have eternally. There are hundreds of rituals in which we participate without thinking very much about them. Some of these rituals reflect our highest hopes and greatest visions and some of them become wooden, even demonic. Protestants, especially in their negative reaction to what they conceived to be the demonic character, for instance, of the sacrament of penance have tended to feel negative about ritual as such. Some of us who have grown up in the Protestant community have prided ourselves on being nonritualistic. We wanted to experience faith directly and not through the power of a priest or the power of a sacrament or rite.

Many Protestants joined the word "dead" with "ritual." We rejected a sacramental system which Catholics and Orthodox curiously retained. We therefore tended to be confused and uncomfortable about the meaningfulness of the two sacraments we accepted. While Catholic and Orthodox communities related the seven sacraments somewhat to the stages of human life and to the human crises and victories of life, Protestants tended to see their sacraments as important to initiate persons into the faith community or to sustain persons in that community but not as much a strengthening of persons throughout the stages of their lives or in the crises of their lives. Moreover, many Protestants have failed to see that as a result of the rejection of the wider use of sacraments they have developed their own rituals which are performing similar functions for persons at the stages of courtship, marriage, birth, child-rearing, relating to society beyond the family, faith-affirming, vocational decisions, dealing with failure and guilt, renewal of one's vision and purpose. This is not to say that the Protestant attempt to reform the unfortunate practices associated with the sacraments was not constructive. It was a signal contribution. However, as is true in most reform movements there were overreactions which are still with us over 400 years later. Fortunately, the recent healthy dialogues among Protestants, themselves, as well as with Roman Catholics and Orthodox concerning the nature of sacramental life auger well for the future. What is needed is more fundamental work on the nature of ritual and the nature of the sacraments in terms of biblical, theological, and ecclesiological sources and how these understandings are related to human and faith development. This must be done in full awareness that we are living in an advanced, fast-moving technological age where the natural symbols and rituals associated with nomadic or agrarian life are no longer as evident or as powerful to us. With this in mind we will look first at the nature of ritual as a way the society projects its vision of the meaning of life to its participants and how ritual is related to sacramental views of life. Then we shall discuss Erik Erikson's understanding of the life-giving power of ritual and his theory of the stages of ritualization in life. Finally, we shall analyze James Fowler's emerging understanding of the nature of faith and the stages of faith development. These analyses will not only open new levels of meaning for sacramental life but also prepare the way for the discussions of specific sacraments in Part III.

The Relation of Ritual and Sacrament

From the point of view of social anthropology, ritual refers to all symbolic behavior and is not limited to actions of people who are associated with religious institutions or traditions. Anthropology studies rituals of greeting, naming, parting, parenting, transition periods in life from birth to death, etc. These rituals express the values of the people involved and tell their story of the purpose of their life together. The rituals are similar from culture to culture but have many unique features which distinguish the particular values and images of each cultural group. In primitive cultures education and ritual are related in much more precise ways to the actual life issues of persons. For instance, there is instruction from parents and wise members of the community concerning many aspects of life which are not dealt with in modern society. Such life issues (which are a part of education and ritual and can be seen in the primitive stories and myths told to the young) include first menstruation, first intercourse, first child-birth, integration into a new family on the part of the female or male, and others. These rites of passage, as Van Gennep called them, are seen in contemporary life as well but often without the natural communication between older and younger members of the community. Much sex education, for instance, takes place covertly and involves communication between more experienced and less experienced members of the youth culture itself. This pattern tends to perpetuate misinformation and destructive "myths" rather than the communication of the positive and deeper meaning of sexuality. Of course, not all primitive images were positive.

There is much research concerning the nature of ritual, symbol, myths, and the interrelationship of these factors in various social structures. There are many agreements and disagreements concerning the nature and meaning of these interrelationships. Victor Turner tends to study the many meanings to be found in a single symbol in a particular ritual depending upon the different situations or contexts in which the symbol is experienced.[1] Claude Levi-Strauss studies the many different symbols which are equated in a single meaning in myth, and he tries to reduce the complex action of a myth to a limited number of recurring themes, to find the basic structures of these themes which have universal application across all cultures.[2] Raymond Firth studies how private symbolism of a unique person who makes a signal contribution can effect public symbolism and conversely how public symbols can change the symbols of private persons. Many social anthropologists would agree with Firth when he says that the symbols involved in various rituals embody mystery and some measure of revelation; but he sees the mystery and revelation as "belonging to the realm of human imagination and human comprehension. Men in their social existence construct and inherit the intellectual and emotional frames in which they set and attribute meaning to the details of the external world."[3]

We are working on a very different thesis: namely, that life is holy at its very base. It is religious in its structures and in the very fabric of the experiences associated with the drama of life from stage to stage. We are saying that the rites of life are not religious because we put religious meaning on them. Rather they are religious because God's spirit is present in all of life; and the sacraments, for instance, are revelatory events illuminating that which *is*.

Such a view is somewhat similar to the position taken earlier by Louis Bouyer. He defined rite as a symbolic action which is religious by its very nature. The rituals of life *are* religious because they participate in the natural flow of God's communication with human beings and in their efforts to have communion with one another, using diverse symbols, myths, stories, and actions to convey their visions of the ultimate meaning of existence. Bouyer says, for instance, that the early church leaders "did not in the least imagine that the rite of eating or of washing was a profane action, bare of any religious significance before Christ's intervention, but upon which He bestowed a particular meaning by a purely arbitrary decision. . . . Truly, traditional theology joins the institution of the sacraments by Christ with the *natural symbolism of washing and eating,* which of itself has a religious significance. . . . The words of institution simply gave a new meaning to rites already charged with meaning. And the new meaning was not forced upon the natural meaning but rather amplified and enriched it."[4]

Bouyer's research in the history of religion and in anthropology brought him to the conclusion that natural rites are the primary stuff of religions and that these rites are the essential *sacraments* on which all later *sacramentalia* (such as the seven sacraments of Christianity with their divine symbolism) are based. Fundamentally, he believed that prayer is the primary human response to the mysteries of life; then, natural rituals of eating, washing, etc. developed. Quickly, myths were developed not to explain the rites so much as to expand them imaginatively. Myths were symbolic of the transcendence already present in the rite. Soon humans felt the need to identify sacred space, places natural or constructed in which they could celebrate their sense of the presence of the deities. Bouyer differs from Van der Leeuw who saw two levels of ritual—one in which a properly divine action was present (mysterium tremendum) and the second in which the ordinary actions of human life were later brought into the sacral sphere (mysterium fascinans). Bouyer sees these two levels as interrelated and inseparable. Bouyer's interpretation of the evidence is convincing when he concludes that "rites are not actions that are themselves more or less indifferent and which have been by sheer compulsion impregnated with a meaning for which they were in no way prepared. They are themselves meaningful actions. A ritual action, far from being a late offspring of a highly intellectualized religion that has to have recourse to gestures to regain contact with the simple-minded, is the most spontaneous and original manifestation of religion. From this ritual action, the later notions about the religion itself are gradually derived. A living rite is not something that has been coldly worked out so that religious ideas which have been put together in the quiet of one's study may have some external manifestations. It is an immediate primordial creation of religiously minded persons in which they have actively realized their effective connection with the divinity before they explain this connection to themselves."[5]

These ideas are similar to those of the Orthodox theologian Alexander Schmemann. As we have noted in chapter 1, he sees our essential human nature to be that of "homo adorans." It is our natural, not supernatural, response to life to see the whole world as a gift from God. Our natural response is to adore God, to receive the gifts of the natural world as a priest who utters prayers of thanksgiving, blesses the gifts, and distributes them justly to all of God's family. The "universal priesthood" has its base in our essential nature. Schmemann sees no spiritual superstructure in life or in the scriptures. To him, the Bible tells a story of God giving human beings the gifts of this world as "communion with God. The world as man's food is not something 'natural' and limited to natural functions, thus being different from, and opposed to, the specifically 'spiritual' functions by which man is related to God. All that exists is God's gift to man, and it all exists to make God known to man, to make man's life communion with God."[6]

This view is not naive concerning the mission of the church to extend God's love to all persons or to reform social structures which have become inhuman or dehumanizing. It does base such evangelical or social efforts on a vision of the religious life which is fully involved in this world as God's eucharist, God's common table to which each of us is a guest and a priest to others in Christ's sacrificial but joyous spirit of love and justice.

The major problem with the thought of these ecumenical thinkers who see God's grace in all of the natural order to which Christ's gift of wholeness and salvation point and in which it is fulfilled is this: We are now living in a technological age in which we are seemingly "creating" new forms of life "artificially." With our research into the very structures of life, the DNA research which is helping us rearrange genetic life, with test-tube babies and attempts to design synthetic forms of human-machine life, we are increasingly separated from the purely natural rituals of life. As Gerard Pottebaum observed at a religious education conference to which persons from other world religions were invited, technological advances were threatening the religious faith of many present. A religious sect, for instance, in Thailand was preparing to celebrate in their liturgical year the season of the Moon-god when they were told the Americans had set foot on the moon. They were angered and distraught. The conclusion of the conference members was that with every technological advance we experience a sense of loss and are forced, as were the members of the Thailand sect, to reinterpret our religious beliefs and find fresh ritual forms to carry our new visions of reality.[7] It is our belief, however, that such reinterpretations will be less traumatic and more enriching of the human pilgrimage of faith if we see God's unfolding purpose and presence in our efforts to penetrate even more of the mystery which is God's universe of infinite love and meaning. If we do not have a sacred-secular, material-spiritual split, we may be less threatened and can see the importance of finding new forms for our widened visions. However, these rites will still have to be grounded in the natural elements of life out of which all new creations themselves will have to come. If not, the rituals will not feed the human family of the future and will become wooden or demonic.

In keeping with the theme that our rituals portray our vision of the values and beliefs of a people and that these rituals are extensions of a sacramental view of the very nature of life, we will now turn to the findings concerning the stages of human and faith development from birth to death and how the rituals of life can be kept healthy. When the rituals cease to reflect a vision of life which is in harmony with the gospel of God's love and care for all of life, they are in need of revitalization so that our vision of the ultimate meaning of life is not lost but kept alive and open to the pulses of change which are coming so rapidly in our world.

The Stages of Ritualization and the Sacramental Nature of Life

The most exciting and innovative work on the stages of ritualization has been done by Erik Erikson. He has studied children at play and in their interactions with their parents and peers. Also, he has analyzed the normal, daily rituals which take place during six major stages of human development from infancy to adulthood. It is his strong conclusion that the human family communicates its various visions of reality, its beliefs, values, and world views via these rituals of life. Such rituals (related to eating, washing, naming, elimination, dress, right and wrong, and others) reveal the way we "look at" or see life. Rituals which are life affirming and which incorporate the purpose of life envisioned by a society point to an underlying sacramental view of life. In this ethos can be found a numinous quality which permeates the group's consciousness and blesses the individual in his or her quest for personal identity and some sense of ultimate meaning. Rituals which become compulsive or legalistic for individuals or the group become hurtful and dehumanizing. Such ritual Erikson calls *ritualism*.

The reason rituals become legalistic and wooden (or dead) is that they have been made into idols. This happens when a sense of playfulness, of leap, or leeway is absent from the ritual. Rituals which cease to carry the humanizing vision of a people should be changed; a playful innovation should take place so that the new situations in which we find ourselves in a "future shock" society can be dealt with creatively and in a way which encourages us not to live in the past or cling to the present, but to sort out and be able to experiment with optional futures. This calls for widening and developing further our world view and the basic values we are seeking to conserve or create. In short, reritualization will always be necessary in order to keep our visions alive and growing—especially in our world of rapid change. Erikson agrees with Toffler that great rituals and festivals which communicate our national visions and dreams are greatly needed in a world where persons are experiencing changes of values, occupation, location, or multiple marriages and changing family patterns. A sense of continuity is required in order for persons to experience a sameness of identity between what the individual thinks and feels about himself or herself and what others in the wider community think. Finally, ritualizations and reritualizations are profound factors in personal development from birth to death.

For this reason Erikson has sought to chart the normal stages of ritualization. He has done this in the belief that we have not recognized both the inevitability and importance of ritualizations in life. Erikson is always aware of the dialectics of social stability and social change and their ongoing impact on personality development. He believes that we communicate our visions of what life means via the simple, unconscious, daily rituals of interplay within the family and in the community's life. Therefore he studies carefully what he calls the "slow laws of ontogeny" which a fast-moving society will neglect at great danger.[8]

Erikson sees the importance of the renewal of society's vision through children who partake of the stability of basic ritualizations, through young people who either confirm the vision or reform it by dissent or revolt, and adults who "participate in a given or an emerging system of political choices between conservation and innovation in productive and generational processes." What is essential is a pattern of feedback "from the newcomers emerging through the generational process; a feedback which supports the established social form if it, indeed, continues to facilitate the interplay of inner and outer structure, or which insists on a reassertion of the spirit where it has fallen victim to an overgrown ritualism."[9] Erikson understands how easy it is for rituals to become desacralizing and dehumanizing. Reritualizations which are required by rapid change, however, must always be in harmony with the deep-running epigenetic development of persons and in harmony with the laws of growth which increasingly we better understand. To be secure, such reritualization, such playful innovation must take place in relation to our major personal and social strengths and problems—never in isolation. The development of a world view, a way of seeing and being seen which includes our sense of ultimate faith, is crucial to human identity, stability, and creativity.

The sacraments came out of these normal, natural, daily rituals and are related in interesting ways to the various stages of human life. Before we look more concretely at the potential meaning of the sacraments to these stages let us follow Erikson's charting of the elements common to each of his six stages and how they contribute to the extension and reform of the greater vision of the meaning and purpose of life.[10]

For persons to become genuinely human in identity, Erikson believes the family has a crucial responsibility. This is so because "in principle and probably within some genetic limits" the newly born species could fit into any number of pseudo-species and their habitats. The newly born, therefore, "must for that very reason be coaxed and induced to become 'speciated' during a prolonged childhood by some form of family"; the child must be familiarized by ritualization with a particular version of human existence. He or she develops a distinct sense of corporate identity, later fortified against the encroachment of other pseudo-species by prejudices which can make very small differences in ritualization "extraspecific and, in fact, inimical to the only 'genuine' human identity."[11] Erikson believes that we are largely blind to our own cultural rituals because more often than not we experience ritualization as "the only proper way to do things; and the question is only why does not everybody do it our way." While the daily rituals do convey a common vision as well as a secure way to identify self and others they also can become "legalistic ritualizations in which develops an orthodoxy of mere social compulsion and compliance subject to 'deals' which sacrifice the spirit to the letter." Ritualization at its best represents a "creative formalization which helps to avoid both impulsive excess and compulsive self-restriction, both social anomie and moralistic coercion."[12]

Erikson has found that healthy ritualization accomplishes a formidable number of things. It elevates the satisfaction of immediate personal needs into the more acceptable context of communal and shared life; it teaches a sanctioned way of doing simple and daily things and makes these acts into a contribution to the joint sense of common destiny; it deflects feelings of unworthiness onto outsiders (within and without the child's culture) "who are excluded or are excluding themselves from knowing the right way"; it helps develop cognitive patterns which, in turn, are put in the service of a general vision (it is for this reason that the ideology and world view of the group is so important to identity); it develops a "ritual sense" which grows with each stage of development (and becomes the ground for a sacramental view, for instance, of all of life's experiences); it helps the person discriminate between good and evil behavior which becomes the seedbed of judicial norms; it helps develop an independent identity which in adolescence is sealed by some form of "confirmation" or second birth which can integrate all childhood identifications in a world view and belief system while making as ideologically foreign all those wishes and images which have become undesirable and evil and are remindful of other "lower" species of persons.[13]

We must be clear at the outset of our discussion of Erikson that he does not take a specifically religious stance concerning the nature of ritual. Rather he sees ritualization from the perspective of ethology. Yet, his views are couched in language which is often in harmony with Christian values. He believes that the human species has a *biological* need to *care*, to contribute to the nurture and guidance of the next generation, to be creative and *generative,* to *love and to be loved* (the need for intimacy), to be *autonomous,* to initiate and to develop *competencies* which give individual satisfaction but which help others in the community, to have a clear *purpose* for life which will enhance the direction of the *will,* to find a great *fidelity,* someone or something to which the person can give himself or herself and in which is found a *world view* and guiding *ideology* which gives wider and deeper identity, and finally, to *trust* self, others, and the universe so that *hope* will be alive and the person will genuinely care for others, for nature, and for the values which make life a precious and sacramental gift.[14]

Now we may be ready to focus more clearly upon the specific stages of development, what the normal ritualizations are, and their meaning in human development. We will be attentive to what Erikson's insights may say to us concerning educational and liturgical life within the church and to the implications for a sacramental approach to nurture. However, more detailed analysis of the specific sacraments of baptism, communion, confirmation, ordination, marriage, etc., in relation to human development will follow in Part III of this book.

We have elected to review the stages of human and faith development by employing the theoretical understandings of Erik Erikson (human development) and James Fowler (faith development). We do this in recognition of and appreciation for the work of many other persons. For instance, we believe that the research of Lawrence Kohlberg on moral development and the findings of Jean Piaget on cognitive development, the refinements of Piaget's work by Ronald Goldman and David Elkind on stages of religious development and the challenge to such views by Gabriel Moran in his religious education developmental theory are all important to the continuing dialogue concerning human development. Many of the insights from such wider research can be found especially in the presuppositions of James Fowler's emerging theory of faith development and our interpretation of its strengths and limitations.[15]

Erikson's seminal thought concerning the stages of human development, while neo-Freudian, are grounded in an awareness both of the importance of the affective and the cognitive. At both levels the rituals in family and community guide persons toward a clear sense of identity and provide a purpose for life and a pervading fidelity around which life is organized and given direction. First, let us be stimulated to further thought by the findings of Erik Erikson concerning his stages in the ritualization of experience. We present these stages with the recognition that empirical research still needs to be conducted to confirm or alter these observations.

Infancy

Erikson gives a very heavy emphasis to the essential nature of the first year in life to subsequent emotional and mental health. He goes beyond this to underscore the relationship of a positive self-regard (which starts in infancy) to the development of a society which has a positive and affirmative stance in respect to all of life and communicates a *vision* of corporate destiny which encourages individual and community growth and a general sense of hope and well-being.

Infancy is not just a time for the rituals of greeting, naming, feeding, elimination, dressing and undressing; it is a period of life when the child develops through such rituals a sense of the *numinous* (an indwelling force or quality which animates or guides—evoking awe or reverence), of seeing and being seen by an affirming presence which is the mother or parent. This sense of the numinous is the stuff of relationship out of which the child develops a positive and benevolent feeling for self and for the other which is the parent. This is the very ground for higher forms of rituals of religious faith in which human beings feel in the living presence of God and "see" the meaning of life in the "face" of God as the child sees the light of the parent's love and affirmation in the luminous eyes and smiling face of the parent.

Erikson says that this sense of the numinous historically has been the domain of organized religion. However, the informal rituals of infancy are the seedbed for these more formal rituals later. The crucial nature of the rituals of "mutual recognition" between child and parents cannot be overstated. It is children who have not had such affirming and loving relationships, communicated through the rituals of greeting and naming, who become autistic and psychotic. Erikson believes that the numinous assures us of separateness transcended and yet also a distinctiveness confirmed, and thus is the very basis of a sense of "I" renewed (as it feels) by the mutual recognition of all "I's" joined in a shared faith in one all-embracing "I am!"[16]

The rituals of greeting are profound in their potential for subtle communication of the parent's feelings of affirmation or fear both of the child or of self (parents with feelings of low self-worth treat their children in ways that transfer their negative feelings from self to child in multifarious ways). The ritual takes place every morning as the mother or parent approaches the awakening infant in a smiling or worried way, speaking in an animated or anxious voice, looking, feeling, sniffing, to discover some source of discomfort. These rituals are highly unique to the style of each parent and yet similar enough to be classified as rituals of greeting or naming from culture to culture. Both the affective and cognitive development of the child are involved in the responses of child and parent.

Parents not only experience joy and affirmation they also experience feelings of anger at having to be confined and limited by the new situation. They have ambivalent feelings between love and warmth and the desire to abandon the child and increase personal mobility. It is not easy for parents to deal with such negative feelings; but they will appear along with the accompanying guilt. Erikson has found that ritualized patterns of care help both parents and the child overcome these negative experiences and return to affirmation of each other and life. It is for this reason that Erikson believes the sense of the numinous is so crucial. It overcomes the fear of abandonment and estrangement and communicates a sense of deep affirmation, acceptance (even of the negative feelings and behavior), and mutuality. Ritualizations which become negative and compulsive can be quite destructive in infancy. Such ritualizations become ritualism (dead and wooden and not life-affirming). These nonlife-affirming patterns between parent and child, in turn, become the distortion of the numinous quality and fall into idolism. As can be easily seen, Erikson's analysis of the rituals of infancy are filled with language which points to religious meanings. For instance, the gaze of the mother or parents has the numinous power not unlike the deity looking "down" upon all of the human family. The child "looks up" to the parent's care and love just as those in the faith community "look up" and seek to be "lifted up" by faith in God. This ritual has, at its base, the power to help the child "see" the vision of life's meaning and to be an accepted, affirmed, loved member of the community. While the infant obviously does not think such thoughts, he or she does have a deep need to be loved, accepted, affirmed, and to trust and be trusted. It is out of the interplay of the rituals of greeting, naming, feeding, etc., that the essential virtue of the first year of life must be born. That virtue, according to Erikson, is hope. A child must leave infancy with an unconscious but life-giving feeling of hopefulness about the future and a responsiveness to the new experiences coming down the road.[17]

Understandings such as those which Erikson has distilled may have great potential for our understandings of education for baptism and for the liturgical life of parents and the congregation.

The Second Year of Life

In the second year of life the child begins to exert more personal autonomy which is experienced by parents via the unwelcome "no" with which the child responds when asked to do something. This "no," of course, is an essential step as the child seeks to differentiate self from parents and to exert his or her will. Erikson sees the development of a sense of autonomy and the cultivation of the will as the ontogenetic arenas around which the ritualizations of right or wrong, good or evil (what he terms the Judicious) take place.

The child begins to identify himself or herself as good or bad via the interplay with parents who communicate acceptance or rejection of certain behavior through their tone of voice or words which point to certain rules or do's and don'ts which have been established. It is somewhat surprising that the sense of justice and morality which we associated with natural social structures has its beginning in the second year of life. Erikson sees the genesis of such judgment in the development of a structure within the self which Freud called the superego and which Erikson calls an "inner self watch." This inner awareness is the source of the feeling that the child is being judged by others to be doing good or bad things and from which the child gets a positive or negative self-image. The stage is related to the psycho-sexual stage of "anality." The process of elimination and toilet training becomes symbolic of the conflicting feeling the child has about his/her own excrement and backside. The rituals around elimination are powerful dramas of the use of "free will" and choice. Parents urge the child to control, to choose to do the right thing at the right time. They communicate many subtle messages concerning their vision of what good people do and what lesser people are like. They sometimes use language and actions which produce feelings of shame and doubt rather than self-worth and affirmation.

"The self-doubt and hidden shame" says Erikson, "attached to the necessity of 'eliminating' part of himself create in the human being a certain subdued rage which eventually must either rebel against the condemning authority or turn to righteous condemnation against others. I point to this matter darkly because here we meet the ontological origin not only of the *divided self* but also of the *divided species.*"[18] Not only does the child have to watch out that the good self wins over the bad self but that he or she will not wind up as a member of a lesser group of human beings. The child, therefore, has a "constant need for new everyday ritualizations of moral discrimination in words and sounds truly corresponding to a shared moral climate which the child can comprehend—and experiment with."[19]

It is not difficult to see that such a personal need for moral discrimination is the ground for the need of society for laws, rules, and institutions which provide the *modus operandi* for delivering just decisions. The law, then, is the watchful presence to keep society true to its own standards, in line with its own vision of "justice for all." The major problem again with these ritualizations within the family and in the public arena is that they can and do become *legalistic.* The letter of the law triumphs over the spirit. Parents and society can dehumanize by their legalistic rituals. Such dehumanization normally results in responses from children all the way from rage to apathy.

Studies in moral development have established the fact that very young children do not have the ability to decenter (get some distance from the self) enough to make decisions regarding the just or fair thing to do for others. Their tendency is to want an "eye for an eye, a tooth for a tooth." This fact appears to be heavily related to the limited level of cognitive development and not to any "moral" failure. Attempts to help children in the second year of life develop their moral sense must recognize their egocentric nature and must focus much more on the feeling level and the simple rituals of "good or bad" behavior as defined by the parents or others in the family. This level is highly significant, nonetheless, and is foundational not only to the person's later response to the legal structures of society but also to the interpretation of the nature of God as a lawgiver and a judge of positive and negative living.

Therefore, the quality of the judicial ritualizations in the second year of life is very important to later moral and religious development. This period of development, for instance, points to the power of preparation for and participation in the sacrament of penance or reconciliation not only for adults but for children and youth in forms appropriate to their life issues, self-perception, and feelings of relationship with others and God.

The Play Age—3 To 5: Dramatic Rituals of Self-Definition

With the use of toys and imagination children experiment with self-images and images of others in order to find out what positive ego-ideal they want to affirm and also to discover what images of self they want to avoid. Erikson sees this period as a particularly important time for ritualizations of dramatic elaboration in which the acting out of good and bad images provides the opportunity for children to begin to find purpose and direction for their lives and to deal with a sense of guilt which comes when their initiatives are rejected by parents or others. The crucial issue is for the playfulness first discovered during these stages to be encouraged and affirmed. This is true because this very sense of playfulness and leeway is the quality which can later become essential in the renewal of life and in the reformation of dead rituals. All through life the dramatic sense is at work in our unconscious and conscious worlds. With encouragement during this early stage children can begin to define themselves in play which helps them avoid "acting out" behavior which can be so destructive and negative. The rituals of play provide a chance for authenticity to develop in a safe environment. Denials of such play can force children (also youth and adults) compulsively to assume the role of shameless evildoers—as preferable to being either nameless or overly typed.[20]

School Age—6 To 11: Rituals of Identity Through Adequacy of Performance

Schoolage children are seeking to discover the adequacy or inadequacy of their abilities. They discover their competence or incompetence in a social milieu in which their interaction with teachers, peers, and parents (largely in relation to the school setting) gives them feedback about their abilities to read, write, spell, manipulate, and classify various symbols in order to communicate, perform physically in sports, etc. Of course, there are many rituals of performance which take place in this process of interplay. There are many rituals of learning which must be appropriated in order to survive in this world.

Erikson understands the schoolage period to be much more important to personality development than others, such as Freud, thought. The rituals of performance translate into some very rewarding experiences of self-affirmation for those who perform well or into some very devastating feelings of inferiority for children who do not perform well, according to those who are making judgments. Feelings of failure and guilt can result. If there are opportunities for second, third, and fourth chances to try, with rituals of support, children can build strong, realistic self-definitions as a result of this interplay.

The point is, however, that schoolage children are not in a "latency period" of less struggle and semi-innocence. Estrangement is a common experience for them. The play life of early childhood is transformed into work. Games can highlight competition or cooperation. Imagination can become "duty to perform." Many children can become so concerned to perform well and to please parents and teachers that they can fall into patterns of overformalization, perfectionism, and empty ceremonialism. They can fall into patterns of works righteousness, "that works make the man and technique the truth."[21]

So, church leaders need to be alert to the very great potential for good or evil that the rituals of performance have for the pilgrimages of the children to whom we are related. Our rituals of faith must be focused much more on the real struggles schoolage children are experiencing. It is not enough for sacraments of communion or penance to be "pious rituals" which are performed by children to please parents and others. The powerful experiences of affirmation, joy, forgiveness and reconciliation, need to be related to the world in which schoolage children are immersed.

Adolescence—Rituals Which Help Bring Together their Convictions and Find a Great Fidelity

The crucial issue for adolescents is to begin to find a great faith— someone or something to which they can give themselves—a faith which will help them to organize themselves and give them a sense of purpose and direction. How this actually takes place depends, says Erikson, on the identity youth bring from childhood interplay with others. New rituals appear in adolescence. Some of these are spontaneous such as rituals related to style, music, special esoteric language, learning to relate to the opposite sex or to drive. These spontaneous rituals help youth relate to one another and to make it clear to adults and children that they are different—no longer children and not yet adults. There are also *formal* rituals which help them celebrate the convictions and beliefs they are coming to affirm. These rituals include formal inductions into groups which are joined and in which various statements of purpose or belief are publicly affirmed. Of course, in relation to organized religion, confirmation education and liturgies become formal occasions for public declaration of conviction. How confirmation becomes genuine and not a perfunctory and outward form will be discussed in Part III. Graduation from high school again is potentially a ritual of joy, symbolizing departure from the world of dependence and entry into the adult world. Erikson emphasizes the need of adolescents to integrate these elements of conviction in "technologically convincing day-to-day activities" and to "engage in periodical rites and ceremonies of a religious, national or military nature" without falling into too much conformity. The rituals should be the channels of communication of a vision of the meaning of life. When the vision is lost, the ritual should be critiqued and renewed. Youth often reject dead rituals but only create counterritualizations to convey new meanings. Some youth seek meaning in these new ritualizations and fall into what Erikson calls *totalism,* a fanatic and exclusive preoccupation with certain ideals within a very tight and legalistic system.

The fact that this move to totalism happens illustrates how great the need of youth is for clarity of faith and how great the potential is for creative church interplay with adolescents. There are some special problems in this period, related to research findings concerning the stages of moral and faith development. We shall address these in our analysis of faith development stages and in Part III. Of course, the great danger in this period is for adolescents to become estranged and become confused about their convictions, act out their feelings in rebellion, mocking present rituals, rejecting societal values in negative behavior which is destructive.

In respect to ritual life, the task of adolescents is to be able "to visualize a future in which they will be the everyday ritualizers in their children's lives and, perhaps, occupy ritual positions in the lives of the next generation."[22] How this can be done will be addressed in our discussion of confirmation education and liturgy in Part III.

Adulthood—Rituals Which Generate New Life Personally and Socially: Becoming Creative Generational Ritualizers

While adults are inevitably ritualizers of the next generation they often are unaware of the nature of their ritual life and the degree to which their informal and spontaneous patterns influence their children and others. Adults are potential ritualizers. Not only through the formal rituals of graduation from college or some apprenticeship, or the ceremonies of marriage or induction into work or community groups but in countless informal rituals of parenting, teaching, producing, caring or curing hurts of body or spirit. An adult is a person who is more or less ready to become a numinous model for the next generation and to act as a judge, however indirectly, of good and evil, as well as a transmitter of certain values which the adult believes to be important.

Such parental, didactic, productive, or curative rituals are enforced by being related with conviction to God who created us or to some other God-like figure who has convincingly proclaimed principles by which persons organize their lives. Again, the potential of sacramental education and celebration needs to be explored in direct relation to the specific concerns of adults (those related to their attempts to be adequate in work, family life, nurturing, and healing or caring). These life issues are the very seedbed for generating new life and for renewing faith. Education and liturgical life in our families and within the faith community should be related with integrity to the actual issues confronted. These issues change from young to middle to older adulthood and in relation to the stages of human, moral, and faith development of adults.

Most adults can develop enough objectivity to be able to critique and analyze the liveliness of the rituals in which they participate. They can be playful and innovative in the renewal of our ritualizations. Many adults have the capacity to act out dramatically the possible results of certain behavior or to "play with" new forms of life which more adequately capture the life-giving aspects of the particular ritual. What we develop as family rituals (which celebrate, for instance, the values of the family, its history, its unique character, its delights in the gifts of individual personalities) can be evaluated and experimented with. Rituals which are becoming meaningless or dead can be renewed and reformed.

Erikson is correct, however, in reminding us that we cannot prescribe rituals or "create" new rituals easily. It is the very nature of ritual to be pervaded with the spontaneity of surprise in the midst of the repetition we associate with it. What is needed is a blending of recognition and surprise which are the result of creative interplay.

Adult rituals are important, not only for individuals, but also for the renewal of our institutions, including the church. The vision of the meaning of our life together is important to share widely. Adults particularly need a sense of being grounded in a world view which unifies all of the aspects of their lives. A religious vision, therefore, is important to the wholeness and health of adults. Erikson sees religious faith and world views as a protection against the most profound threat—that of nonexistence. He is critical, however, when groups, including churches, politicize existential human needs of this depth "and come to live off human aloneness and death" rather than serve with integrity.[23]

We are employing Erikson's insights while at the same time recognizing that his findings have not been confirmed through empirical research. Moreover, some of his basic assumptions, such as the pervasive organizing principles of identity, generativity, and life cycle are being analyzed for their adequacy.[24] Nevertheless, we think that there is very genuine depth of understanding in his view of psycho-social development and very real potential in a dialogue between his view of the stages of ritualization and the sacraments. We hope the dialogue to follow will both celebrate the richness of Erikson's insights and also identify problem areas in need of further study.

The Stages of Faith Development

Much of the discussion of the nature of sacramental life in the past, as we have stated previously, has been only casually related to the stages of growth from birth to death. Erikson's thoughtful work in recent years has been employed rather often to identify the expected normal crises in life and has been illustrative of the positive and negative results of the presence or absence of supportive, humanizing trust, love, and faith at each of the stages of life. Especially in respect to baptism and confirmation, Erikson's observations concerning trust vs. mistrust in the first year of life and his discussion of identity vs. role confusion in the adolescent years have been used as a part of various denominational rationales for the importance of the sacraments in the life cycle of persons.

Still more recently, James Fowler has focused clearly upon what he is calling the stages of faith development. He is seeking to describe the essential nature of faith and the structures of the development of faith from birth to mature years. Starting at Harvard Divinity School in 1972 and continuing today at Candler School of Theology at Emory University, Fowler has done research on the specific elements which are present in faith and how these elements or structures change and grow in relation to the experiences persons have within the family, their wider social relationships and cultural setting. Fowler has made a signal contribution in his emerging theory of faith development stages. His findings have very real potential for our discussion of the importance of life-giving rituals at various points in the pilgrimage of life and for our exploration of the sacramental nature of life itself. Let us turn, therefore, to a more detailed analysis of Fowler's faith development understandings and to the stages he believes he has evidence enough to posit.

Let us mention at the outset that Fowler has drawn his theory from hypotheses he has established from his reflection on the theories of Erik Erikson (psychosocial development), Jean Piaget (mental development), Lawrence Kohlberg (moral development), and to a lesser degree Robert Selman (on perspective taking). Also, he recognizes his indebtedness, in the definition of the nature of faith, to Cantwell Smith, Paul Tillich, H. Richard Niebuhr, Richard R. Niebuhr, Michael Polanyi, and others. He has tested his hypotheses by interviewing 359 persons of both sexes and of various ages from 3.5 to 84 years. Fowler is very honest about the largely Christian (84.1%) and largely white sample (97.8%) he and his associates employed. He is beginning to embark upon serious cross-cultural studies which he hopes will bring balance and perspective to his theory. We have decided to employ Fowler's categories for the stimulus that may take place both in refining the relevance of his findings for the meaning and use of the sacraments throughout life and in identifying the strengths and limitations of his views in the process of this discussion. Not only will Fowler's own continuing research expand our understandings but also the work of other persons and groups. For instance, the findings of the ecumenical group supporting the Faith Development in the Adult Life Cycle Project will increase understandings and serve as a point of reference for independent but cooperative evaluation of Fowler's views.[25]

While Fowler is primarily interested in defining the stages of faith through which all persons potentially progress (with or without a particular religious tradition) he is also interested in finding models and methods of developing what he calls "good" faith upon the earth. He is interested in discovering how churches and families can nurture healthy, life-giving, humanizing, socially aware, liberating faith in the lives of persons at each of the stages of life. He is interested in identifying and putting into operation "rites of passage" or experiences of intensification which have educational, celebrative, therapeutic, and meditative potential in persons' lives from stage to stage. It is in relation to this concern that we wish to discuss Fowler's faith development stages. We shall outline his major assumptions and findings at this point in the book, but we shall again dialogue with his findings as we discuss specifically each of the sacraments and the education and liturgy needed for them to become relevant to persons at the various stages of life.

Fowler is also quite concerned that the church find ways to sponsor and support persons as they struggle honestly and freely with their own faith constructions. This issue, of course, focuses on qualities of caring needed by leaders, parents, and other members of the faith community. While this concern will be more implicit than explicit in what we explore, it will be present and is very important. Now, on to Fowler's view of the nature of faith and the stages of faith development.

The Nature of Faith

To Fowler, faith and belief are quite different and distinct realities. He sees faith as "a way of knowing and seeing the conditions of our lives in relation to more or less conscious images" we have of the ultimate meaning of life. It is a dynamic, active way of approaching life and organizing ourselves around values and commitments which we think and feel are most important for us.[26] Our real faith is revealed not only by what we say we really care about but by the way we act, the decisions we have made or are making. In this sense, every person has some kind and quality of faith. People have very different contents for their faith. These may come from religious traditions into which they have been born (Christian, Jewish, Hindu, etc.) or from various values to which they have been exposed (the importance of money, power, position, or social justice). Faith always involves the self in relation to others in relation to some values or realities which we regard as ultimate. In this sense, faith is always structurally triadic. Fowler recognizes that there is such a thing as human faith (which everyone experiences) and Christian faith (which has a particular faith story, set of symbols, history, rites and practices, relationships—a particular content). While he is aware that the content of faith is often crucial to the quality and "goodness" of faith, he has not focused on the *content* of faith but rather on the *structure* of faith as it develops from stage to stage. He is influenced in his descriptions of the elements within the structure of faith by Piaget and Kohlberg as they have defined the structures of mental and moral development as ways of knowing. Fowler recognizes that faith is a much wider and deeper reality than a way of knowing. So, he sought "to incorporate the structuring of affective, valuational and imaginational modes of knowing that Piaget and Kohlberg have sought to avoid."[27] Fowler sees faith as a by-product of the interaction the person has with his or her total environment. It must, therefore, be the result of "the relations of reasoning to imagination, or moral judgment making to symbolic representation, of ecstatic intuition to logical deduction." Faith has to do with the holistic approach the person takes to all of life, the way the person constructs and reveals what he or she sees to be most meaningful in life. This faith stance, while always somewhat changing and dynamic, provides the basis for making decisions about personal and ethical life. Some of the faith stances persons construct are rather self-centered and self-serving. Others are more oriented to the care of a wider circle of family or neighbors, a very few seem to be genuinely oriented toward persons or communities which are universal. Fowler's research actually found one person out of 359 who was a Stage VI person with a genuinely universal faith which profoundly organized the self around ultimate concern for justice and love for all persons of whatever situation, racial, national, or religious background. This is what Fowler means by good faith. While it was his original intent to *describe* the stages of faith development, he admits that the six stages he discovered do become somewhat *normative*. They do describe progressively better and more fully matured qualities of faithfulness. How these six stages of faith are related qualitatively to the various contents (beliefs, symbols, master faith stories, rites and practices of the various faith traditions) is not known at this time. Fowler believes the content is important and that each person must be specific and particular about his or her faith stories, symbols, and rituals. The relation of the structure of faith to the various contents of faith (in developing a good faith which moves toward universal love and justice) will also be a part of later research.

Fowler follows Piaget in his views about how the structures of faith change. Piaget said that mental growth takes place when the person's mental constructs fall into disequilibrium as the person encounters experiences with which previous ideas or understanding cannot deal. The mind grows through what he called assimilation and accommodation. When the child has experiences with the mother around a basic need such as elimination the child assimilates various early "concepts" of the mother, taking the initiative to change the diapers, to put on a dry, warm diaper instead of a wet, cold diaper which was causing the disequilibrium. The child learns how to get the attention needed from the parent. But as the child grows the parents expect that the child will be able to control the process of elimination and will be toilet trained. The child, of course, does mature physically and becomes capable of controlling his or her own bladder and bowels. However, a new disequilibrium sets in when the parents do not act as they have in the past. Mental growth takes place slowly in this new disequilibrium as the child's mind develops a new structuration by accommodating itself to the idea that "toilet training" is possible and is the way to deal with any subsequent disequilibrium caused by bladder or bowel pressure. The mind of a two-week-old child could not be accommodated to such an idea; but, the mind has grown enough by the second year to do so. With the new construction in the mind about behavior related to elimination the child's mind can assimilate new suggestions from the parents which will make for more autonomy, happiness, and a sense of well being. Remember this illustration as we discuss the process of faith development later. We shall then explore why some persons find equilibrium at Stage II or III in adolescence for instance, and stay at this stage all the rest of their lives while other people experience disequilibrium at Stage III and because of positive new experiences find their way of knowing and valuing growing to the next stage of faith development. In other words, such persons find a new accommodation, a new way of seeing and organizing life and its meaning which will help them find a fresh and more satisfying equilibrium—a sense of balance and perspective by which to assimilate new experiences which come to them.

In faith development the accommodation is in the total self, not just in the mind as in cognitive development. Fowler gives attention to the transformation in consciousness which takes place from stage to stage or which is experienced in conversion which can take place within a particular stage without the person necessarily growing to the next higher stage. Fowler also takes seriously the past, that persons are formed in communities and are shaped by past actions and decisions, by stories and images which are rich and unique. He also seeks to relate the six stages of faith to the predictable crises of human growth as well as the transitional periods between the psychosocial stages of development identified by Erikson or Levinson.

The Stages of Faith Development

Fowler starts his description of the stages of faith by identifying a pre-stage which takes place from birth to two years. He refers to this period as *Infancy and Undifferentiated Faith*. While the first two years cannot be studied via the interview pattern Fowler has employed, observations and reflections on them reveal that this period is very basic to faith development. As Erikson has pointed out the issue of trust is the fundamental one for the infant. Because of the quality of the relationships and care the child experiences during these momentous days a sense of trust of self, others, and the environment either develops or a sense of mistrust and basic anxiety emerges. The "seeds of trust, courage, hope and love are fused," during the period, "in an undifferentiated way."[28] The period is crucial because the quality of mutuality and the strengthening of the above virtues are either developed in a beginning but very important way or are undermined. In any case, the seedbed for faith is laid by parents and significant others in ways so subtle but profound that later steps in faith can be taken with much more ease or difficulty as a result.

The great danger of this period is an excessive narcissism in which the experience of being "central" continues to dominate the child's way of relating. If a sense of mutuality does not grow the child can leave this period with patterns of isolation and without a sense of hope. The transition to Stage I begins when the child begins to have a sense of self and is relating language and symbols to life through ritual play.

Stage I—Intuitive-Projective Faith

This stage of faith is appropriate for children ages 3 to 7 but is sometimes seen in persons who are older. In this stage the child is unable to separate fact from fantasy very well. The child is able to grasp powerful images and stories which communicate intuitively the feelings and concerns of the primary adults in his or her life. The visible actual faith of these adults can be caught in powerful if somewhat necessarily egocentric ways. Gabriel Moran correctly questions the use of the word *egocentric* in view of the fact that the young child must be centered in the self in order to discover and affirm the self. He agrees with Fowler, however, when Fowler projects an image of growth which helps the child develop the capacity to decenter while at the same time becoming a deeply centered person.[29]

This is the stage of the first self-awareness of sex and death. The beginning and end of life are perceived along with the strong taboos by which we tend to insulate children from these powerful areas of experience.

The structures of thought are preoperational in that the child thinks with his or her perception and imagination rather than logically. Some very important images and feelings about self, others and ultimate reality are intuited during this period. These images, feelings and stories depict good and bad ways of living which children take with them in their conscious and unconscious life. The power of the fairy tale is a sign of the child's way of appropriating images of life's meaning and destiny. Images about God are more general (God is everywhere!)

Children who have poor relationships and negative experiences can find their imaginations possessed by images of terror or can be exploited through pressure from adults to conform to moral or doctrinal expectations which they do not understand and have not lived enough to relate concretely to their own lives.

The transition to Stage II is precipitated by the "child's growing concern to know how things are, to clarify for him or herself the bases of distinctions between what is real and what only seems to be."[30]

Stage II—Mythic-Literal Faith

This stage is appropriate for children of elementary school age (7-11 or 12) but again is often found later. This stage correlates with the concrete operational stage of mental development (Piaget) in which the child begins to think logically in relation to the concrete experiences of life. However, the child tends to take everything at face value or literally. This means that children are greatly interested in learning the stories, beliefs, and observances that are a part of belonging to a community. Children are also interested in the moral rules and attitudes but do not contest these in terms of their value but only if they are not fair at a personal level. Symbols of their tradition are taken literally and are one dimensional.

The desire to make sense out of things and the power of concrete operational thought leads children to want to order and classify things and to develop a faith story which conveys some coherent meanings.

Images about God are much more anthropomorphic than in Stage I, curiously. Fowler was surprised by this finding. God is described with human characteristics rather than a description of general intuitive qualities or abstract concepts. Persons in this stage are people of the story. They carry the meaning of life in stories and myths which they do not seek to get behind or understand symbolically or to convert to propositions of truth. They do not seem to have the capacity to step back from the story and to formulate reflective, conceptual meanings or to critique these meanings for their consistency with other aspects of their lives.

Fowler thinks advantage should be taken of the capacity of Stage II persons for narrative and story as the primary way of finding and giving meaning to life.

The danger of this stage is the tendency to remain wedded to the literalness of the stories, beliefs, and practices and not to want to get behind them to their deeper meanings. Another danger, Fowler thinks, is in the tendency to think in terms of individual fairness or reciprocity and then to rely on this principle excessively so that the person can become perfectionistic or given to "works of righteousness" or can have a sense of badness, "embraced because of mistreatment, neglect or the apparent disfavor of significant others."

Fowler found adolescents and adults who were primarily in this stage—persons who equilibrated in their faith development in childhood and did not grow in this dimension of their lives. He illustrated this with an interview with a woman public school teacher who was very literal about saints, prayed to a God who would reciprocate when she or her children needed help, who enjoyed the mythic elements in her faith and took the stories literally. While an adult in other arenas of life she had a child's way of knowing and seeing life's ultimate meaning.

The transition period to a Stage III faith is the person's recognition of the implicit clash or contradictions in stories that leads to deeper reflection concerning their meaning. The transition also to formal operational thought (which usually comes in early adolescence) makes it possible for the person to do the abstract thinking which is required and necessary. The previous literalism is questioned and the person is more open to new ideas and images.

Stage III—Synthetic-Conventional Faith

While this stage is usually entered by adolescents it is the most common stage of faith that is found in the adults in most of our churches in America. As young people move out beyond their families and as they seek a more independent identity they experience diverse values, patterns of life, behavior, and loyalties. Faith is a way of providing a coherent perspective or center for their lives in the middle of all of these conflicting norms. Fowler agrees with Erikson that the adolescent period is the time for finding a great fidelity, someone or something to which the adolescent can give him or herself in order to give the self a sense of identity and in relation to which the person can get a sense of direction and purpose. Erikson sees the rituals of driving, installation into groups, sexual practice, confirmation into a faith community, graduation from high school as important to the process of finding such a center of fidelity. Fowler's research findings differ to some degree with Erikson's views. Fowler has discovered that adolescents seem to be reworking and critiquing their commitments and values, using their formal operational mental powers, but in a limited way. Most often, they discuss their values, are introduced to certain beliefs and commitments, voice serious questions about the adequacy of these faith commitments, but end up affirming for the most part what they have been nurtured into. Their critique, says Fowler, is at the personal level and is in relation to the questions having to do with identity (who am I?) rather than a critique of the system "as a system." Stage III faith is synthetic (in that it tends to bring things together from various sources) but it is conformist and conventional (in that the person tends not to be able to step outside of the system of values, beliefs, or practices long enough to do genuinely autonomous reflection and reevaluation).

This is the reason that many young people more or less quit the church soon after they are confirmed—even though they made public declarations of strong and intelligent belief. Here is a clear illustration of the difference between belief and faith. Their actual, operational values, way of knowing and seeing life, their stance (faith) is often rather different from their conventional beliefs. Also, youth really do not have the wider experience with alternative systems of value and commitment in order to do individual reflective thinking. It is like a father of one of the writers said about his decision to become a Christian as an adolescent. His father was interested in world religions and had various books on the subject around the house. So, the adolescent son read and discussed other world religions in comparison to Christianity. Then, he joined the Methodist church next door in a small town in Missouri because it was really the only option he had!

It is for this reason that Fowler's studies say that beliefs are tacit (basically unexamined) in Stage III faith. They may be deeply felt and even tied to an emotion-packed conversion experience, with very real meaning for the person's sense of direction and purpose. Authority is still located outside of the self in the persons who represent the beliefs offered or in the consensus of some valued group.

The concern for matters of justice and peace on a world scale are usually not really high on the list of values, except in a most general and conventional way.

In relation to getting behind the symbols and faith stories of the tradition into which the person has been initiated, the Stage III person really does not seek to demythologize the stories or seek to get behind them to deeper personal and social meanings. Fowler's research makes this quite clear. Again, this finding is very important for religious educators, pastors, and parents to know. Piaget has demonstrated that adolescents generally have the abilities of formal operational thinking (namely, to do abstract thinking, to get behind the symbols to do conceptual work concerning their meaning in various propositions or generalizations about the truth revealed, to critique, analyze, invert, reconstruct, etc.). Fowler finds that while the abilities are there they are used in a rather narrow, personal way and usually leave adolescents (early and middle adolescents especially) in a conventional, more conformist faith stance. Fowler sees the more rigorous critiquing of the symbols, beliefs, rites, and practices of the faith community to be a later activity—seldom found before late adolescence and more commonly found in young adulthood (when their experience has been greatly widened). In fact, Fowler believes that one reason so many church people equilibrate in Stage III faith and stay there all of their lives is that their experiences are more limited in respect to genuine diversity and they are in communities which continue to reinforce their Stage III faith. Moreover, this quality of faith is very satisfying and significant for many.

Fowler's view now is that Stage III persons are "not so much locked into their particular symbols in a kind of fundamentalism of symbolic forms. Rather, symbols of the sacred—their own and others—are related to in ways which honor them as inseparably connected to the sacred. . . . Any strategy of demythologizing, therefore, threatens the participation of symbols and symbolized and is taken, consequently, as an assault on the sacred itself."[31] We find Fowler's work is stimulating and generally helpful. However, he seems not to be totally consistent here. He gives illustrations from persons who came out of adolescent conversion experiences in a charismatic group and of an older woman who as an adolescent was brought up in a Unitarian Church. It seems that the Unitarian was in a faith community where the norm was to demythologize. The norm was not to do so for the person with the adolescent conversion experience. Both persons were clearly bright intellectually and were persons with formal operational thinking powers as adults. Fowler saw the woman to have been in Stage III faith when she was confirmed at 13 as a Unitarian because she was really only doing what was conventionally offered. Later, however, the woman left the Unitarians, moved out into life in a much wider way as an actress and writer, became a Quaker and moved into Stage IV or Stage V faith stances. The question which needs to be pursued more in additional research is whether demythologizing activity should not be undertaken with early and middle adolescents (but wait until late adolescence and young adulthood) or whether it should and can be done if there is community support for it. This question is also related to the findings of Piaget (that adolescents do have, for the most part, the mental ability to do so) and to the findings of Ronald Goldman in England concerning the stages of religious thinking (that the thirteenth year was the beginning of such critical thinking is respect to religion).[32] In many of our faith communities within the Christian church, Fowler's findings no doubt apply. The findings on this issue will have very significant ramifications for relegous education, liturgical life, and preparation for ministry (both lay and professional). We shall return to this discussion in our chapters on confirmation and ordination.

The transition to Stage IV, Fowler finds, is brought about by serious clashes or contradictions between valued authority sources, e.g., when officially sanctioned leaders (such as in Vatican II) make marked changes in beliefs, policies, and practices previously thought to be sacred and unchangeable, (an experience that leads persons to discover how relative beliefs are to a particular group) *or* when one experiences leaving home for work, study, or marriage and discovers that one's conventional faith stance is inadequate.

Stage IV—Individuative-Reflective Faith

This is a quality of faith which persons develop when they begin to take seriously the burden of responsibility for their own commitments, beliefs, attitudes, and style of life. Such a forward movement tends to be taken by a very few late adolescents (5.4% in Fowler's sample— although 28.6% were in Stage III-IV transitional) and young adults (40% of the 21 to 30 age group studied). A substantial number of the latter age group were in Stage III-IV transitional (33.3%), however.[33]

The tendency of Stage III faith persons to critique their beliefs and loyalties largely at a personal level now moves out to critiquing their faith "as a system." A certain ability to step outside of the beliefs, symbols, faith stories, and practices begins to develop. The effort is related to what Erikson calls the quest for an ideology, a philosophy of life, a world view which embraces the realities of the wider community of power, position, and competing social, political, and corporate institutions. All of this wider effort is related to the quest for intimacy and love relationships at a very personal level.

Stage IV faith seeks to get behind the symbols of the faith community into systems of meaning related to life issues, to demythologize the symbols and master faith stories without "losing faith"; it is beginning to be more alert to unconscious factors which function in our decision making about beliefs and values, is beginning to think of the importance of social relationships well beyond the personal realm, is concerned about "laws, rules, and standards that govern social roles," is able to see that rituals and symbols, after critical analysis, are meaningful at a new level.[34]

The transition to Stage V faith is ususally triggered by a certain restlessness within, certain disturbing inner struggles with the recognition of the relativity of values in life; by an awareness that even though individual decisions were reached concerning commitments, world view, and lifestyle, there is concern that these decisions do not deal completely with all of the paradoxes in life or with all of the attractive optional lifestyles or beliefs or by disillusionment with compromises that have been made in one's values. Persons raise new questions, also, because of stimuli from the wider world of political crises, disparity between the rich and the poor, the recognition that laws can be unjust, etc. In this transition persons move away from the clear distinctions of Stage IV to the more dialectical and multileveled approach to truth found in Stage V.

Stage V—Conjunctive Faith

Stage V faith is ready to have encounters with alternative beliefs and traditions in a qualitatively different way than Stage IV. Persons in Stage V are willing to try to relate to other traditions (religious or secular) or philosophies of life in a dialogical manner, seeking to relate to others as though they may, in fact, have discovered truth about life which will alter and strengthen commitments held to be dear. Other persons are invited to speak their truth in their own way, with their own language. The listener is willing to hear without imposing his or her meaning on the other.

Stage V persons come to believe that the symbols, stories, doctrines, and liturgies offered by their own or other traditions are limited and partial. The awareness can cause frustration for some Stage V persons, but it can inspire others to increase the dialogue and to celebrate the power behind the mystery. Stage V persons can take this wider stance while continuing their commitment to a particular faith community.

Stage V persons become aware of the necessity to integrate conscious and unconscious forces in their lives. This awareness moves them to look for great faith symbols and stories which meet their deepest needs but which may come from various traditions with power to ground all persons in meaning.

Stage V persons do see the relativity of our laws and social norms, as Kohlberg has discovered, and are interested in humanizing laws and finding social norms which are more equitable for all races and classes of people. They are also more able to stand against an unjust law in civil disobedience if necessary.

Stage V persons see a certain interconnectedness in life. They move to a "second naivete," as Paul Ricoeur says, "to believe in the organic unity of all things and become able to resubmit to the initiative of the symbolic. Interestingly, such persons begin to distrust the separation of symbol and symbolized, sensing that when we neutralize the initiative of the symbolic, we make a pale idol of any meaning we honor."[35]

Fowler thinks that Stage V faith is seldom reached before middle adulthood. He found no Stage V persons in his 21 to 30 age sample; the age 31 to 40 group had an increase of Stage IV-V transitionals, but a large group of Stage III persons (37.5%); the 41 to 50 group had 34.4% Stage IV-V transitionals and Stage V with a very large percentage of Stage IV persons (56.2%); the 51 to 60 age group had 23.5% in Stage V with 29.4% in Stage IV and 35.3% in Stage III and a few in Stage II. The 61+ age group shows a distribution from Stage II-III transitionals (long equilibrated) to a lone Stage VI person.[36] His findings open up a vast new arena of important ministry with adults—persons who have tended too often to think they were not in need of faith development.

Fowler believes that Stage V faith is for many persons and not just for theology professors! He illustrates with a woman of 78 years who moved through many crises in life to a Stage V faith where she was involved in service to others and had worked through her Quaker community to believe that she had found a new grounding for her Christian faith which transcended the symbols of her own faith. She said to the interviewer that she had discovered somewhat painfully "that it doesn't matter what you call it, whether you call it God or Jesus or Cosmic Flow or Reality or Love, it doesn't matter what you call it. It is there. And what you learn directly from that source will not tie you up in creeds . . . that separate you from your fellow man."[37] Fowler saw this woman (who was renting rooms to graduate students to continue her service and writing) to be a person growing in her faith in a way most of us should gladly emulate. Here we see a person who had a social consciousness and was interested in finding unity in the midst of the paradoxes in life.

The transition to Stage VI faith is precipitated by the awareness of the somewhat divided nature of Stage V faith, not in terms of desire for unity, but in terms of the actuality of universal love and justice. Such transitional persons perceive the possibility and really the imperative to create an inclusive community. The disequilibrium caused by living between two worlds motivates some—the untransformed world in tension with a transforming vision. Some move on to actualize the dream in definitive ways. Others see the dream but fall back to Stage V for lack of courage.

Stage VI—Universalizing Faith

Fowler describes the structures of a mature faith not the content of such a faith. He happens to believe that Christianity, when fully embraced, leads persons to such a faith and that Christian beliefs, symbols and practices lead to the radical love and justice for all persons and nature which Stage VI reflects. He does cite other than avowed Christians as illustrations of Stage VI faith such as Abraham Heschel and Gandhi.

Stage VI faith is a quality of faith which goes beyond the paradoxical situation of Stage V with its loyalty to the present order and its various compromises with universal love and justice. Stage VI persons such as Martin Luther King or Mother Teresa of Calcutta risk the security found in the partial justice of the present order for a more inclusive order in the future. Stage VI persons seek to overcome the paradoxical situation through words and actions which incarnate universal love and justice for all beings. Such persons risk going against individuals and institutions wedded to proximate and limited arrangements in order to be spent for the transformation of the present unjust situation "in the direction of a transcendent actuality."[38] The actions of such persons reveal the truth of the Golden Rule, as Kohlberg's research maintains; "to do unto others as we would have them do unto us" is indeed very rare in actuality and is very costly to the person who dares to do so—not just at the personal private level but in relation to the whole human family and all of nature. Such persons often threaten the false security of others and are finally rejected by many.

A Stage VI faith, however, is contagious and does create "zones of liberation" to which other persons are drawn. People do not set out to be Stage VI persons. They are usually the result of nurture into a particular faith community which gives them the vision, but the exigencies of history help create the conditions which call forth such an expansive response. As Fowler says, "It is as though they are selected by the great Blacksmith of history, heated in the fires of turmoil and trouble and then hammered into usable shape on the hard anvil of conflict and struggle."[39]

Stage VI persons are very rare and usually do not come to such a faith until middle to later adulthood. Such persons are not perfect persons. They often have blind spots in their perceptions and behavior. However, they respond to the need for universal love and justice with abandon and total commitment. They show the rest of us the hard and narrow pathway to the universal community which we call the kingdom of God on earth.

From the Christian perspective, Fowler believes the content of God's grace and love through belief in Jesus Christ and through the call to be members of the kingdom of God will lead us to Stage VI faith. It will be a witnessing approach to faith and not a judgmental one. He believes that Christians are called to be true to the vision of the kingdom of love and justice for all and to act upon that vision. Christians are not called to require all people, dedicated to God as they are as Jews or Hindus, to become Christians. Rather, we witness to the radical monotheism revealed through the Judeo-Christian tradition and fully in Christ. This is a monotheism which transcends our ability to symbolize it and order it fully. It is a belief in relation to which all images, symbols, rites, and practices are relative. In this sense Fowler seems to agree that the ultimate, while revealed clearly in history and in Christ, is still a mystery. Stage VI faith seeks to be true to its vision, but humble before the mystery which is the ultimate reality, open to be taught the truth from within and beyond the community of faith in which the vision was caught.

Stage VI faith is able to go to the deepest level in respect to conscious and unconscious motivations. It is able to see not only the other person's situation but the situation of persons in other groups, religions, and cultures. It has a quality of empathy which is rare and also painful for the person who senses the needs of others and seeks to respond personally and socially. It is a faith which can see the symbolic nature of all of our theological or philosophical statements of belief and can demythologize them—and yet see the deeper power of the symbols and rites to create community. It is a faith which is open to leading from the ultimate mystery from which the vision of universal love and justice comes. It is a faith which resides genuinely within a particular faith community. While the living out of this vision radically may be a judgment on that particular community it is not the goal of Stage VI faith to denounce and reject that community but to help it fulfill its own vision. Jesus said that he came not to abolish the law and the prophets but to fulfill them (Mt. 5:17). This is characteristic of Stage VI persons.

Fowler at first sought, not to make a judgment about which of the stages of faith was most adequate, but rather to describe the structures of faith at different ages and stages. He, however, now believes that it is somewhat self-evident, without judging the meaningfulness of the content of the faith of persons at Stages II, III, IV, or V, that Stage VI faith is normative. It is a mature faith for which other stages are developmentally prior or preparatory. How this belief will be confirmed or altered in subsequent research remains to be known. If we were to take Stage VI faith to be normative, we would have to change our goals for education and liturgy markedly.

It must be stated, however, that persons live out the Christian faith dynamically and powerfully at each of the stages of faith development. Moreover, it should be a goal of religious education to stimulate learners to experience the depth dimensions associated with each stage with integrity while at the same time enabling learners to confront issues which open the door to growth to the more mature forms of faith associated with later stages. For instance, considerable research is available about the rather profound religious insights children can express intuitively prior to their development of more mature forms of faith.[40] Such findings illustrate the need to not classify persons in their religious lives in ways that demean the seriousness of their commitments. The joys of the Christian pilgrimage can be celebrated at each point of the journey while, at the same time, recognizing the fact that the journey is not finished.

Notes

1. Victor W. Turner, *The Ritual Process* (Chicago: Aldine Publishing Co., 1969); Victor Turner and Edith Turner, *Images and Pilgrimage in Christian Culture* (New York: Columbia University Press, 1978). Turner distinguishes sign from symbol, saying that there cannot only be a multiplicity of meanings for a single symbol but that there is a likeness between the thing signified and its meaning. This is not so with signs. Symbols are semantically "open." The symbol's meaning has continuity but it is not fixed. Dominant symbols have *exegetical meanings*, supplied by those inside the ritual system, *operational meaning* derived from the use made of the symbol, and *positoral meaning*, discovered as the symbol is interpreted in relation to other symbols in the total ritual system. Some meanings are discerned quite broadly, some are latent, some are hidden.

2. Claude Levi-Strauss, "The Efficacy of Symbols," *Structural Anthropology* (New York: Basic Books, 1963).

3. Raymond Firth, *Symbols—Public and Private* (Ithaca, N.Y.: Cornell University Press, 1973), p. 196.

4. Louis Bouyer, *Rite and Man: Natural Sacredness and Christian Liturgy* (Notre Dame, Ind.: University of Notre Dame Press, 1963), p. 196.

5. Ibid., p. 66.

6. Alexander Schmemann, *For the Life of the World* (Crestwood, N.Y.: St. Vladimir's Seminary Press, 1973), p. 14.

7. Gerard A. Pottebaum, *The Rites of People* (Washington, D.C.: The Liturgical Conference, 1975), p. 33.

8. Erik H. Erikson, *Toys and Reasons—Stages in the Ritualization of Experience* (New York: W. W. Norton, 1977), p. 118.

9. Ibid., p. 173.

10. In Erikson's basic identity scheme he normally has eight stages. The major difference is to be found in his single category of adult rituals. He has young adult, middle adult, and older adult identity stages in his basic pattern.

11. Ibid., pp. 79-80.

12. Ibid., pp. 80-82.

13. Ibid., pp. 82-83.

14. See several of Erikson's works in which these themes are developed: *Childhood and Society* (New York: W. W. Norton, 1963); *Identity and the Life Cycle* (New York: International University Press, 1959); *Insight and Responsibility* (New York: W. W. Norton, 1964); *Young Man Luther: A Study in Psychoanalysis and History* (New York: W. W. Norton, 1962); and others.

15. See L. Howard Grimes' excellent review of these theorists in "The Bible and the Teaching of Children," in the *Perkins Journal* (Fall, 1977), pp. 10-26.

16. Erikson, *Toys and Reasons,* p. 89-90.

17. See Erikson, *Insight and Responsibility.*

18. Erikson, *Toys and Reasons,* p. 95.

19. Ibid.

20. Ibid., p. 103.

21. Ibid., p. 106.

22. Ibid., p. 107.

23. Ibid., p. 125.

24. See Gabriel Moran, *Religious Education Development* (Minneapolis: Winston Press, 1983). Moran raises important questions which lead to further research while also affirming Erikson's contribution.

25. Kenneth Stokes, *Faith Development in the Adult Life Cycle* (New York: W. H. Sadlier, 1982). This is a report of an early symposium (in which Fowler participated). A wide-ranging study of adult faith development will be reported after studies of adults in the United States and Canada have been completed.

26. James W. Fowler, *Stages of Faith* (San Francisco: Harper & Row, 1981), p. 93.

27. Ibid., p. 99.

28. Ibid., p. 121.

29. Moran, *Religious Education Development,* p. 111.

30. Fowler, *Stages of Faith,* p. 317.

31. Ibid., p. 163.

32. See Jean Piaget, *Six Psychological Studies* (New York: Random House, 1967), and Ronald Goldman, *Religious Thinking in Childhood and Adolescence* (New York: Seabury Press, 1964).

33. Fowler, *Stages of Faith,* p. 317.

34. Ibid., p. 180.

35. Ibid., p. 177.

36. Ibid., p. 319.

37. Ibid.

38. Ibid., p. 200.

39. Ibid., p. 202.

40. See Edward Robinson, *The Original Vision* (Oxford: Religious Experience Research Unit, 1977) and Maria Harris' interpretation of such findings in "The Original Vision: Children and Religious Experience," in *Family Ministry,* ed. Gloria Durka and Joanmarie Smith (Minneapolis: Winston Press, 1980), pp. 56-77.

Part III

Sacramental Life: A Basic Model and Its Integration in Religious Education and Liturgy

Chapter 7

Toward a Basic Model:
Integrating Sacraments,
Religious Education, and Liturgy

New Models

Every perspective on the sacramental life of the church is the creation of some sort of model. These are primarily *theoretical* models, meaning-schemes, built to advance fresh understanding or show logical relationships between ideas, but they are also usually to some extent *physical* models because people who address themselves to the questions posed in the *idea* of sacrament, as an issue for theology, do this seldom out of a narrow theological concern, but out of an involvement in the church's worship and pastoral life.[1] Even the most theoretical of studies of sacraments, such as George S. Worgul's, *From Magic to Metaphor*,[2] concludes with a model of sacrament as celebration, the farthest thing from an abstract theoretical definition.

Worgul's celebration model emerges out of critiques of what he calls the "scholastic" model with its mechanistic-physical presuppositions about the cause and effect of God's grace in the world; the "mystery-presence" model (Casel) in which "inspiration was more valuable than content"; and the "interpersonal-encounter" model (Schillebeeckx) which posits the presence of God but doesn't say how this comes about.[3] Worgul's argument for a celebration model assumes that the reality being celebrated is not created in the event, but is already present. He sees the "reality event" of sacrament, God's gift of grace in Christ, as celebrated but not created in our liturgies. For Worgul, celebrations are personal and corporate. They allow internalization through listening and acting, "a turning in" to discover the reality-event in human consciousness and a "turning out" where worshipers reach out to one another, becoming living, acting symbols of the meaning the celebration is manifesting.

Worgul's model is a construction quite similar to that implied in the definition of sacrament given by Tad Guzie. As we have seen, Guzie sees the eucharist as the central "festive action" and the other sacraments grouped around it in celebrations of initiation, healing, and ministry.[4]

New models abound. Sacrament is: "God's self-giving" (White),[5] "doors to the sacred" (Martos),[6] "visible words" (Jenson),[7] "presence of God calling us to presence" (Duffy),[8] "life in all its totality—returned to man, given again as sacrament" (Schmemann),[9] "the celebration of our new enlightenment and interpretation . . . translated into gestures and signs that signify our discovery" (Segundo),[10] "Spirit-filled signs that actually effect here and now for us the very thing we are celebrating" (Bausch).[11]

These image-models have some different emphases but their common presuppositions are more obvious and important. They all in various ways see: (1) All of life as sacramental. (2) Sacraments as symbols of the fact that the entire world belongs to God and is the gift of God to us, uniting us to creation and all people in celebration of the sacredness of all life and of our belonging to one another in the Spirit. (3) God's grace made visible in many ways, but uniquely in Jesus Christ. (4) The church as the sacrament of Christ. (5) Sacramental events as a presence of Christ in the church and world. (6) Sacraments as *power now* in church and world—not mere thoughtful recollection or emotive soliloquy but present Spirit energy evoking human commitment and action. (7) Sacraments as kingdom events and as such signs of the future. (8) Sacraments as truly human events, natural to the life cycle, nurturing in the evolution of faith, and responsive to real human need.

Mysterion-Sacramentum

Our model of sacrament as *mysterion-sacramentum* is consonant with this modern consensus of overlapping motifs. We articulate these agreements in a defining model which (1) affirms the root of sacrament in God's word in scripture, (2) acknowledges the logic and validity of evolution of sacramental life in the dynamic tradition of Christian people, (3) understands sacrament as God active and inspiring in our world, animating discipleship in events of human commitment framed in the human community of faith but directed outward to service in the world, and (4) is naturally ecumenical because its formulation is shaped within an ongoing interconfessional conversation, reaching beyond the dividing histories of denominational argument and practice to some common history and some seminal affirmations.

Our model of sacrament as essentially *mysterion-sacramentum* is neither arcane nor archaic; it is simply foundational, based upon origins of sacrament in primary Christian language and idea, and in beginning and continuing historical practice. As *mysterion*, in a New Testament vision, sacrament is:

1. Christ as God's kingdom sign and	"Unto you is given the *mysterion* of the Kingdom of God" (Mk. 4:10-12).
2. Christ with his people.	"a *mysterion* hidden for ages . . . but now made manifest" (Col. 1:26).
3. Universal activity of God redeeming the world of which we are stewards and servants.	"This is how one should regard us, as servants of Christ and stewards of the mysteries of God" (1 Cor. 4:1).

Sacrament as *mysterion* is thus created out of biblical substance. It is also, as *sacramentum*, created out of ecclesial strategy. As *sacramentum*, sacrament is:

4. Sign or symbol

The sign-acts which are symbols of *mysterion* in church and world are of quite different kinds—as substantial as bread, and as spiritual as a vow. (The sign-symbols are water, bread and wine, touching, oil, forgiveness, and different vows of commitment.) They are the core of common liturgy events by virtue of ecclesial decision. The sign-acts we acknowledge are supplied to us variously by Jesus' practice, by apostolic practice in the early church or by later common practice in the church.[12]

5. Commitment

The sign-act liturgies of Christian people are commonly agreed upon gestures of commitment, where the signs of *mysterion* touch us as moments of choice where we decide for Christ, for one another, and for the world.

An "Essential" Vision

The model we present is not a definition. We do not think it necessary nor particularly helpful to advance a definition. We have tried to explain the model, in chapters 2 and 4 exactly, not as a definition, but rather as a kind of primary vision, relating sacrament simply and basically to *mysterion* in the New Testament, to parable with Jesus, and to *sacramentum* in the early church where *mysterion* translates into commitment in the culture where Christians must witness to it, become part of it and bear it forward.

If we have been this "essential" and "primary" in our framing of a model, it is not because our interest is theoretical. We have wanted to think in a primary way in order to make the focus of commitment as plain as possible. What in fact is essential is the existence, the liveliness of Mystery-Present in our real lives in the real world. So our interest is very much in the normal ritualizations of life as identified and clarified by Erikson and others and the development of the stages of faith in human experience as described by Fowler. These things are a matter of ordinary, daily lives of faith and of momentous events of personal, cultural, and historical crisis. It is certainly essential in the church that we find genuine meaning, honest redeeming encounter with our Lord, with other persons, and direction and mission in our participation in the symbols of God's work in the world, communicated to us in the particular sacraments. They relate to our struggles, to our fulfillments, to our crises and failures, and to our wholeness and our success. Individual sacraments cannot correlate precisely with our *kairos* moments, either developmentally as we move through different "stages" of life or uniquely, personally in the unfolding of each person's pilgrimage. But they do relate to the stages of human development and they are at least potentially flexible enough to relate to the unique experience of individuals. It is their power that they can address and absorb us personally and include us in a worshiping people with a common sense of purpose and a corporate ministry within and beyond the congregation. These action-parables of God's kingdom, giving blessing and demanding decision are essential to our lives of faith. They both nurture and give precise dramatic and numinous content to faith. And they should be the kind of exercise in Christian life which is necessary to us, because it is their purpose to relate faith to actual issues in life.

We turn now to discover some of the ramifications of the model for particular sacraments in a design which relates them to the stages of human and faith development discussing understandings, attitudes and behavior in the ministries of education and liturgy.

Integration and Creative Tension

One of the trends identified in chapter 1 was the current tendency to integrate religious education and liturgy and see the life of the church more wholistically. It is now generally affirmed that persons learn what it means to be faithful Christians by participating with members of the faith community in the full range of experiences at the center of the community's life.

There is no doubt that a powerful religious education takes place as persons incorporate the values, master faith stories, formal and informal rituals, characteristic behaviors, and visions of the meaning and purpose of life manifested in the sacramental celebrations of the community. However, as noted in chapter 1, religious education and liturgy should not lose the creative tension essential to the integrity of their respective functions. In the sacraments there needs to be integration. The inclusion of children, for instance, at the communion table can be a profound education as well as liturgical experience for the child. Such an experience can bring identification with faithful persons, a strong sense of being loved and embraced by God as the center of life. This experience takes place prior to the child's ability to articulate the meaning of communion or to reflect on central elements in communion historically or theologically. However, a religious education is needed which constructively engages parents and the congregation, and increasingly, the children themselves, in exploration of their perceptions of the nature of communion, their feelings about the "aliveness" or "deadness" of the experience, their questions about the meaning of the action parables, the stories, and ritual expressions, and the relation of the celebration to other aspects of their lives. Also, in order to keep the sacramental celebration true to the gospel, the liturgical expressions need to be evaluated, critiqued, and in some cases, revitalized. In this way religious education makes its best contribution by being in creative tension with liturgy. Of course, it is also true that liturgical life which is dynamic and genuinely revelatory of God's life of love, trust, and justice is a judgment upon religious education which is barren, lifeless, and unrelated to the sense of the sacredness of all of life. Here again we see the interrelation of liturgy and religious education.

In order to be more precise about the unique aspects of each, however, let us look more closely at the guidelines which will be operative as we reflect on the religious education and liturgy needed in relation to each of the sacraments being discussed in Part III.

Religious Education, Sacramental Life, and Mystery

The discussion of religious education and sacramental life has been extended and made visible especially by those interested in catechesis. An example of this approach is the helpful volume, *Liturgy and Learn-*

ing Through the Life Cycle, by John Westerhoff III and William Willimon. Westerhoff, here and elsewhere, employs the concept of catechesis because he believes that persons in our secular society need to see life through the Christian world view and perspective revealed by Christ and the church. In order for persons to see their lives in relation to God's love and will, they need to be enculturated into the community of faithful members of the body of Christ. Children, youth, and adults enter the Christian community through baptism and are socialized into the beliefs, values, practices, and perspectives on life through participation in the drama of the church year, the celebration of the community's vision of life, and the church's story which becomes the frame of reference for the individuals to tell their own stories of faith. Westerhoff and Willimon have made a significant contribution interpreting how faith can be experienced and finally owned within the church as a pilgrim community in which the memory and vision of the church is acted out and celebrated in sacramental life.[13]

Faith enculturation, to Westerhoff, is seen as much more than a conserving and corporate activity. It should involve persons in doing critical analysis as well. Catechesis, he says, is "concerned with both continuity (conserving an authoritative tradition) and change (making a prophetic judgment on its understanding of that tradition). It is a process intended to both recall and reconstruct the church's tradition so that it might become conscious and active in the lives of maturing persons in community. . . . Catechesis, therefore, intends to help us understand the implications of Christian faith for life and our lives, to critically evaluate every aspect of our individual and corporate understandings and ways, and to become equipped for and inspired to faithful activity in church and society."[14] Catechesis, he maintains, should be a community activity which shares its beliefs, values, and story with individuals in order to help them catch the faith but also to use the essential vision of God's love and justice as means of critique, judgment, and finally of transformation of both individual and corporate life in line with the vision.

While Westerhoff's view of the nature and purpose of catechesis is commendable and certainly supportive of our basic model of sacramental life in the church, it could profit from more attention to the concept of mystery. A genuine Christian religious education can be developed which celebrates the "identified mystery" which Christ's revelation makes possible without forgetting that God is an "identified mystery which still remains a mystery," as Schillebeeckx says. The strength of the concept of catechesis is that it makes more probable a

Christian pilgrim with a very clear sense of identity, a strong commitment to Christ and to ministry and mission in the world. The possible weakness of catechesis is that it may be less open to dialogue with God's actions and presence in the wider life of the world, including the possibility that Christianity could be judged by God's revelation of truth via persons and institutions other than the church. This wider perspective is really more consistent with the biblical witness. This is true because God often uses the simple faithfulness of those who "give a cup of cool water" to those in need (whether or not within the church) as an illustration of behavior which really pleases God's sense of love and justice. Or, as Amos records concerning God's will, "Seek good and not evil, that you may live . . . Hate evil and love good; enthrone justice in the courts. . . . I hate, I spurn your pilgrim feasts; I will not delight in your sacred ceremonies. When you present your sacrifices and offerings I will not accept them. . . . Spare me the sound of your songs; I cannot endure the music of your lutes. Let justice roll on like a river and righteousness like an ever-flowing stream" (Amos 5:14a, 15a, 21-24). We are inclined to pause when we see what the biblical witness is concerning how God works in history and in our personal, social, and corporate lives.

One of the major problems in religious education today is the quest for certainty evident in both conservative and liberal communities. The fastest growing communities are those which have codified "the truth" into certain truths on which persons can base their beliefs and in which they can find unity as selves. By seeking the truth to teach they have been tempted to eliminate the mystery of the kingdom of God which is a central tenet of the biblical witness.[15]

We shall indicate our view of Christian religious education which celebrates the good news in Christ and the firmness of the call to ministry within the body of Christ without discounting "the mystery which still remains a mystery" and which, while calling for high commitment and individual decisions in concrete forms of ministry, is still open to God's presence in the very structures of life and is thereby less judgmental, hopefully, of how God's love and justice may break in upon our lives.

In earlier research and writing we have distilled four basic models of religious education: (1) assent to correct beliefs, (2) rebirth into new life in Christ, (3) nurture into Christ-like living, and (4) participation in the ministering community of faith.[16] In each model the relation of religious education and liturgy (especially sacramental life) is different. In the assent model the sacraments are defined much more precisely and become substantialistic means of grace to those who have agreed with the beliefs essential for salvation. In the rebirth model the sacraments are interpreted in the light of the need to confess one's sin, repent, and surrender to God. Baptism and communion are channels of surrender (dying to sin) and rising with Christ in new life. In the nurture model, with its emphasis on God's unconditional love, the sacraments are seen in relational and symbolic terms. Persons are baptized into the body of Christ, into the accepting, loving, caring community of faith. Communion is seen as a sharing in the fruits of God's supreme gift of love as Christ gave his body and blood that we may live the life of love and trust fully. The final model, participation in the ministering community of faith, sees the sacraments to be powerful communicators of the good news in relation to the life issues of persons within the ministering community. Word and sacrament, religious education and liturgy are interrelated and wholistic. Moreover, the sense of mystery is at the heart of this model. While there are important elements in each model which need to appear in any fully developed approach to religious education we shall highlight the participation model and show how it broadens the concept of catechesis and becomes a constructive framework for our discussion of religious education and liturgy in Part III.

Religious Education As Participation in the Ministering Community of Faith

Persons learn to be Christian by participating fully with others who are incarnating the life of love and justice which Christ revealed and which the church continues (as the sacrament of Christ). Persons learn to be faithful to God by hearing and recreating the story of the love of God for all creation and the agony of God when the human family rejects or distrusts this love. The vision of God's life of love and justice is made known to learners as they experience the rituals, faith stories, actions, lifestyles, and creedal statements of the faith community. However, in order to appropriate the vision, the individual must not only be socialized but must make decisions which protect the integrity of the self and which genuinely integrate the faith with all of the experiences he or she is having beyond the faith community. Education which is honest must explore the wide range of options which have been or are being formulated as answers to life's basic questions.

In our participation model of religious education there is a recognition that God is the creator of all of life and that God's grace is present not only within the faith community but in the very structures of life. The faith community is called to be stewards of the good news of God's love and justice; but, the faith community does not control

God's grace nor does the community dispense this grace in ways not possible beyond the community. The faith community is not satisfied to share the vision, to bring persons to the decision to affirm the vision and to reenact it. The faith community is to prepare persons to be in ministry within and beyond the community, to be firm in their beliefs and actions, but to be open to ways in which God is mysteriously moving to bring love, peace, and justice alive in persons and places which use interpretive codes other than our own.

This wider setting for religious education is based on two basic concepts: (1) Human nature is finite and yet capable of responding to and participating in God's infinite vision, and (2) God's nature is fundamentally grounded in mystery. God is manifested in nature, history, and personality (supremely, we believe, in the person of Christ); but, because of the finitude of persons, all of our formulations about God are limited and subject to error. Therefore, we can never capture God's will or way perfectly. Such a stance makes us much more cautious about socializing persons into our version of the Christian vision of life as *the* ultimate truth or as *the* approach to renewal, or as *the* way to be related to one another and God in love and trust.

This approach celebrates the joy and confidence of the "identified mystery" through Christ and the church but is more aware that God, by nature, transcends the versions of the good news we teach. God's love and justice are active within the ministering community, but God is acting in the world and universe in ways that the faith community only dimly perceives or faintly understands. Consequently, a sense of humility is integral. We have the vision. We celebrate that which we have experienced of God's forgiveness, acceptance, and call to ministry; but we do so knowing that there is much that is unknown. We, in fact, see through a glass darkly (1 Cor. 13).

Since God is active in all of life, all events and phenomena which confront persons can be seen as religiously significant and as a call to faithfulness. In fact, we say yes or no to God in these everyday decisions. From this perspective, there is no split between the sacred and the secular. The *content* of our religious education, therefore, cannot merely be the stances of faith which come from the biblical witness or from the history of the faith community's life together, as central as this is. The content must include God's actions today in the wider life of science, law, the humanities, and stories of people in other faith communities who are seeking to discern the nature of God's life of love and justice. Such a stance moves us beyond catechesis to a religious education which celebrates its convictions and participates actively in the ministries of love, truth, and justice in the world. Such a religious education is joyously Christ centered ("the identified mystery") but is open to the manifestation of God's activity in the wider life in the universe ("the identified mystery which still remains a mystery"). Moreover, in this interpretation a unique task of religious education is not only the communication of the great beliefs of the Christian community but the persistent pursuit of God's truth wherever it is incarnated in the universe.

Participation in the ministering community of faith is a model which seems very similar to the assumptions behind catechesis. In several ways it is. The major difference is the self-understanding of the faith community itself. Catechesis draws a rather tight circle, focusing as it does on the unique life of the Christian community—its stories, beliefs, rituals, festival actions as the primary educative experiences. Catechesis flows from a practical theology which is defined from within the circle of faith. Religious education from the faith community which is focused on the "identified Mystery which still remains a mystery" is just as firm about the importance of sharing the faith stories, rituals, and concrete forms of ministry and mission but is turned out in order to be open to God's actions in the world beyond the church. This means that Christian religious education can celebrate with appreciation the insights and truth which come from the social sciences as well as from the Christian tradition. When we find love, trust, acceptance, and justice we discover that they are epiphanies of the sacramental nature of all of God's creation to which the Christian gospel is a witness. The uniqueness of the Christian revelation in Christ (the primordial sacrament of God) can be taught and lived without the temptation to fall into self-righteousness or idolatry of belief or form.

Such a stance greatly affects the attitudes teachers and parents will take to religious education. It will affect the outcomes we have in mind for the learners of whatever age or condition. It will influence our openness to creative methods. Especially such a stance will influence the content and processes we build into our curriculum. And, certainly, this more open stance calls for a liturgy which is turned out to the world while celebrating the glorious good news which is the unique message of the gathered community in Christ.

Concern for Liturgy

In an ecumenical study on sacraments there is obviously no specific discussion about liturgy which can be universally helpful since we all operate under widely different rubrics regarding what is fixed and what is free. Some general studies have appeared which have been successful in offering liturgical guidance, speaking to us across denominational lines, such as *Liturgy and Learning Through the Life Cycle*, by John Westerhoff III and William Willimon[17] or *Visible Words*, by Robert Jenson,[18] and most of the churches provide specific help in companion volumes to their liturgical books, such as the *Manual on the Liturgy*[19] of the Lutherans, the *Commentary on the American Prayer Book*[20] of the Episcopalians, or the volumes which have accompanied the appearance of the alternate liturgies of the United Methodists.[21] We have no wish to duplicate these resources but will utilize them to help us all become more aware of general directions and options.

The best thing to read about leadership in worship remains Robert W. Hovda's *Strong, Loving and Wise*.[22] It is not a book about sacraments but is richly insightful about the doing of liturgy.

Our concern about the liturgical action of sacraments is in fact the same subject matter we encountered in trying to understand sacrament theologically and historically. We shall frame the concern in a somewhat different way.

1. How is the grace of God as Mystery Present signified? Is the fundamental symbol at the heart of each sacrament clear and eloquent? Does it articulate the fundamental parable which is the sacrament?

2. Is the liturgy-event a family of God celebration? Is it a true meeting, relating people to one another and in Christ? Is church a reality here?

3. Is commitment made, and clearly made, for primary participants and all present? Is the commitment understood and entered into openly with appropriate word and gesture?

4. Is the sign-event as clear as it can be about God's rule in the world? Is the kingdom of God, which is in our midst and which is coming, made manifest?

5. Is the sign-event faithful to scripture, to the history of sacrament in the church, and is it framed in a suitable dramatic logic?

A Kingdom Scene

We will, from the standpoint of these primary interests, make limited commentary upon current liturgical practice. We will do this as we consider the several sacraments, but one of the criteria probably needs at least some expanded comment at this point. The fourth criterion asserts that a sacrament should be an affective sign of the kingdom of God. We have established in chapter 4 our understanding of sacraments as action parables of the kingdom of God. The idea that a primary purpose of sacrament, or of Christian worship in general, is

the creation of a kingdom scene and kingdom vision has specific implications. A great deal of Christian worship exists, as Jürgen Moltmann
points out,[23] as "refreshment" in the midst of the purposive, accom-
plishing, ordered world of work. As a "pause that refreshes" along the
way, interrupting momentarily our determined work toward calcula-
ble goals, worship is something tied to the work-cycle within which it
provides refreshment and consequently is easily replaced by competing respites and entertainments. Thus is the holy time of liturgy captive to the worldly time of work and the accomplishment of purposive
ends. The model Moltmann apposes to worship as refreshment is
worship as festival. Feast, of course, is not an instrument to another
purpose. It is its own reason. This is perhaps hard for us modern
people to grasp with our things to do and places to go. Play in its many
forms is simply too idle a matter for us. Moltmann remembers how
"the farmers in Northern Germany used to stand outside the church
on Sunday morning and chat about business, while their wives and
children were singing and praying in the church. The men came in
only when the sermon began. The "play" of worship has no serious
purpose for serious people.[24] Participation of serious people waits
upon serious purpose. But worship is not something that finds its real
reason for being outside itself; it is its own reason; it is in itself meaningful. This is not immediately clear to all of us. Moltmann understands that when what we *have* and what we *do* to get what we have are
the things that give life meaning, we may not be able to see useful
purpose in the festivity of worship. "The reproduction of life through
work puts a stop to the festival renewal of life from a transcendent
source."[25] So Moltmann invites us to worship as feast, not respite from
work and therefore defined by work. As feast, worship is not refreshment within a cycle of work but an alternative to the tyranny over us
of what we have and what we do to get what we have. Worship as
alternative introduces us to new life and the discovery that we are, and
that we are in God. "Feast introduces an as yet unknown freedom into
the midst of unfree life."[26]

The new life Christian faith has to celebrate as alternative is the new
time of the kingdom of God: time redeemed by the holy kairos of
Jesus, surprising us with a radical alternative indeed—a different life.
So sacrament is the creation of a kingdom scene. This does not mean
the creation of an unreal dream, but it does mean making room for
fantasy—the actual vision of an *alternative.* Praying is always living out
of hope, out of what is not, but what may yet be. It names what is not
in order to break the spell of what is. Sacrament must be visionary in
this sense and call us into the new life which is not but which is God's

future for us and our world. The substance of this summons is especially embedded in the word of Jesus in parable and story. These
pictures of what the time of God is like should be allowed space in the
alternatives which are our sacraments. But we should not be satisfied
that the kingdom of God is manifested in sacrament as vision. The
qualities of God's time should, of course, be present in the event itself.
If the action-parables are not embodiments they are simply advertise-
ment, but then what will they advertise if they are not embodiments?
There must be a congruence between what is spoken and what is
signified.

We may be instructed at this point by the realization that the situation of Christian worship as "alternative" to values dictated by a materialistic culture is something often best understood and realized by
poor people. The colorful worship characteristic of Latin people and
black people is case in point. As James Cone puts it, concerning black
worship: "Black people who have been humiliated and oppressed by
the structures of white society six days of the week, gather together
each Sunday morning in order to experience another definition of
their humanity."[27] He describes this as a kingdom scene of worship
where people are "no longer named by the world but named by the
Spirit of Jesus."[28] Is not this eschatological "alternative"—life not
bounded by oppressing strictures but liberated by the freedom of
newness in Christ—a *sine qua non* of Christian worship? The creation
of this vision and the means to experience it together is an essential
part of the art of liturgy. It should not surprise us that the poor should
find this easier to accomplish than the affluent. Jesus told us that it was
hard for the rich to enter the kingdom of God.

There is no simple formula for the achievement of this kingdom
time. It cannot be coerced; it can only be invited. If we will invite
Jesus and in turn humble ourselves to let him invite us, we have to find
ourselves in situations where he invites us. Sacraments are intended as
particular moments for this invitation because they are small dramas
of Christian decision. Some things are necessary for these action-
parables to work as kingdom-scenes. In the first place we have to
present the kingdom Word and trust it. The role of the minister and
leaders is not manipulation-coercion, but effective presentation and
trust. Sometimes the appropriate Word is prescribed, if not, it needs
to be found and presented. How the Word is presented *says* a lot. The
clear presentation of the kingdom Word needs to demonstrate not
only its importance, but its indispensable centrality to the liturgy of
sacrament. This means, of course, good lucid reading,[29] and a significant role in the liturgy for the reading of scripture. This may mean the

highlighting of reading with the "accompaniment" of praying, singing, and perhaps moving—as when gospel lessons are read "among" the people. A great deal of scripture has been set to music; the use of the music can be a powerful illumination of the Word. In some way reading needs to be brought to the affective level of prayer. The uses of music (vocal, choral, organ, hymns), dance, vocal prayer, and silence, are needed to give reading a resonance in the lives of the people who assemble to worship.

In the second place we have to present the kingdom-Word and its sign in an action-event in which all are included. The sacraments are different kinds of events in this regard. The eucharist intends the uniform participation of all present. A wedding or a baptism focuses on some very few persons among us, and we cannot all be "primary" participants in these sacraments. It is nevertheless possible for weddings and baptisms to take place in ways that include our participation and promote our identification with the faith-dimension of what is taking place. All Christians who find themselves witnesses to these kingdom-signs have something to sing about and something to long for concerning the covenant which is at the heart of these events. In prayer and song, and perhaps in witness we need to participate. The promises of God and the promises of people which are the substance of weddings and baptisms are not the narrow concerns of the people being married or baptized. No, these repeated covenant-events have continuing significance for all of us because they speak vital things to us about our life together and our mission in the world. We will only know this when the liturgies involve us convincingly. This does not necessarily mean some massive and thereby intrusive role of the congregation in these events. It does mean that some things happen that make the point. It should make a difference, for instance, in the celebration of baptism, if we would all join in singing Fred Pratt Green's hymn.

> Lord Jesus, once a child,
> Savior of young and old,
> Receive this little child of ours
> Into your flock and fold.
>
> You drank the cup of life,
> Its bitterness and bliss,
> And loved us to the uttermost
> For such a child as this.

So help us Lord to trust,
Through this baptismal rite
Not in our own imperfect love.
But in your saving might.

Lord Jesus, for his/her sake,
Lend us your constant aid,
That he/she when older, may rejoice
We kept the vows we made.[30]

In the third place, if a sacrament will be understood as a kingdom-sign it needs to happen as a kingdom-action which leads us from the sanctuary of our worship out into our world with renewed vision and commitment. This can happen in prayer and song, but it is also a primary purpose of preaching. The Word which is heard in our liturgies is ordinarily couched in words which need and deserve interpretation. Preaching should not be an absolute rule of sacramental celebration. It is easy to conceive of isolated events where it would be unnecessary or inappropriate, but it should be a normal expectation within sacrament, and it should be a larger part of the function of such preaching to point us toward the wider meaning of the sign we celebrate as a reminder of how God's kingdom is invading our world and making us servants of the mystery of God in the world.

In the fourth place, it is exceedingly helpful, if not necessary to the whole direction we are indicating, if the lives of the ministers of sacrament are themselves signs of God's kingdom. It has been established long since that the validity of the ministries of the church does not depend upon the piety of the ministers (Donatist controversy). But let us not kid ourselves; the piety of the ministers has a lot to do with what is communicated to the believers. More often than not, the medium is the message. The lives of the ministers—of all who witness to the kingdom—speak more eloquently than the text of any liturgy or sermon about the reality of God's kingdom in the world. What we bring to the sign-event that is sacrament is more than a faith-sign, an official church-word, a biblical Word, and our special understandings and skills; it is also the sign-event of our own lives as confirmation or denial. This is a fact which is hard to live with. It is uncomfortable. We would like to forget it. But forgetting it is wrong. Christian faith is an exactly incarnational occasion. It is not finally concept, but who we are and what happens. All this is to say, never abstract yourself from the kingdom-sign that is sacrament.

Words

From a concern with sacrament as kingdom-sign we turn now to consideration of sacrament as words. What we call sacrament, and indeed all liturgy, is always more than a text. It is a congruence of Word, sign, words, people, sounds, sights, gestures—multiple dimensions, whose unity comprises actual liturgy. But it is a text. It is an accurate commonplace in current discussions of sacrament to observe that, being unclear about symbol and uncertain about the capacity of symbol to communicate, we often obscure or even bury the potent primary symbol of a sacrament in an avalanche of words. This is true, and no more important critique about sacrament is before us. It is natural for us, with our many books, to assume that sacrament is simply text. Much of our mechanistic-legalistic sacramental life flows from this assumption. This is not helped by the practice of many ministers to annotate the official text with their own commentary.

Liturgical theology sometimes follows the same wordy path. Study of sacrament can become a matter of textual analysis. Liturgical theology as textual analysis is almost always too ideological and authoritarian. The method, seen in theology[31] or in popular liturgical tour guides,[32] instructs us as to how matters should be. Strangely, we are often satisfied to know this. It is necessary though to take the humble and often troublesome step and inquire how things really are. Theological-liturgical analysis of texts of worship will usually tell us what certain norms are and how liturgical celebration should create the prayer of worshipers and form their spirituality, but it will not tell us whether or not, nor how, it actually does these things. This is a more elusive matter. Inquiry at this level is much more difficult than the heady theological work of establishing norms. But we need to work at this "affective" level. Specifically, we need to know more about how symbol functions in human experience, and we need to be asking the people in our churches what is happening to them in worship.

Just because it is so legitimate for us to react against overemphasis on text we may be tempted to underestimate or even misunderstand the indispensable role which text plays in sacrament. Words are vital in the sign-event which is sacrament. The gestures and symbols are eloquent, but their *meeting* with words in the common experience of worshiping people is the crucial point where sacrament as meaningful and moving human action is created.

St. Augustine, preaching on John's Gospel puts the matter clearly in a commentary on the text, "Now you are clean because of the word which I have spoken to you" (Jn. 15:3): "Why does he not say 'You are clean because of the baptism with which you have been washed,' but 'because of the word which I have spoken to you,' unless the reason is that even in the water it is the word which cleanses? Take away the word and what is the water but (plain) water? But when the word comes into association with the material element, a sacrament comes into being, as though the word itself took visible form. For when the Lord washed the disciples feet he had said, 'A man who has bathed needs only to wash his feet and he is altogether clean' (Jn. 13:10). Whence does the water acquire such power that by touching the body it is able to cleanse the heart, if it is not through the action of the word: and not because the word is spoken but because it is believed."[33]

Martin Luther makes the same point referring to another sacrament: "For as soon as Christ says: 'This is my body' his body is present through the Word and the power of the Holy Spirit. If the word is not there it is mere bread, but as soon as the words are added they bring with them that of which they speak."[34]

Following Luther, F. J. Leenhardt compacts the thesis in a single, telling sentence: "What is essential in this bread, which Christ gives, declaring that it is His body, is not what the baker has made out of it, but what Jesus Christ has made of it when he gives it and declares it is his body."[35]

Words in our liturgies may be misused, abused, and overabundant, but there is an essential word. In sacrament the symbol and gesture which the eye sees meets the word—the Word of God, the word of our faith-formulas,[36] and the word of our responding commitments. Sacrament comes to us as multimedia and is received by us in a multisensual way. No part is more vital to this event than the word of meaning. So the words need our loving care: clear expression, illuminating gesture, and convincing personal involvement.

The heart of our commentary about the liturgies of sacrament will concern the five questions we have posed at the beginning of this section. We hope that our special comment here upon the question of sacrament as kingdom-sign and the particular significance of words will be a helpful background to our continuing discussion. We turn now to a consideration of the baptismal liturgy. In our study we have approached infant baptism, adult baptism, and confirmation as separate subjects. They are, of course, not separate subjects but dimensions of one subject, Christian initiation.

Notes

1. Cf. Bausch, *A New Look at the Sacraments;* Segundo, *The Sacraments Today;* Duffy, *Real Presence;* McCauley, *The God of the Group;* White, *Sacraments as God's*

Self-Giving; Schmemann, *For the Life of the World;* Guzie, *The Book of Sacramental Basics;* Martos, *Doors to the Sacred;* Jenson, *Visible Words.*

2. George S. Worgul, *From Magic to Metaphor* (New York: Paulist Press, 1980).

3. Ibid., pp. 201-213.

4. Tad Guzie, *The Book of Sacramental Basics* (New York: Paulist Press, 1981), pp. 53, 66ff.

5. James F. White, *Sacraments as God's Self-Giving* (Nashville: Abingdon, Press, 1983), pp. 9-12.

6. Joseph Martos, *Doors to the Sacred* (New York: Doubleday, 1981), pp. 10-27.

7. Robert W. Jenson, *Visible Words* (Philadelphia: Fortress, 1978), pp. 3-25.

8. Regis Duffy, *Real Presence* (New York: Harper & Row, 1982), p. 3.

9. Alexander Schmemann, *For the Life of the World* (Crestwood, N.Y.: St. Vladimir's Seminary Press, 1973), p. 20.

10. Juan Luis Segundo, *The Sacraments Today* (New York: Orbis, 1974), p. 34.

11. William J. Bausch, *A New Look at the Sacraments* (Notre Dame, Ind.: Fides/Claretian, 1977), p. 16.

12. Cf. James F. White, *Sacraments as God's Self-Giving* (Nashville: Abingdon Press, 1983), pp. 70-92. White calls the signs dominical, apostolic, and natural.

13. John Westerhoff III and William Willimon, *Liturgy and Learning Through the Life Cycle* (New York: Seabury Press, 1980).

14. John Westerhoff III, *Building God's People in a Materialistic Society* (New York: Seabury Press, 1983), pp. 49-50.

15. See Thomas Groome, *Christian Religious Education* (San Francisco: Harper & Row, 1980), in which Groome presents a shared vision/praxis model of Christian religious education which keeps the mystery of the kingdom of God alive and central while highlighting the essentials of the "identified mystery" revealed in Christ. Groome sees education for the kingdom of God as the metapurpose of Christian religious education.

16. See Robert L. Browning, Charles R. Foster, with Everett Tilson, *Ways Persons Become Christian: Harmonizing Different Views of Church Education* (Nashville: Abingdon Press, 1976). Cassette tapes and guide.

17. Westerhoff and Willimon, *Liturgy and Learning Through the Life Cycle.*

18. Jenson, *Visible Words.*

19. *Manual on the Liturgy,* (Minneapolis: Augsburg Press, 1979).

20. Marion J. Hatchett, *Commentary on the American Prayer Book* (New York: Seabury Press, 1980).

21. Cf. *A Service of Baptism, Confirmation and Renewal* (Nashville: United Methodist Publishing House, 1976).

22. Robert W. Hovda, *Strong, Loving and Wise* (Washington, D.C.: The Liturgical Conference, 1976).

23. Jürgen Moltmann, *The Open Church* (London: SCM Press, 1978), pp. 65-69. For a fuller exposition see his *The Church in the Power of the Holy Spirit* (New York: Harper & Row, 1977), pp. 108-114.

24. Ibid., p. 65.

25. Ibid., p. 69.

26. Ibid., p. 71.

27. James M. Cone, "Sanctification, Liberation and Black Worship," *Theology Today* 35 (1978), p. 140.

28. Ibid.

29. A good text to use in training readers is Charlotte I. Lee, *Oral Reading of the Scriptures* (Boston: Houghton Mifflin, 1974).

30. *The Hymns and Ballads of Fred Pratt Green* (Carol Stream, Ill.: Hope Publishing Co., 1982), p. 35f.

31. Pierre Grelot et al., *Liturgie et Vie Spirituelle* (Paris: Editions Beauschesene, 1977).

32. An old but apt example is *This Is the Mass,* by Henri Daniel-Rops (New York: Hawthorne Books, 1958).

33. Quoted by E. C. Whetaker in *The Baptismal Liturgy* (London: SPCK, 1965), p. 5f. Migne, PL 35. 1840. *The Nicene and Post-Nicene Fathers,* Vol. 7, p. 344 (Tractate LXXX, ch. XV., 1-3).

34. *Luther's Works* (Philadelphia: Muhlenberg Press, 1959), p. 341.

35. F. J. Leenhardt, *Essays on the Lord's Supper* (Richmond: John Knox Press, 1958), p. 48.

36. The faith-formulas found in our different sacraments, the great thanksgiving of eucharist, blessing of water and questions of faith in baptism, etc., constitute a body of affirmation analogous to our creedal formulas.

Chapter 8

Infant Baptism: Initiation

Infant baptism is a powerful sacramental experience when it is seen in relational rather than in substantialistic terms. It can be affirmed biblically and theologically but also social scientifically in relation to human and faith development.

The clear direction of recent thought about baptism is to reclaim an earlier pattern of initiation of persons into the body of Christ—a pattern which unified baptism by water, confirmation by the laying on of hands (or anointing with chrism), and participation in holy communion. This threefold initiation can be discerned in the scriptures, in history, and in present practice—both in adult baptism and in infant baptism.

This current trend toward the unity of initiation was predicted in 1969 by Geoffrey Wainwright when he said that the movement toward a unified rite of initiation was the only way he could see that the church could solve the problem of the relationship of baptism to confirmation and to communion. The classic conflicts concern such problems as (1) the nature of baptism and whether it symbolized a radical decision to die to sin and to rise anew with Christ by one who has reached the "age of discretion," or whether it is the sacrament which represents God's acceptance and love as the infant is engrafted into the body of Christ and nurtured to service in the universal priesthood, (2) the nature of confirmation and when it should take place in the life pilgrimage of those baptized as infants, (3) the nature of communion and whether persons can come to the Table before or after baptism, before or after confirmation. The Eastern church has not had these problems because it has had a unified approach to initiation all along. Infants are baptized by immersion, confirmed with

138

the laying on of hands and anointing with oil as symbols of the presence of the Holy Spirit, and given first communion. In other words, the Eastern church has engrafted the child fully into the body of Christ, into the ministering community with full rights.

Wainwright foresaw that there were only two directions to go. He said: "May it be that there is no satisfactory answer to the Western problems apart from the restoration of a unified initiatory complex of which baptism is the key? The choice would be between (1) bringing the other events [confirmation and communion] into infancy to join baptism and (2) postponing baptism until it could once more hold the other events together as whole."[1]

Wainwright's prognosis is fascinating because the dominant solutions which emerged have gone precisely in these two directions. The Roman Catholic Church, after reflections coming out of the Second Vatican Council and subsequent studies concerning adult initiation, has returned to the unified pattern of initiation found in the catechumenate of the second to fifth centuries. While infants were sometimes baptized with adults within a household, the primary focus of the catechumenate was on preparation of adults (through catechesis, ethical review, liturgical participation, and election) for baptism, confirmation, and the eucharist, usually on Easter Sunday. A current mood concerning Christian initiation within the Roman Catholic Church is to affirm a return to the second of Wainwright's options—namely, a postponement of baptism from infancy and an urging of the faith community to affirm adult initiation as the norm. Wainwright himself recommended this solution in 1969 because he believed that the church was in a post-Christendom era when much sharper definitions were required and much higher commitment needed in order for Christianity to penetrate the secularized culture. To him, infant baptism tends to deemphasize the quality of decision making essential for a vibrant faith centered in Christ—a faith which will take the risks necessary.

Our position is to affirm Wainwright's first direction for the children of those *within* the faith community (with infant baptism, confirmation, and communion as a unified initiation) while affirming the second option for persons who are responding to the gospel from *beyond* the faith community (i.e., a strong ministry of authentic evangelism, education, liturgical, and ethical life eventuating in a decision to die to the values of a secularized culture and to rise with Christ in baptism, confirmation, and communion to become a full member of the body of Christ in ministry in our contemporary world).[2] This second option is discussed more fully in chapter 13.

Infant Baptism in the Early Church

Recent studies have made it increasingly clear that infant baptism was practiced in the New Testament church and during the early centuries in the life of the church. There was, of course, a strong emphasis on adult repentance and conversion and, in turn, on adult baptism. However, several references to baptizing children with adults imply infant baptism. For instance, Peter's words at Pentecost point to this probability: "Repent and let each of you be baptized in the name of Jesus Christ for the forgiveness of your sins, and you shall receive the gift of the Holy Spirit. For the promise is for you and your children, and for all who are far off as many as the Lord our God shall call to himself" (Acts 2:38, 39). There are several references to the baptism of entire households: of Stephanas (1 Cor. 1:16); the call of Cornelius for Peter to come to save persons "and all your household" (Acts 11:13); the baptism of Lydia and her household (Acts 16:15a); and other similar illustrations. Because marriage took place at a very early age there is every reason to believe that the children in many households were quite young—certainly before any age of discretion in contemporary terms.

Wainwright's study recognizes these accounts of infant baptism in the New Testament church but emphasizes the possibility that infants were baptized because persons believed that the second coming of Christ was at hand and that such children would be lost if unbaptized. Karl Barth and Joachim Jeremias both put some weight on this view. When it became reasonably clear that the eschaton (the end) was not at hand there was still evidence of infant baptism. During the patristic period infant baptism was probably practiced widely. Irenaeus (120-202 A.D.) reflects the state of affairs when he states "He came to save all through Himself—all I say, who through Him are reborn in God—infants, and children, and youth, and old men. Therefore he passed through every age, becoming an infant for infants, sanctifying those who are of that age, and at the same time becoming for them an example of piety, of righteousness, and of submission, a young man for youths, becoming an example for youths and sanctifying them for the Lord."[3] Origen (185-254 A.D.) recognized that infants have not sinned. Nevertheless he recommended baptism for them because no one is free from defilement (Job 14:4). Of course, such a point of view reflects the emphasis on original sin into which many early Christians believed the child was born. Scholars see little reason to doubt the authenticity of Hippolytus' words in the *Apostolic Tradition*, "And first baptize the little ones; and if they can speak for themselves, they shall do so; if not, their parents or other relatives shall speak for them."

However, at best infant baptism can only be inferred in the early church. The real issue is: Are children included within the body of Christ or not? Are they the recipients fully of the grace and love of God or are they to be put "on hold" as preparatory members, or enrolled as catechumens,[4] or be seen as half members (until confirmation "completes" baptism), or dedicated and nurtured until a decision is made at the age of discretion, followed by baptism?

As Oscar Cullman says in his classic study, the story of Jesus receiving the children and comparing their openness to the kingdom of God (Mt. 19:13) "is quite rightly adduced as a legitimation of infant baptism, in which nothing else is at stake than the reception of children into fellowship with Jesus Christ: 'Forbid them not!' "[5] Cullman sees the great power of the church as a community of faith into which circle the child is received and nurtured. He maintains that "all humankind, in principle, has received Baptism long ago, namely on Golgotha, at Good Friday and Easter. There the essential act of baptism was carried out, entirely without our cooperation, and even without our faith. There the whole world was baptized on the ground of the absolutely sovereign act of God, who in Christ first loved us (1 John 4:19) before we loved him, even before we believed."[6] Cullman transcends the question of whether or not a conscious decision to surrender to Christ is essential prior to baptism when he states that baptism actually confers a new status upon the infant or adult, a new set of realities just as at the moment of naturalization a person has conferred upon him or her many rights of the state. "This act gives a quite precise and decisive direction to the life" of the person whether or not he or she perseveres in it, or whether or not he or she understands it.[7] Cullman sees the high potential in infant baptism for engrafting of the child into the community which awakens, nurtures, and gives content and direction to the faith resident in the child's life.[8]

Infant baptism is much more than the giving of a new status. It is a commissioning for participation in the ministering community. It is an ordination of the child into the universal priesthood. And, as any parent knows, the spontaneous life of the child quickly ministers unto us as much as we minister unto the child.

The Current Situation

There is a strong trend toward the unity of infant baptism, confirmation, and communion within ecumenical circles. This trend is defensible in terms of human and faith development as well as biblically and theologically. Baptism is a one-time event in which the person is received into the body of Christ as a full member. The two additional symbols of full membership are: (1) the laying on of hands or the anointing with oil (confirmation) which symbolizes the presence and power of the Holy Spirit in the child's life and the commissioning of the child for ministry within the body of Christ, (2) participation in the eucharist, the reception of the bread and wine by the child symbolizing full acceptance by the members of the body of Christ.

The Eastern church continues the unity of the initiation by celebrating infant baptism as a major event within the life of the total church. The sacraments of baptism, confirmation, and communion are integrated with a positive sense of high joy and illumination. As Theodoret of Cyrus (393-466 A.D.) wrote, "If the only meaning of baptism were remission of sins, why would we baptize newborn children who have not yet tasted of sin? But the mystery of baptism is not limited to this; it is a promise of greater and more perfect gifts. In it are the promises of future delights; it is the type of the future resurrection, a communion with the master's passion, a participation in His resurrection, a mantle of salvation, a tunic of gladness, a garment of light, or rather it is light itself."[9]

The commitment of the entire congregation is seen in the high expectations for sponsors, parents, and the worshiping community. The baptismal liturgy is a major event in the congregation and not a few moments stuck in between a scripture and an anthem, as is often the case in many churches.

The Episcopal Church has moved in this direction as have several other faith communities (such as United Methodists and Lutherans). Recognizing the need for various stages of growth in faith and the need for the repeatable nature of communion and confirmation Daniel Stevick concludes, "The unified rite of baptism, consignation and eucharist is here set forth as the standard. Whenever the rite is administered (except in emergency conditions) and to whomever, all of it should be administered."[10]

The Roman Catholic study of the nature of Christian initiation, coming out of the Second Vatican Council, has produced a document, the Rites of the Christian Initiation of Adults (R.C.I.A.) in which the unity of baptism, confirmation, and eucharist is reclaimed.[11] This unity was a part of the Eastern church from the earliest days but also of the Western tradition. The focus today is upon the evangelization of adults who are living lives which are centered in the values of a secular culture. The process of penetrating our secular society in a post-Christendom age is a major concern.

Nevertheless, many Roman Catholics prefer the unity of initiation in infant baptism for children within the faith community. This is strongly affirmed because children (as well as adults) are persons of faith.

They quickly develop a sense of what is trustworthy, of what makes sense. What is needed is for the child to be brought into the faith of the Christian community, to be affirmed as a sacred gift from God with potential for sharing love and creating trust and goodness.

Mark Searle, demurring at the resistance of some Roman Catholics to include children in the total life of the church, asks why some regard children as incapable of active participation. "Why else should children, alone of all the baptized, be barred from confirmation and eucharist?" Searle goes on to underscore the fact that the child ministers to parents and others in profound ways. A child summons parents and others to a "deeper understanding of the mystery of grace and of the limitations of human abilities. . . . All this is merely to suggest that, in its own way, a child in fact plays an extremely active, even prophetic role in the household of faith, if we let it. The obstacle is not in the child, but in the faithlessness of the adult believers. If there is any reason for not admitting an infant to faith and baptismal life in the household of faith, it is only that the child's own God-given household is not faithful."[12]

One of the major events of our time has been the publication of the document of the Faith and Order Commission of the World Council of Churches, entitled, *Baptism, Eucharist, and Ministry*, sometimes called the "Lima text." This document has had very wide ecumenical discussion and is heralded as a major breakthrough. As the document states, "That theologians of such widely different traditions should be able to speak so harmoniously about baptism, eucharist, and ministry is unprecedented in the modern ecumenical movement. Particularly noteworthy is the fact that the Commission also includes among its full members the theologians of the Roman Catholic and other churches which do not belong to the World Council of Churches itself."[13] While this document focuses on the baptism by water and the mutual recognition of "one another's baptism as the one baptism into Christ," it also emphasizes that the gift of the Spirit can be signified in additional ways," by the sign of the laying on of hands, and by anointing or chrismation" and for some churches "participation in holy communion."[14] This most significant position paper again recognizes the existence of a trend toward the unity of initiation among the church bodies represented at the World Council of Churches meeting in Vancouver, British Columbia, during the summer of 1983.

Infant Baptism and the Development of Faith

Since we are not talking about infant baptism as an infusion of God's love into the life of the child, we can look more carefully at the quality of the relationships between the child, the parents and sponsors, and the congregation. It seems self-evident that God loves all children, because of the goodness of creation, whether or not they are baptized. The love of God which *is*, and which we do not control, is pointed to, celebrated and, we believe, experienced relationally when young children of faithful parents are engrafted into the body of Christ through infant baptism. The way we as parents, sponsors, congregation, and pastors relate to the child reveals the nature of our faith, the direction and purpose we affirm for our lives. As Fowler has said, the values and commitments which we put at the center of our lives will reveal the quality and content of our faith to the child. This is a fact which challenges us to look closely at whether or not we ourselves are baptized in the spirit of Christ and the integrity of the church as the sacrament of Christ, truly making Christ's life of love, trust, and justice visible in the world.

When infants are baptized, confirmed, and given communion in Christ's church they are part of the community of faith which seeks consciously to support and nurture the child into the quality of life which the community celebrates.

Children in the first two years of life—the period Fowler calls undifferentiated faith—need to experience unconditional love and acceptance in a way which comes to earth in the nitty-gritty rituals of feeding, caring, holding, exploring things and persons in the environment, etc. In this interaction between the child and the parents and others, the seeds of faith are sown, and pre-images of what the world is like are developed. A later profound faith in a loving and just God has its genesis in the trusting attitudes the child develops in a family which is trusting and in a church which demonstrates trust, love, forgiveness, and many opportunities for renewal.

Erik Erikson sees very deep meaning in the quality of these trusting and loving rituals. Fully recognizing the frustration and possible negative feelings that parents bring to the constraints of child-rearing, Erikson supports parents in their effort to develop positive, life-giving rituals of naming (the positive tone of voice when using the child's name and when naming the objects and persons in the wider world), feeding, elimination, clothing, while at the same time admitting their negative feelings and avoiding the destructive guilt which can come back in the form of life-denying rituals. The numinous quality in the way the mother or parent looks at the child and is present in the child's life is not unlike the quality of faith and trust which is communicated through the life-giving rituals in our religious community.

The quality of "mutual recognition" between the child and parents is of central importance because it makes possible a "separateness transcended" and yet a "distinctiveness confirmed." Erikson sees these relationships within the family and within a faith community to have great potential for communicating the meaning and purpose of life. The priesthood of parenthood is clearly implied when Erikson reminds us of the power of the loving eyes of the parents to communicate a sense of ultimate well-being and acceptance—not unlike God looking down lovingly into our eyes as we look up for affirmation and acceptance.

What Christian parents and sponsors and members of the faith community are doing as participants in infant baptism is committing themselves to the extension of this quality of trust and love to the child and to accept the presence of a new creative member of the ministering community who will make a profound difference in the way the church expresses herself. Confirmation is the sacrament which commissions the child to find and use his or her talents for ministering in the universal priesthood. Sponsors and the congregation join the parents in commitment to nurture the child in ways that his or her full resources will be discovered and freely and joyously shared. Participation in communion is the symbol of being a full member of Christ's body, with an ongoing avenue of depth acceptance and communication with God and other members of the body in thanksgiving and celebration.

It is within such a community of honesty and yet support that parents can deal with the struggles related to the child's beginning definition of self as good or bad. As the parents seek to free the child to be autonomous, while also seeking to instill values consistent with respect for persons and property within and beyond the family, there are inevitable clashes and moments of self-doubt. To be a member of a faith community which affirms honest sharing of burdens and joys, which recognizes the necessity for forgiving attitudes and many opportunities "to try again," is to be strengthened as a baptized person for life's pilgrimage. (See chapter 6 for other possibilities from the thought of Erikson or Fowler.)

Religious Education of Parents, Sponsors, and the Congregation

It is clear that persons learn to be faithful to the vision of the meaning and purpose of life revealed by Christ, by participating in the total life of the faith community. However, more explicit counseling and education are required to deepen the meaning of baptism and to provide the nurture and support parents and sponsors need.

Just as adult catechumens of the past prepared themselves for baptism through study of the basic beliefs of the church, participated in the life of mutual ministry with their sponsors and other members of the community of faith, looked carefully into their honest values in relation to the new life in Christ, learned how to celebrate faith in God through the sacraments and worship, *so* today parents and sponsors can be greatly strengthened and enriched by opportunities for counseling and education regarding the meaning of infant baptism and their responsibilities in the process.

The particular forms such sensitive counseling and education take depend considerably upon the denominational or local church traditions and expectations. These realities must be respected as persons are invited to explore the unified approach to Christian initiation being affirmed. A great deal of listening is required on the part of pastors and lay leaders as parents and sponsors are asked to share their hopes and expectations, their honest questions, and their central beliefs. The symbolic nature of language must be kept in focus in order for persons to be able to get behind the actions and words which come out of past experience to possible common concerns, feelings, and meanings.

Through *individual visits* to parents who are expecting a child the pastor or other professionals or lay leaders may help the parents affirm the opportunities for further preparation for the birth of their child and for the baptism of the child into the body of Christ. Informal religious education could follow such counseling sessions on a one-to-one basis in situations where only a very few parents are expecting at a similar time.

Group sessions with parents and sponsors can be developed during which some of the issues can be explored in more depth. Such sessions need to be scheduled flexibly to meet the varying needs of those involved. Parents should be consulted about the persons they wish to have as sponsors. Then, the sponsors can be a part of the more specific sessions which deal with their roles as sponsors. Such group sessions should deal with some of the following issues:

1) *The Priesthood of Parenthood.* Parents can be brought into a supportive community where they can share their anxieties, areas of confidence, hopes, honest needs. The creation of such an affirming atmosphere is important in order for mothers and fathers and their sponsoring friends to be able to see the unique strengths they can bring to the ministry of love and trust with their children. The nature of the church and ministry within the universal priesthood of all believers can be discussed in relation to the unique priesthood parents and sponsors can have as the newly born child is engrafted into the

body of Christ. Just as the church is the extension of Christ's ministry—his eyes, hands, feet—meeting needs in the world, so the parents and sponsors become "Christs" to the child, helping the child to experience full acceptance, genuine love and affirmation, and the beginning of the sense of justice for all as the child discovers helpful limits in his or her environment and begins to develop a sense of right and wrong.[15]

2) *The Child, the Unique Gift of God to the World.* Parents usually express feelings of hope and "great expectation" about the new life to be born. Group sessions should build on this reality and set it in a Christian frame which views the child as a unique gift not only to the parents and the church but to the world. God has even greater hopes and expectations for the child to be a refreshing breeze, bringing life and vitality to the world. Such study and sharing can focus on the baptismal step of naming or the pre-baptismal ritual of naming which takes place in Orthodox communities especially. The rite of naming points to the unique expectations parents bring to the new life in their midst. As our former colleague Charles Foster says so well, "Children look upon their names as among their most treasured possessions." Names locate children in a specific place, Foster maintains. The name we choose locates the child in a specific family, in a given set of relationships in the community and in a "set of relationships transcending the finite and historical boundaries of our specific geneologies." The Bible projects the importance of the personhood of individuals by using the name of Moses or Samuel to reveal God's call to specific ministries in the world. Foster sees children as persons with great ministries to perform, however unconsciously and spontaneously. Children are called to be the bearers of our culture—our values and traditions—and they are a means of God's gracious activity in our lives. Foster agrees with Erikson that the early rituals of life, including especially the sacrament of baptism, communicate the vision of the meaning and direction the child's life may have.[16]

3) *Family Ministries Through Rituals Which Affirm the Child's Sacred Destiny and Unique Gifts.* The group sessions should look ahead at the subtle but profound messages of hope or rejection which are communicated by parents in the daily rituals of caring, feeding, clothing, touching, talking to and with, naming, exploring, etc. Such conversations can open the door to a discussion of the normal stages of growth, the expected stages of ritualization as outlined by Erik Erikson, and the new and promising insights concerning the stages of faith throughout life. This work should be done dialogically in careful relationship to where the parents and sponsors are in their concerns and interests

and in a way which sensitizes them to the high potential for growth in faith which can result from the priesthood of parenthood during the early years of life. Moreover, such discussions can help parents and sponsors see growth in faith to be a lifelong process. Self-assessment of parents and sponsors concerning their own growth in faith, their own rituals (and their life-affirming or life-denying qualities) can be an important by-product of such reflection and testing.[17] (See chapter 6.)

4) *Education Concerning the Unity of the Initiation of the Child Through Infant Baptism, Confirmation, and Communion.* Again, it is important to recognize early in this discussion the nature of the sacraments so that the dialogue can get past certain tight legalisms which we sometimes bring to the discussion (See Part I). Likewise, it is important to listen to the differing views which parents and sponsors bring with them, to create an atmosphere which affirms explorations of alternate views of infant baptism, and to share the rationale for the unity of the sacraments of initiation which is emerging ecumenically. (See chapter 13 on adult baptism as well as this chapter for this trend.) In this discussion, help the parents and sponsors to see how baptism, confirmation, and communion are symbols of the total acceptance of the child into the body of Christ, that there is no partial acceptance, awaiting a later confirmation or a fulfillment in a later communion. Here is an opportunity to show how the child is baptized into the faith community which is repeatedly dying to self-worship, corporate evil, and dehumanization and is rising to new life in Christ. Help parents and sponsors discern the meaning of the laying-on of hands, the confirmation of the child with the seal of the Holy Spirit. Especially are baptism and confirmation of the child calls to ministry in the univeral priesthood— not in some global abstract way but in the concrete, intuitive, and spontaneous ways that children minister to all of us, disarming us with their wonder, awe, joy, and teachableness. Here we can explore in what ways the child is "ordained" through baptism, confirmation, and communion in the ministering body of Christ.

Perhaps the most controversial aspect of the unity of initiation of the child is the participation in communion. The Eastern Orthodox Church climaxes the dramatic service of infant baptism with a symbolic procession around the table (after the immersion of the naked child in water three times, the anointing with oil, clothing the child in white) and the serving of the elements of bread and wine (mixed together in the chalice) to the child with a gold spoon. Such participation of the child in the central act of devotion of the worshiping body of Christ truly symbolizes the child's full acceptance into the body and further symbolizes the child's strengthening for ministries within the body.

Such views are fresh and somewhat unusual for persons in many of our churches, even those which practice infant baptism. Therefore, time to share initial reactions, more serious questions, and unexpected affirmations needs to be planned. Such discussion may be related fruitfully to an orientation of parents and sponsors to the liturgy to be used in the initiation of the children. Honest and rigorous analysis should be encouraged. Differing views should be respected.

5) *Orientation to the Unified Service of Initiation*.[18] The liturgy itself is a profound educator. Prior to participation, parents and sponsors should discuss the elements of the liturgy, review their roles and functions, become aware of how they can make creative contributions to the service (such as baking the bread, writing letters to the child to be read at the annual anniversary of the baptism, making hangings or banners, planning a celebration for the congregation, etc.). The nature of the responsibilities of parents and sponsors can be clarified in relation to the vows they are to take. The opportunities for ongoing growth in faith can be explored in terms of participation in Christian family life education, liturgical life, and ethical concerns within the home, in religious education for not only parents and sponsors but for all adults as they progress through life, in the relogous education of the child, deliberate and formal as well as indirect and informal, and also participation in the sacramental and service life of the church at every stage of growth in faith.

The Preparation of the Congregation

One of the most powerful "educators" is the participation of the congregation in an infant baptism in which the congregation has been prepared through liturgy and sermon and then led sensitively to experience a unified liturgy.

A young couple in our classes at Methesco, having studied and experienced a unified liturgy of infant baptism, confirmation, and eucharist, asked one of the authors to participate in the baptism of their newborn son. They were co-pastors in a small-town United Methodist church in Ohio, near the theological school. Meeting with them to discuss the meaning of the experience and to plan the service it was decided to hold the service on the lawn of the parsonage, set up a communion table under a large tree, place a liturgical hanging, designed and made by the wife, on the tree behind the table. The couple invited the congregation to participate in the baptism of their son and selected several members of the congregation to participate as sponsors, ushers, persons who would be involved in bringing the water forward for baptism as well as bringing the elements of bread and wine forward for the child's first communion.

The congregation in this small-town church participated eagerly and with much affirmation in this celebration of the child's engrafting into the body of Christ. Considerable education took place informally as the parents prepared various members of the church to assist in the liturgy in the ways already mentioned. The parents and the celebrant learned much as they wrote the service together. The parents got much enjoyment in studying the meanings associated with their son's name and in writing these meanings into an *act of naming* in the liturgy as follows:

LITURGIST: A name has power. It is the sign of a person. It will represent that person to us. His or her life and character will be symbolized before us by the name chosen. A name brings with it a history. Others of us have borne that name. It will represent our life and tradition to the child.

FATHER: The name we have chosen is William John Lakota. William is the name borne by his father, his grandfather, his great-grandfather, and it was the name of his great-great grandfather before him.

MOTHER: John was the name of his maternal grandfather and great grandfather. Lakota is the maternal family name which carries the meaning of Peace.

FATHER: William is a teutonic name meaning "Defender of Many."

MOTHER: John is a Hebrew name meaning "Gracious gift of God." In giving this name we remember the writer of the gospel of John, Jesus' beloved disciple.

FATHER AND MOTHER: You are William John Lakota.

LITURGIST: You are William John Lakota.

PEOPLE: You are William John Lakota. May you become known to us, and we to you, through the love and grace of God our Creator.[19]

The service moved with a sense of intimacy and caring through the naming, the baptism, and the confirmation, with congregational participation at each level. When the Table was ready and the people were coming forward to receive the bread and wine, it started to rain. Soon, the clouds opened widely and the entire congregation was "baptized" during the eucharist! Retiring to the safety and dryness of the parsonage, we concluded the service by serving William John communion with a silver spoon. The members of the congregation smiled as the child licked his lips in response! There was a feeling of inclusion and family which was genuine and pointed to the quality of Christian community already in existence but also a community which welcomed the child who had been ordained to fresh expressions of the universal priesthood.

While the members of this particular church had not experienced a unified initiation before, the response was positive and supportive. There is little doubt that such a response was the result of careful preparation and planning and wide involvement of the members of the faith community in the celebration. Such an approach is a convincing and powerful way to educate the congregation concerning the integrity of full initiation of infants.

Another important way is through the preaching which takes place in relation to the initiation rites. Preaching and teaching about the meaning of baptism and especially the rationale for the unified pattern can be done with great meaning with attention to the renewal of baptismal vows for all members. Such preaching or teaching can take place before or after the liturgy. Cyril of Jerusalem did his interpretations of baptism after the Easter celebration, presenting what came to be known as the Mystogogic sermons or lectures. Cyril delivered five sermons or lectures on baptism, confirmation, and communion the five weeks *after* Easter (during which the baptism had taken place). His reasoning was sound. He said, "Knowing well, that seeing is far more persuasive than hearing, I waited till this season; that finding you more open to the influence of my words from this your experience, I might take and lead you to the brighter and more fragrant meadow of this present paradise; especially as ye have been made fit to receive the more sacred mysteries, having been counted worthy of divine and life-giving baptism. It remaining therefore to dress for you a board of more perfect instruction, let us now teach you exactly about these things that ye may know the deep meaning to you—word of what was done on that evening of your baptism."[20] The time between Easter and Pentecost can be a rich time of reflection on the meaning of incorporation into the body of Christ and the power of the action parables of baptism, confirmation, and communion to strengthen persons for ministry.

Liturgy: A Comprehensive Sacrament

Anyone who reads any of the literature of baptism discovers an action/concept which is comprehensive. It subsumes Christian self-identity. Through it we are brought into *the faith*, and by it we are continually reminded that Christian life is life *in Christ*, that to be a Christian is to be baptized with the baptism which is his. But baptism as many Christians experience it is something not comprehensive at all. It is often "relegated" to the "back seat of the bus" of liturgy and appears hardly to be on the agenda of real events. The worship practice of Christians is widely divergent when it comes to baptism. Surely if baptism is to function for us as *real* initiation and primary sign of Christian self-identity it demands a central focus in our worship. This means that when baptism is celebrated it should itself be the heart of the liturgy. The worship of the day, the preaching, the praying, the singing, should all tend toward the baptismal event and baptismal meanings. Let us underline that this is needful because baptism is a comprehensive event. It is not something exclusively for the newly baptized. Baptism is always something which involves us all. "Officially," Christians understand this. So the ecumenical document of Lima, *Baptism, Eucharist and Ministry* (1982), declares, "At every baptism the whole congregation reaffirms its faith in God and pledges itself to provide an environment of witness and service. Baptism should, therefore, always be celebrated and developed in the setting of the Christian community."[21] But we don't always function this way, or we function this way perfunctorily. The congregation reads together its little formula of acceptance of the baptized and that is that. Much more is possible to make the baptismal event a comprehensive one in which all celebrate our one baptism.

At the outset of the baptismal liturgy itself there is provision now in the ritual of many of the churches for the participation of lay people in introducing and presenting the candidates for baptism and their families. It is important for persons of the family of the church to serve this function who are not themselves candidates or immediate family of candidates. It represents simply and eloquently to all that there is a bond between those who are to be baptized and all of us who have gathered for worship. A rubric of the new United Methodist liturgy says "A representative of the congregation presents the candidates."[22] This could, of course, be several representatives and could be sponsors or godparents, as called for in the same new liturgies.[23] These people need to be deeply involved in the whole process of baptism, with the families of those being baptized, and should have a visibility to the congregation. They not only stand for, but they function for the whole people in the process of inviting and blessing new members into the family of the church. They need to be recognized, appreciated, and encouraged. It is possible for them to be acknowledged with the families weeks before the baptismal event itself so that the whole congregation can know what is happening and participate as they are able in the nurture of families preparing for baptism. When *we* are perceived as having a significant role in the baptism itself, then we will naturally understand baptism not as an addendum to normal worship or a "sentimental" corner within it, but as primary focus.

Baptismal Renewal

There are some other things that can advance this sensibility. Baptismal renewal is becoming a feature of liturgical reform in a growing number of denominations. It is a liturgical event particularly appropriate as an accompaniment to baptism itself. Sometimes congregations are exhorted at times of baptism to participate vicariously by renewing their baptisms in the baptism of others. There is probably more reality in following baptism with a service of baptismal renewal where the minister steps before the people and puts directly to them questions like, "Do you turn to Christ?" "Do you repent of your sins?" and "Do you renounce evil?"[24] and hears the people respond, "I turn to Christ," "I repent of my sins," "I renounce evil." These typical vows (Anglican *Alternative Service Book*) with perhaps the kinds of affirmations which may follow them (e.g., "Do you believe and trust in God the Father, who made the world? *I believe and trust him.*") can be signified with water. Water may be sprinkled toward the entire congregation. A large bowl of water can be carried around the room by an acolyte or other person while the minister sprinkles water toward the congregation using a small evergreen branch, repeating the words, "Remember your baptism and be thankful" (New United Methodist liturgy).[25] The invitation to baptismal renewal can also be made in a manner which anticipates the response of individuals to come forward and renew their baptisms. This is analogous to the eucharist, where people come forward to be blessed or for their commitment to be recognized. In this kind of baptismal renewal the minister will lay hands upon each person or make the sign of the cross on the person's forehead with water and say, "Remember your baptism and be thankful."

The experience of baptismal renewal can be a truly moving event in the life of a congregation. In the anticipation that this may be so we need to bear one fact in mind. Many people in our churches do not have a very clear image of what baptism is all about. One year a student in the basic course in worship at our seminary brought a layman from her parish to several sessions of the class. The man was very interested in the material on the eucharist, but he was amazed when we got to baptism and he found himself in biblical, historical, and theological territory which was utterly unknown to him. One of our colleagues has written liturgical dramas on the sacraments. The first, on the eucharist, was easily and enthusiastically received in the churches where the students took it. The second one, on baptism, was well received, but one could detect puzzled looks and wonder on the faces of some people at the services. Lay people knew enough about the Lord's supper to be able to "decode" a liturgical drama which presented it out of primary imagery from the Bible and from its history. The same could not be said about baptism. It is entirely possible for us to create a beautiful event for baptismal renewal and have it languish before our eyes in the assembly of the Christians because people are unable to connect their lively everyday reality with the imagery presented before them inviting their involvement. If baptism is to be the central focus of our worship when it is celebrated, and if we all are to enter into the baptismal event acting in the knowledge that it is always about our reality, a prerequisite is necessary. There must be enough common understanding for the liturgy to be received and acted out with integrity and enthusiasm.

A central Ohio Catholic priest some years ago introduced an innovation in the liturgy by parodying the well-known advertizing of a local evangelist ("The church of what's happening now") saying, "Brothers and sisters, this is St. Mary Catholic church, the church of 'now what's happening.' " There has indeed been in the last twenty years (a period of basic reform and a great deal of experimentation) plentiful opportunity for the people to chorus, "What's happening now?" This cry, and the frustration that produces it can only be avoided by careful preparation. Concerning baptism, we probably should begin preparation with a simple axiom: Baptism will not be a comprehensive action/concept unless and until it is on the agenda of a congregation's life at times *other than* the liturgical occasions of baptism. Regularly, in preaching, teaching, and planning, the comprehensive images of our life which are baptismal images (dying and rising with Christ [Rom. 6:3-5; Col. 2:12]; washing away of sin [1 Cor. 6:11]; new birth [Jn. 3:5]; enlightenment by Christ [Eph. 5:14]; reclothing in Christ [Gal. 3:27]; gift of the Spirit [Acts 2:1, 38; Titus 3:5]; salvation [1 Peter 3:20-21]; freedom from bondage [1 Cor. 10:1-2]; liberation to a new humanity [Gal. 3:27-28; 1 Cor. 12-13])[26] need to be before us and be perceived as Christian baptismal identity. If we cannot establish a clear relationship between Christian baptism and Christian life, then baptism is a kind of fetish in the church, precious, maybe, because it is traditional, but actually a ritual existing in a ghetto of sentimentality where with "oohs and ahs" we rejoice with a family as their new arrival is properly "done." There is no need to despise the value of this "recognition," but it is not baptism.

Baptismal Seasons

Another way in which we can raise consciousness concerning baptism is to baptize at times which naturally amplify the meaning of baptism. These have been in our history the festivals of Easter (the resurrection time of new life), Pentecost (the time of Spirit power), and Epiphany (the time of the baptism of Jesus). Each of these days should be times of the celebration of potent, primal Christian self-understandings. When baptism is made a natural part of the story/meaning that a festival day naturally jubilates, its connection to doctrine and life can be simply and lucidly demonstrated. Practical problems sometimes intervene to prevent us from doing this. Consider, for instance, the difficulties in the way of thinking about Easter as a primary time for baptisms. It sounds right historically, theologically, but logistically it sounds wrong. Easter is the time when the congregation of worshipers is swollen with numbers of people, many of whom have nominal or no relation to the church. Since baptism is initiation and a special Christian "family" celebration, isn't this "day of strangers" exactly the wrong day for this sacrament? Some Christian communities are working around this problem through the institution of Easter Vigil services as unique "family" celebrations of Resurrection. Churches which are encouraging Easter Vigils (services which begin late on Holy Saturday night and continue into the beginnings of the Easter day) and providing liturgies for them are also suggesting these services as special times for baptism.[27] This can be a good solution where the Easter Vigil becomes an established worship of the people. It is a poor solution where the vigil is a poorly attended preserve of only a few.

One way or another, though, we need to let Easter again become known among us as a day of the "new life" which is baptism. Not only does baptism need the infusion of meaning and inspiration which is Easter, but Easter needs to have, in our whole celebration of it as a day and a season, the vitality of baptism. Frank Senn's observation that, "we have yet to discover what Easter is all about, largely because we have divorced it from its baptismal context," is all too accurate. "The prospect of fifty days of continuous celebration of the Lord Jesus' resurrection just boggles the mind."[28] It does, of course, and the evidence is that we don't manage to celebrate resurrection very well.

Crucifixion we can identify with for a season, but not resurrection. Some may conclude that this is because resurrection is more difficult to believe. This is so, but it is probably not the reason we do Easter poorly. We can identify better with crucifixion than with resurrection because we believe more in our difficulty, our pain, and our need for salvation—and that of the world—than we do in our new creation and the transformation of the world. But the message of resurrection is not isolated news about Christ Jesus; it is human news: "For as in Adam all die, so also in Christ shall all be made alive" (1 Cor. 15:22). This triumph of life is not simply a future to hope for. Its quality, the *Christ-quality*, is the life offered to us now. St. Paul calls it a transcendent life ("we regard no one from a human point of view" [2 Cor. 5:16]), an empathic life ("if anyone is in Christ" [2 Cor. 5:17]) and something novel, radically changed ("a new creation" [2 Cor. 5:17]). Resurrection then, like kingdom of God, is not something postponed; it is something available. The resurrection of Christ, like God's new time, is not something into which Christ enters alone. The rising of Christ is also the rising of those who are Christ's; God's reign is a sovereignty we can choose now. Resurrection and kingdom of God are events which belong to one another.

Easter is the festival of our new creation. It is thus *the* great day for baptism. One way or another it needs to be reclaimed for this purpose. It is a wonder and a great thing that people flock to church on Easter. True, it is something of a pagan spring rite, but it is also testimony to the compelling authority of Jesus. Whatever we make of the outpouring of people and however we cope with it, this abundance should not lure us away from making Easter the focus of faith for the Christian community. To "tailor" Easter to the novel situation created by the influx of a crowd of "strangers" is to ignore the real and, indeed, essential novelty which Easter is for Christian faith. Baptism can help us "redeem" Easter, as a day and as a season. When we baptize on this festival day, and organize the "great fifty days" from Easter to Pentecost as a special time of postbaptismal education and training, which focuses upon the newly baptized but involves us all in tending and spreading the holy view of a new creation, rather than one great "blow-out" followed by the "hangover" of "low" Sunday and some nondescript Sundays on our way to Memorial Day, Mother's Day, graduation, and the relief of summer.

What Signs?

Most of the people who have written about baptism in the recent past have challenged the church to restore eloquence to the sacramental sign of baptism. This means bringing back water, its visibility, its audibility and its real application to a human body. No one has stated this more forcefully than Robert Jenson in *Visible Words:*

Most urgent . . . is that we in fact start *baptizing* again. Mere moist-
ening is tolerable only on superstitious and unbiblical assumptions:
that some sort of "mana" is transferred by blessed water. Otherwise,
baptism's ability to speak, to be a visible word, depends altogether
on the function of washing in everyday human life; baptism that is
not in fact a washing is just not a possible Christian sacrament. Even
after scholasticism had provided a sophisticated version of the superstitious rationale for sprinkling, the practice was so generally
perceived as contrary to baptism's essential character that it was
resisted for centuries. Thus Martin Luther rejected it precisely
because baptism must *mean* what it *is*.[29]

Baptism is a washing. This is *an* undisputed meaning. Should not
the sign of this meaning strive to be adequate? As Luther put it,
shouldn't it *mean* what it is? The acceptance of this principle will mean
radical change in baptismal practice in a great many churches. It
means that we shall have to have baptismal fonts large enough to hold
a significant amount of water and large enough to be a practical vessel
for the human activity of washing. How extensive an action of washing
is envisioned? Without being overly prescriptive, we might conclude:
extensive enough to require some toweling. In the case of infants this
probably means that some baptismal garments be used which could be
removed at the moment of baptism so that the diapered infants could
be baptized and then toweled and then vested again with the baptismal garments. This requires, of course, more activity than usually
goes on in the baptizing of infants. This is bound to seem to some an
unnecessary literalization and too much going on. The point, of
course, is not to complicate ritual but to have an evocative symbol.
Surely one of our problems, in every way, with baptism is that it is not
effectively on our agenda. It is unthinkable that we wouldn't do it; we
do it, but minimally. *Significant* ritual action is but one good way to
bring baptism unmistakenly before us. Water, after all, remains a good
symbol in our culture. Many of the symbols Christians have employed
in the past do not speak to us any more. Water is necessary to life, and
human thinking and activity seeking sources and adequate stores of
good water is a constant of our life. Water has meaning; it can be as
powerful a symbol now as it ever was. We should let it speak.

The Water

One of the innovations in most of our new baptismal liturgies is the
prayer of thanksgiving over the water. Like the great thanksgiving of
the eucharist, it is, in addition to thanksgiving, essentially *recollection* of

meanings of water in the history of the people of faith, and *invocation* of the Holy Spirit in the baptismal event. In most liturgies this prayer comes after the baptismal commitments and just before the baptism itself. In fonts not usually flowing with water, water can be poured into the font just prior to this thanksgiving. This "offertory" of water gives the symbol visibility and audibility just as the prayer following points us toward its meaning. Many good versions of this prayer are available in new denominational liturgies and there is a particularly good one in Laurence Stookey's *Baptism: Christ's Act in the Church.*[30] Like the Great Thanksgiving of the eucharist this prayer can and should vary some from occasion to occasion.

The Laying on of Hands

Water is not the only sign in baptism. Water symbolizes the cleansing from sin, the negative turning from evil which is part of our baptism in Christ. The positive enlivening, the gift of the Holy Spirit is symbolized by the laying on of hands. This second sign is not part of the baptism ritual of all denominations, but it is becoming more common. Some postpone the sign of Spirit power until confirmation. This implies, at least, that the gift of the Spirit is not part of the meaning of baptism, and few Christians would be willing to agree to that. Of course, where sprinkling is the usual mode of baptism, the sign of baptism is more the laying on of hands than anything else. One might say that in the sprinkling ceremony a certain fusion of the two signs takes place, were it not for the fact that the washing sign simply disappears.

The status of the sign of laying on of hands is in a peculiar situation in the present time. The ritual of the United Methodist Church is a good example of what we mean. In the old liturgy baptism was followed by a commending of the baptized to the congregation who responded with a pledge to uphold the new "children" in the faith. A prayer and benediction concluded the service. In the new liturgy baptism itself, in the name of the Father, Son, and Holy Spirit is followed by a rubric which reads, "As hands are placed on the head of each person receiving baptism, the minister says to each." The words which accompany this sign are, "The power of the Holy Spirit work within you, that being born through water and the Spirit you may be a faithful witness of Jesus Christ. Amen."[31] This is exactly the "confirming" sentence which appears in a section of United Methodist ritual called "Confirmation and Other Renewals of the Baptismal Covenant." We might describe what is happening here, in the difference between the old and the new liturgies, in two ways. The service of baptism is absorbing into itself the sign and meaning of what has been called confirmation and confirmation is becoming rather than a "one-time" liturgy of "church membership," a repeatable sacrament of baptismal renewal which, while always a sign of baptismal identity, is appropriate for many different kinds of occasions, including the sort of rite we have traditionally called confirmation. Put another way, we could say that the laying on of hands, the sign of the gifts of the Spirit, is becoming a regular part of the baptismal liturgy, and that it is a part of that ceremony which can be repeated in the baptismal renewal we have called confirmation and other services of baptismal renewal.

Two conclusions are being pushed here which are directions of the thinking of many Christians but which are not the polity of all denominations: 1. What we have called confirmation is not an independent sacrament; it has no independent meaning. It belongs to baptism as its reaffirmation and, logically, it is repeatable. 2. Baptism is belonging; it is the sign of the Christian reality and our inclusion in it; the baptized are *real* Christians, not "preparatory" Christians. Liturgy sometimes gets ahead of polity. That is surely a healthy thing.

When these signs are acted out before the congregation, and they normally should occur only at times of public worship, all the people should be able to see what is happening. This obvious principle is often frustrated simply because there are so many people involved in the ceremony, and gathered around, that the view of the congregation is blocked. The difficulties involved here sometimes defy adequate solution. Thought needs to be given to this problem though and the best solution sought, which will be suitable to the event and the architecture.

Other Symbols

There are three additional symbols which need to be considered: chrism, special garments, and a baptismal candle. Chrism, anointing with oil, is at the same time a common Christian practice and an utterly unknown one. It is an ancient sign of God's blessing which antedates a specific meaning. It is an appropriate symbol of Spirit *within* because it is a substance which "penetrates." Anointing with oil, though, while common among many Christians, is not the ordinary cultural phenomenon it once was, and it is a question whether we should try to revive it. Robert Jenson makes the case against: "Anointing's capacity for meaning depended, like that of washing, on a function in the whole of life. But anointing's function has mostly ceased; and nothing can be done about that."[32] This conclusion is debatable on two grounds. There is more anointing going on than one supposes, as shelves of emollients in drugstores testify. Many people experience unction as a new sign in liturgy and find it a something meaningful and moving. This is particularly true in services of healing. A group of our students recently participated in such a liturgy and we were surprised, as were they, at their positive response to the service as a whole, and especially to the anointing with oil. Unction may still be a useful gesture in worship. Those of us who have never experienced it should at least experiment. It does, of course, involve the laying on of hands, or at least the act of touching. This is certainly primary and it may be enough.

Is baptismal chrism distinguishable from the chrism of confirmation? This question is just part of the confusing relationship which exists between baptism and what we have called confirmation. The laying on of hands and the chrism sign which may accompany it has identification with the *baptismal* meaning of Holy Spirit gift. In the present Catholic liturgy of baptism the text read by the celebrant at the anointing begins, "God the Father of our Lord Jesus Christ has freed you from sin, given you a new birth by water and the Holy Spirit, and welcomed you into his holy people."[33] To the usual Western formula, "I baptize you in the name of the Father . . . Son . . . and Holy Spirit," this text adds specifically the meaning of baptized by the Holy Spirit. What is said at the laying on of hands in the Catholic confirmation liturgy is more extensive, but it adds no new meaning nor confirms any new gift:

> All-powerful God, Father of our Lord Jesus Christ,
> by water and the Holy Spirit
> you freed your sons and daughters from sin
> and gave them new life.
> Send your Holy Spirit upon them
> to be their Helper and Guide
> give them the spirit of wisdom and understanding,
> the spirit of right judgment and courage,
> the spirit of knowledge and reverence.
> Fill them with the spirit of wonder and awe in your
>   presence.
> We ask this through Christ our Lord.
> Amen.

The anointing formula is, "be sealed with the Gift of the Holy Spirit."[34]

The classic argument for confirmation is presented in the Apostolic

Constitution which accompanies the rite: "In baptism, the newly baptized receive forgiveness of sins, adoption as sons of God, and the character of Christ, by which they are made members of the Church and for the first time become sharers in the priesthood of their Savior (see 1 Peter 2:5-9). Through the sacrament of confirmation, those who have been born anew in baptism receive the inexpressable Gift, the Holy Spirit himself, by which they are endowed . . . with special strengths."[35] In this understanding, then, confirmation is the completing of Christian initiation,[36] in the *marking* "with the character or seal of the Lord" so permanent and indelible "that the sacrament of confirmation cannot be repeated."[37] The conclusions this formulation opens to criticism and reformulation in our time are the ideas that confirmation "completes" baptism (How does the gift of the Holy Spirit in confirmation complete a baptism where the gift of the Holy Spirit was already an affirmation and a celebration?) and that confirmation is a single, unrepeatable action. Confirmation is coming to be seen as baptismal renewal, a sacrament which does not impose an indelible character but which is an occasion celebrating and intensifying the meanings of Christian life already signified in baptism.

A second ancillary symbol is the white garment which signifies the new creation in which a Christian is "clothed." If infants are, in fact, to be washed in baptism, a simple garment easy to remove and put on is a very practical aspect of the ceremony as well as a useful symbol.

A third symbol sometimes used is the lighted candle. In the alternate rite of baptism (1980) of the Church of England, immediately after baptism the priest or another designated person lights a candle from the paschal candle or another candle used in the service and presents it to the baptized or their parents or godparents saying, "Receive this light. This is to show that you have passed from darkness to light." All the congregation respond, "Shine as a light in the world to the glory of God the Father."[38]

It is sometimes objected that these additional signs clutter the baptismal rite and obscure the primary sign of worship.[39] It is probably the case, though, that because baptism bears such multiple meanings, that the cluster of symbols—washing, laying on of hands, anointing, candle, white garment—helps us to celebrate the richness of the sacrament.

Commitment

After presentation of baptismal candidates, the baptizing ceremony itself usually begins with vows of commitment. These have two emphases: the renunciation of evil and fidelity to Christ. In ancient formulas the former meant specifically the renunciation of Satan. In some contemporary liturgies this is a formulation which does not use the devil image but speaks of the turning from evil and sin. In the new rite of the Episcopal *Book of Common Prayer*, the commitment is framed in the traditional three questions about the renunciation of evil and three about adherence to Christ. They are strong in their direct, concrete imagery. The questions calling for rejection of evil are:

Do you renounce Satan and all the spiritual forces of wickedness that rebel against God?

Do you renounce the evil powers of this world which corrupt and destroy the creatures of God?

Do you renounce all sinful desires that draw you from the love of God?

In each case the candidates or parents and godparents respond, "I renounce them." The questions of faith are:

Do you turn to Jesus Christ and accept him as your Savior?

Do you put your whole trust in his grace and love?

Do you promise to follow and obey him as your Lord?

Those to be baptized respond, "I do." The rich themes of these repudiations and affirmations provide the substance for the kind of critical inquiry into the nature of Christian life which needs to surround the whole process of initiation in the faith.

In most of the new rites, the baptismal vows are followed by the general recitation of the Apostles' Creed as response to questions about belief in Father, Son, and Holy Spirit. This return of the creed to its point of origin is a significant reform. The framers of the Episcopal rite have added after the creed a powerful set of questions to the congregation:

Will you continue in the apostles' teaching and fellowship, in the breaking of bread, and in the prayers?

Will you persevere in resisting evil, and, whenever you fall into sin, repent and return to the Lord?

Will you proclaim by word and example the Good News of God in Christ?

Will you seek and serve Christ in all persons, loving your neighbor as yourself?

Will you strive for justice and peace among all people, and respect the dignity of every human being?

After each question, the people answer, "I will, with God's help." In this straightforward way the people are brought directly into the experience of baptism as commitment in faith. Most churches provide some kind of a text for people to welcome the new initiates into the fellowship. Most of these have been reconsidered and strengthened in recent years.[40] To these have been added the recitation of the Apostles' Creed as a congregational response. The further addition of these simple, fundamental questions greatly strengthens the character of the sacrament as commitment.

Into the Name

Baptism was apparently, initially, into the name of Christ and, as the rite and the affirmation grew together, soon came to be into the name of Father, Son, and Holy Spirit. In the act of baptizing, the name of the person begins the declaration: "(name) I baptize you . . ." The name pronounced should be only the given name or names (first and middle names) and not the surname (last name). The "family" name has, historically, not been used and this is because at this occasion "family" is the family of Jesus. Every time we speak or hear a name and the baptismal formula which follows it we should be reminded of Mark 3:35: "Whoever does the will of God is my brother, and sister, and mother."

The Baptismal Formula

Most Christians are unaware that the baptismal formula in the Eastern church is different from our familiar Western, "(name) I baptize you . . ." The formula of the East reads, "The servant of God (name) is baptized in the name of the Father. Amen. (Immerse) And of the Son. Amen. (Immerse) And of the Holy Spirit. Amen. (Immerse).[41] We believe that the baptismal formula of the Eastern church more accurately represents the truth about baptism than do the words of our own tradition, because baptism, strictly speaking, is not something that we do but something we recognize as done. It is finally Christ's act in the church, and like Laurence Stookey in his fine study on baptism, we recommend that, where there is no compelling reason to use the Western formula, a simple version of the Eastern baptismal words be used: "(name) is baptized in the name of. . . ," or "(name) you are baptized in the name of. . . ."[42]

Reconciliation

One of the meanings given to baptism at Pentecost, the primal baptismal scene, is the forgiveness of sins. "Repent and be baptized every one of you in the name of Jesus Christ for the forgiveness of your sins" (Acts 2:38). Sometimes this meaning is muted in our liturgies of baptism. If not within the baptismal rite as such, then at some time during the service which includes it there ought to be a time of general confession and a hearing of the word of reconciliation. An excellent prayer and declaration of pardon (based on 1 Peter 2:9-10) with congregational response, for this purpose, is supplied in *Baptism* by L. Stookey (p. 159f.). Most denominations have liturgies of corporate confession of some kind. They do not specify these for use in the service of baptism. To be baptized is to be brought into the community of reconciliation and given an identity as someone whose life is a process of repentance and finding forgiveness, of hearing repentance and speaking the word of forgiveness, which is the divine rhythm of reconciliation. This reconciliation of God into which we enter should be celebrated significantly at every baptism.

The Gift of the Spirit

The other meaning given to baptism at Pentecost concerns spirituality. "Repent and be baptized every one of you in the name of Jesus Christ . . . and you shall receive the gift of the Holy Spirit" (Acts 2:38). Baptism is the sacrament of freedom. Liberated from damning pasts, in God's great, loving forgiveness, we are free and this freedom is not something passive in us. Because it is God's gift it is a positive quality, a liveliness which we call Spirit; and we call it a Holy Spirit because it is not what we have created, but is God's gift in Christ. So every occasion of baptism—in movement, in song, in word, in visual beauty—should be a *spirited* occasion, alive with the liberating joy which is, and always has been, irrepressible evidence of God's new creation. Sometimes our attempts to create a joyful occasion result rather in the fabrication of a kind of effervescent silliness. Trust the Word and trust the liturgy. Let the texts dictate the kinds of holy vitality of movement, of sights and sounds, which can enliven our celebration, and our joy—the Spirit's liveliness among us—will not be forced, but a genuine expression of our faith, of the song that wells up in us, and of our hearts desire.

The Whole Rite

The direction of thinking about baptism, as historical study, creative theology, or pastoral-liturgical practice, is tending to see it as part of a whole initiation which includes the washing, the laying on of hands (sometimes with anointing), and eucharist. There are exceptions to this building ecumenical consensus, but they are definitely exceptions. This means, in terms of our past, typical identification of rites, that what we have called baptism and confirmation become one event with two signs, washing and laying on of hands, and that these symbols are prelude to the eucharist in the same service. This kind of "unified" initiation has always been the pattern in the Eastern church and it is now strongly advocated in the West, with the liturgies of many denominations now encouraging the practice. There is some confusion about this because what new liturgies allow and in some ways promote is always ahead of usual pastoral practice and sometimes of denominational polity.

In churches which practice infant baptism, the inclusion of baptismal candidates (infants) at the eucharist may seem ludicrous, if not impossible. If we understand that these, our children, are in fact a real part of our body of Christ then the eucharist does belong to them and they to it and then inclusion in the holy meal at the time of their initiation is logical and important. In the Eastern church this has been managed by the intinction of a tiny amount of bread with the wine in the chalice, and this then given to the child with a small spoon. This is easily possible (but subject to the usual resistances people sometimes put up on such occasions) and can be done in the service right at the beginning of the people's communion.

The putting together of what we have known as baptism, confirmation, and eucharist in one service may seem to some a terrible complication in a service that promises to go on forever. The service need not be complicated. Baptism itself is very brief and the laying on of hands is but a simple gesture with usually very few words, "The power of the Holy Spirit work within you, that being born through water and the Spirit you may be a faithful witness of Jesus Christ. Amen." (United Methodist rite) The eucharist which follows this new beginning is not another sacrament artificially coerced into the occasion. It is rather the holy meal of the family of Jesus to which new members are naturally, immediately invited.

Notes

1. Geoffrey Wainwright, *Christian Initiation* (Richmond: John Knox Press, 1969), p. 40.

2. We disagree with the reasoning of Laurence H. Stookey in his book (*Baptism: Christ's Act in the Church* [Nashville: Abingdon Press, 1982], p. 48) when he argues that because children need a covenant community before they can be baptized, it follows that adult baptism should be the norm. We agree with James White (*Sacraments As God's Self-Giving* [Nashville: Abingdon Press, 1983], p. 47, when he wants the firm covenant community but reasons that "to include children in the Christian family and yet to exclude them from membership in the body of Christ seems inconsistent. . . . Baptism goes much deeper than intellectual cognition alone. . . . Rather, it changes our whole life within a context of loving community relationships, expressed both in family and in the church."

3. Irenaeus, *Against the Heresies II*, 22:4.

4. See Aidan Kavanagh, *The Shape of Baptism: The Rite of Christian Initiation* (New York: Pueblo Publishing Co., 1978), pp. 174-175. Kavanagh proposes adult baptism and the catechumenate as the norm but encourages the enrollment of children as catechumens and the extension of baptismal life with the climax of a unified initiation coming later, "at some more appropriate time."

5. Oscar Cullman, *Baptism in the New Testament* (Philadelphia: Westminster Press, 1950), p. 7.

6. Ibid., p. 23.

7. Ibid., p. 53.

8. Cullman's argument here may be too neat. However, the direction of his views is defensible and undergirds the integrity of infant baptism.

9. In, Anthony M. Coniaris, *These Are The Sacraments: The Life-Giving Mysteries of the Orthodox Church* (Minneapolis: Light and Life Publishing Co., 1981), p. 45.

10. Daniel B. Stevick, *Holy Baptism* (New York: Prayer Book Studies 26— Church Hymnal Corporation, 1973), p. 88.

11. See *The Rites of the Catholic Church* (New York: Pueblo Publishing Co., 1976).

12. Mark Searle, "Childhood and the Reign of God: Reflections on Infant Baptism" in *Assembly* 9, 2, Notre Dame Center for Pastoral Liturgy (November, 1982), p. 187.

13. *Baptism, Eucharist, and Ministry* (Geneva: Faith and Order Paper No. 111, World Council of Churches, 1982), p. ix.

14. Ibid., p. 6.

15. John H. Westerhoff III and William H. Willimon, *Liturgy and Learning Through the Life Cycle* (New York: Seabury Press, 1980), pp. 9-27 for more ideas.

16. See Charles R. Foster, *Teaching in the Community of Faith* (Nashville: Abingdon Press, 1982), Chapters 2 and 3 are especially helpful as a resource for this section of the discussion.

17. See Erik Erikson, *Toys and Reasons: Stages in the Ritualization of Experience* (New York: W. W. Norton, 1977). Also see James Fowler, *Stages of Faith* (San Francisco: Harper & Row, 1981).

18. Resources for parents and sponsors for use in this discussion are:
William J. Bausch, *A New Look at the Sacraments* (Notre Dame, Ind.: Fides/Claretian, 1977). (A Roman Catholic source.)
James F. White, *Sacraments as God's Self-Giving* (Nashville: Abingdon Press, 1982). (A United Methodist interpreter.)
Anthony M. Coniaris, *These Are The Sacraments: The Life-Giving Mysteries of the Orthodox Church* (Minneapolis: Light and Publishing Co., 1981), pp. 19-51. (A full description of the drama of infant baptism in the Orthodox Church which has united the three sacraments in the initiation of the child over the centuries.)

19. The parents, William and Carol Eastin, are now co-pastors in a United Methodist parish in Joy, Illinois.

20. F. L. Cross, ed., *St. Cyril of Jerusalem* (Lectures on the Christian Sacraments) (Crestwood, N. Y.: St. Vladimirs Seminary Press, 1977), p. 53.

21. *Baptism, Eucharist and Ministry*, p. 4.

22. *We Gather Together*, Supplemental Worship Resources 10 (Nashville: The United Methodist Publishing House, 1980), p. 13.

23. *The Book of Common Prayer* (New York: Seabury Press, 1978), p. 298ff.

24. From *the Alternative Service Book* (London: SPCK, 1980), p. 276.

25. *We Gather Together,* p. 16.

26. *Baptism, Eucharist and Ministry,* p. 2.

27. *From Ashes to Fire* (Nashville: Abingdon Press, 1979), p. 176ff. *Lutheran Book of Worship* (Minister's Desk Edition; Augsburg, 1979) p. 152.

28. Frank Senn, *Christian Worship and Its Cultural Setting* (Philadelphia: Fortress, 1981), p. 69.

29. Robert Jenson, *Visible Words* (Philadelphia: Fortress, 1978), p. 170.

30. Stookey, *Baptism: Christ's Act in the Church,* p. 163ff.

31. *We Gather Together,* p. 15f.

32. Jenson, *Visible Words,* p. 171.

33. *The Rites of the Catholic Church* (New York: Pueblo Publishing Co., 1976), p. 235.

34. Ibid., p. 309f.

35. Ibid., p. 292.

36. Ibid., p. 289.

37. Ibid., p. 298.

38. *The Alternate Service Book,* p. 233.

39. Cf. Stookey, *Baptism: Christ's Act in the Church,* p. 169.

40. Cf. The United Methodist Rites of 1964 and of 1976 in *The Book of Worship* (Nashville: The United Methodist Publishing House), p. 8, and *We Gather Together* (Nashville: The United Methodist Publishing House), p. 17.

41. Paul Lazor, ed., *Baptism* (Latham, N. Y.: Orthodox Church in America, 1983), p. 56.

42. Stookey, *Baptism: Christ's Act in the Church,* p. 165.

Chapter 9

The Eucharist: The Lord's Open Table

A Sign of the Kingdom

The eucharist has been the subject lately of vast reform, and the impulse for this historical and creative work has not abated. The primary lines of the reform may be clear, but the work continues. One basic line of reform has concerned the fundamental character of the rite.

The inherited liturgical imagery common to most Christian traditions characterized the supper of the Lord with particular emphasis upon:

1. The cross and the death of Jesus.
2. Sacrifice as the theme of the atoning, saving death of Jesus.
3. Memorial and recollection as modes of our participation.
4. The past and our sin and guilt which are relieved by Jesus' sacrificial death.
5. Communion as personal meeting with Christ.
6. The supper as a somber event where we recall death on the cross, our sin, and costly salvation.

Historical research and comparative liturgical theology has recovered and introduced imagery of the holy meal which exactly contrasts this inherited "picture" and characterizes the supper as:

1. Resurrection, emphasizing the risen Christ.
2. Banquet of joy and festivity.
3. The presence of Christ as the host of a present celebration.
4. The future and the coming kingdom of God.
5. Communion as fellowship, our meeting together in Christ.
6. The supper as a luminous, happy event where we celebrate in a festive mood.

This apparent revolution of primary meaning represents the discovery of eschatology as a key to understanding the essential character of the Lord's supper. Eucharist (thanksgiving) is a term we have all applied to the meal for centuries, but it has not been the main term. More typical have been the title of *mass, Lord's supper,* and *communion.* Eucharist becomes more and more the common name for our holy meal, as we understand it eschatologically and find thanksgiving a prevailing theme of the liturgy and an appropriate name.

It is important to understand that the introduction of eschatology as an interpretive principle has produced the sharp contrast in the six points listed above. It is equally important to realize that the six new and contradicting themes do not cancel the six "traditional" themes we first enumerated. The cross, sacrifice, memorial, human guilt, personal relation to Christ, and sober reflection, are not dimensions of meaning in the eucharist which will disappear or which anyone advocates should disappear. The new and contrasting emphases express the discovery of *other tradition.* Mainly they represent the discovery that there is more in the New Testament that discloses the character of our holy meal to us than the accounts of the last supper, and the decision, which we have mentioned earlier, on the part of many contemporary Christians to let the worship of the early church have a great deal of authority over the creation of liturgy for our own time. To say, for instance, that resurrection is a primary theme of eucharist does not cancel out the cross as a primary theme. Indeed, resurrection and crucifixion, rising and dying, are inseparable primary themes of Christian self-understanding. They belong to one another, yet they require of us some different things in liturgy as we enter into cross and resurrection in our own experience.

No one meaning or conceivable set of meanings can exhaust the significance of the eucharist. It is an inexhaustible symbol, and it certainly encompasses the contrasting sets of themes we have listed above. Having said this, in part as reassurance to those who fear the loss of certain "traditional" values in the eucharist, we need to account for the "new" eschatological emphasis and underline its impact on liturgical celebration today.

The evaluation of a conception of the nature of the eucharist grounded in the idea of the kingdom of God begins with the publication by Hans Lietzmann in 1926 of *Messe und Herrenmahl (The Mass and the Lord's Supper).*[1] Lietzmann identified two distinct types of eucharistic liturgy in the early church, one dominated by the death of Christ and inspired by the "words of institution" of the upper room (Hippolytus) and one dominated by themes of the return of Christ and of community (Didache and ancient Egyptian liturgy). This distinction was dramatized, with special emphasis upon eschatology, by Oscar Cullmann in a brief but important and influential monograph published in 1936 and translated into English only in 1958.[2] Cullmann's essay relates the eucharist to the resurrection appearances of Christ and demonstrates the eschatological significance of eating and drinking with Jesus and the relation of messianic meal to the evolving Christian liturgy. In so doing he showed that much more in the New Testament informs us about the character of our eucharist than the accounts of the upper room. He isolated the emphasis upon death and sacrifice as a *particular* and especially Pauline emphasis, and underlined the continuing relevance for our worship of the ancient prayer, "Lord come! *Maranatha!*" Cullmann concluded that this prayer "ought to assume again the eucharistic reference that it originally had, and it should express the double desire, which was realized for the early Christians, of seeing Christ descend into the midst of the faithful gathered in his name and of discovering for themselves, in that coming, an anticipation of his final messianic return."[3]

These emphases have become by now familiar lines of interpretation of our meal liturgy. They have been most fully developed and best organized, perhaps, in Geoffrey Wainwright's *Eucharist and Eschatology* (1971).[4] Wainwright presents an understanding of the relation of kingdom of God to the eucharist in the exploration—in scripture, liturgy, and early Christian literature—of three images: the messianic feast, the advent of Christ, and the first fruits of the kingdom.

New Testament Witness

We might characterize the nature of the new eschatological awareness of the eucharist in a consideration of two passages from the Gospel of St. Luke. In Luke 14:7-24 Jesus, at table, tells two parables about banquets. They are about who will sit where and the place of honor and who is invited and who will come. Hearing that the exalted may be humbled and the humble exalted, one of those eating with Jesus exclaimed, "Blessed is he who shall eat bread in the kingdom of God!" (14:15). Jesus continues the storytelling indicating that there may be great surprise at who finally comes to the banquet and concludes, "None of those men who were invited shall taste my banquet" (14:24). The new time of God is a banquet, and a feast where our common values may be turned upside down.

Luke 12:35-37 is another illustration of the kingdom of God using again the imagery of a meal. Jesus cautions that the time of the kingdom's advent is unknown. We should be ready because our invitation to the banquet may come when we do not expect it. Surprisingly, the prepared ones who find themselves at the kingdom table will also find that the master of the feast will "gird himself and have them sit at table, and he will come and serve them" (12:37). The new time of God is not only a banquet, and a feast where common values may be turned upside down, it is a meal where the messiah waits upon the tables.

These are but two of many examples which could be given to illustrate the point that the kingdom of God was imaged by Jesus and his hearers as a happy fulfillment, as food and drink enough, a banquet where the Christ serves, a banquet hosted, strange to say, by the one who serves.

When our Christian ancestors made a meal the central event of their worship they had several things besides the upper room in mind. In the first place they had in mind Jesus' teaching about the kingdom of God and the meal imagery this involved—the metaphor of the messianic banquet. Second, they had in mind that Jesus was *present* in the meal, as one invited and paradoxically as the host and, more paradoxically yet, as the one who serves. Relevant to this understanding are the accounts of resurrection appearances, especially John 21:10-13, Luke 24:30-35 and Acts 10:41, as well as passages like Luke 12:35-40 which we considered above, and evidences outside the gospels, like Revelation 3:20: "Behold, I stand at the door and knock; if any one hears my voice and opens the door, I will come in to him and eat with him and he with me." They thus had the memory, not only of Jesus' teaching, but also of actually eating and drinking with him in meals which brought to reality the images of which he had spoken.

Jesus and his disciples were, as the evidence indicates, an eating and enjoying people. His teaching about the kingdom and its banquet was more than theology, it was life. "Why do John's disciples and the disciples of the Pharisees fast, but your disciples do not fast?" This sober question elicits from Jesus a "kingdom banquet" reply: "Can the wedding guests fast while the bridegroom is with them?" (Mk. 2:18-19). Jesus seized the kingdom sign of future for the present. He was a utopian who did not hate the present in the name of the future; he appropriated the joyful kingdom time for his present and therefore faced the criticism typical of puritanical moralists of every age, that he had too much fun and associated with the wrong people. "The Son of Man came eating and drinking, and they say, 'Behold, a glutton and a drunkard, a friend of tax collectors and sinners!' " (Mt. 11:19).

When our early ancestors in the faith made a meal the central act of Christian worship and called it eucharist (thanksgiving), they were recalling, not just the upper room, but all of their experience of eating and drinking with Jesus. This included private events, larger group meals, and feedings of multitudes, where Jesus took bread, blessed it and gave it to them to eat. Obviously, nothing was more precious in their memories than eating and drinking with Jesus. This powerful presence with whom they had lived had been put to death, but death could not contain him. They proclaimed his resurrection, his continuing life, and they claimed this living Christ as a new life in them—as their new living center. The banquet of the Lord, the feast of the Messiah, became the festival of their sharing together in the living, continuing Jesus—the Christ—the host of the meal, and even its very substance.

The Open Table

The emphasis upon eschatology as key to the understanding of eucharist has resulted, for some, in the conclusion that the table of Christ's kingdom is an open table, that is to say that the holy meal is available to *all* without a single condition, not even the condition of baptism. This judgment out of an eschatological interpretation is clearly formulated in the volume to which we have already referred, Geoffrey Wainwright's *Eucharist and Eschatology*. Wainwright quotes with approval the affirmation of J. C. Hoekendijk, the Dutch missiologist, that, "Communion as an eschatological sacrament is the representation of the kingdom in the *world*; it is impossible to lock up the kingdom in the Church, it is equally impossible to make this sacrament of the kingdom a purely churchly event."[5] For Hoekendijk, he points out, "the new overpowers the old," and since at the eucharist we celebrate God's new era in Christ's presence, our sacrament is the "first fruit" of the newness God gives, the "promised feast for the nation," all guests from wherever they may come are to be welcomed.[6] Wainwright concurs that the eucharist is finally of Christ before it is of the church. We cannot aspire to be more than the first fruit of what is God's kingdom. This means that "no one should be refused communion who has been moved by the celebration of the sign then in progress to seek saving fellowship with the Lord through eating the bread and drinking the wine."[7] This includes the unbaptized, but he believes that persons so "moved" should "be brought to baptism and soon."[8]

Wainwright differs with Schillebeeckx, Semmelroth, and Rahner, while appreciating their contribution to a new model. He does not move from Christ as the primordial sacrament, to the church as the sacrament of Christ, to the sacraments themselves. He believes we must move from Christ as the sacrament of God to the sacraments directly. "The sacraments," he states, "remain the Lord's entirely, and may be used by Him, even when (at the purely human level) defectively performed, as the vehicle of His presence to bring His Church to a more obedient acknowledgement (and therefore greater enjoyment and more faithful proclamation) of the kingdom of God. In the light of this eschatological purpose, no obstacle of ecclesiastical discipline dependent on a sinful state of Christian disunity must be allowed to block the Lord's invitation to all penitents . . . to gather round His table whenever it is set up and receive His forgiveness for sins that have led to disunity and be filled through his transforming presence with the love that unites."[9]

Jürgen Moltmann arrives at the same point of view in a focus upon eschatology which is primarily pneumatological rather than Christological. In his book, *The Church in the Power of the Spirit*,[10] Moltmann presents the Holy Spirit as the key to an understanding of what he calls the "glorifying of the Father and the Son through the Spirit."[11] He realizes that Christian doctrine, specifically the trinitarian tradition, has put forward a history of Christ which stressed incarnation, baptism, ministry, and passion much more than transfiguration, resurrection, exaltation, and what he calls "the consummation of the lordship of God."[12] There has been, in other words, a lopsided interest in origins and the past and a neglect of Christ's future. The Holy Spirit is, for him the central concept of the way forward, that is, of eschatology. "Glory" is an idea at the heart of this conceptualization. Glory is the unfolding splendor and beauty of God. Christ was taken into the glory of the Father. For the glory of God the Father he was exalted after he had humbled himself to death on the cross and was made Lord over all things (Phil. 2:11). We are all familiar with this language in relation to Christ. Moltmann's contribution is to point out that glorification is also at the center of the history of the Spirit in the light of its future. The power which glorifies humanity in the glory of God is the Holy Spirit. "It is the Holy Spirit which glorifies Christ in believers and unites them with him. Through union with Christ in the Holy Spirit the coming glory already becomes efficacious in the present life."[13] For this reason the Holy Spirit is called the first fruit and a guarantee of glory (Rom. 8:23; 2 Cor. 5:5). The theological conclusion then, of immense practical significance for Moltmann, is that, "the Spirit glorifies the Son and the Father in creation."[14] This simple formulation "points the trinitarian history of glorification towards the glorified Trinity at the end."[15] This means "the unity of the triune God is the goal of the uniting of man and creation with the Father and the Son in the Spirit. The history of the kingdom of God on earth is nothing other than the history of the uniting of what is separated and the freeing of what is broken, in this being the history of the glorification of God. If the unity of God were described in the doctrine of the Trinity by *koinonia* instead of by *una natura*, this idea would not seem so unusual."[16]

When Moltmann considers sacrament in the light of this eschatological understanding, where the Spirit is a kind of principle of divine freedom within the Trinity, he concludes: "Even if Christ is termed the one, unique mediation of God, yet this mediation presses forward to its self-mediation in the world. . . . That means that Jesus as the Messiah is open for the messianic era and that as the Christ who has come he is open for the future of his rule. Even if the church is termed the 'fundamental sacrament,' the thing that makes it so points beyond itself. 'The eschatologically victorious grace of God' leads the church beyond its own present existence in the world and drives it toward the perfected kingdom of God." Because this is so the Holy Spirit must be a primary element in our understanding of mystery or sacrament, since "the presence of the kingdom of God and the revelation of the divine mystery of the last days are to be found in the eschatological gift of the Holy Spirit. He reveals Christ and creates faith. Proclamation, fellowship and the emblematic messianic acts take place in the power of the Holy Spirit. He is the power of the divine future and the one who completes the divine history. He glorifies Christ in believers and in the power of the new creation of the world. Not Christ for himself but Christ in the Holy Spirit, not the church for itself but Christ's church in the Holy Spirit, must be called the mystery or 'sacrament.' "[17]

At this point the logic of Moltmann's argument meets that of Wainwright: The eucharist is "in Spirit" the Lord's supper. "What is true of theology applies to church discipline as well. The Lord's supper is not the place to practice church discipline; it is first of all the place where the liberating presence of the crucified Lord is celebrated."[18] Around this table, as he understands it from the perspective of his Christ-glorifying doctrine of Spirit, one can place no barriers at all. "The Lord's supper takes place on the basis of an invitation which is as open as the outstretched arms of Christ on the cross. Because he died for the reconciliation of 'the world,' the world is invited to reconciliation in the supper. It is not the openness of this invitation, it is the restrictive measures of the churches which have to be justified before the face of the crucified Jesus."[19] This point of view extends, of course, beyond "intercommunion," that is, openness to the churches. It is, straightforwardly, openness to the world.

We agree with this point of view and, along with Wainwright and Moltmann, believe that it is a logical conclusion of a theology which understands eucharist eschatologically, that is, as a sign of the kingdom of God.

To say that the table is open to all means that it is open to children. This fact gives the eucharist a special place in our thinking about education, and our understanding of the evolution of faith.

Communion and the Stages of Ritualization and the Stages of Faith

Communion symbolizes the life-giving, joyous faith of the community. To share this sense of mutual concern and love with very young children can have powerful effect. The rituals of sharing, feeding, touching, lifting up can say, "We love you. All of the people here love you. You are a part of all that we think is important in life." The child learns through the actions of the community. This is existence education. The child becomes incorporated into the body of Christ before he or she can understand what God, Christ, the church or the sacraments are. Such understandings can and do take place as the child is led to reflect, intuitively at first, then concretely, and finally abstractly, on what he or she is experiencing.

In relation to the stages of faith, young children in the undifferentiated faith period, during the first two years of life, and during the Stage I Intuitive-Projective faith of early childhood, have deep need for trusting relationships, for a joy concerning existence itself, for a growing sense of who the child is as a "good or bad person," for taking initiative and making a difference as a person. Communion, when experienced as a joyous sharing of love from another and from God, is a profound paradigm through which young children can see life and themselves. At each of the stages, new levels of meaning can grow in relation to the same event. For instance, in Stage II Mythic-Literal faith, school-aged children are those who learn through stories. The stories of Jesus' life, the lives of biblical characters who revealed the nature of love, the actual story of the Lord's struggle to be faithful which led to the crucifixion and the mystery of the resurrection—all of these stories can give new content and meaning to the eucharistic life of the parish. Also, family and parish celebrations of communion should take place with much relational warmth and high enactive involvement of parents and children in the drama of God's love of all. We should not expect too much understanding of the *concepts* associated with communion or the nature of a symbol, etc. That level of learning and experience is to come in Stage III development more appropriate to the abilities of adolescents and above.

The nature of communion can be discussed, criticized, questioned, and compared to other rituals in other world religions. The result will be very important decisions to affirm some version of the meaning of communion which is rather similar to what is expected by parents and elders. Fowler calls this a Synthetic-Conventional faith (Stage III). It is one in which the self is centered in meanings that the person works out honestly but which are fairly local and conventionally acceptable. Nevertheless, when couched in the worshiping congregation in joyous celebration these views are strong food for both Christian faith and action.

If persons grow in their faith beyond Stage III they will experience and share the same eucharistic table but they may well see communion in wider and deeper ways.

Persons in Stage IV Individuative-Reflective faith could begin to perceive communion in a more honest, personally critiqued, and corporate way. Persons expressing a Stage IV faith will begin to evaluate communion as an element in the whole Christian system of belief and action. The young adult or adult who is working honestly at this level of faith will try to put the concepts associated with communion into a somewhat larger, overall framework. He or she will try to work out an ideology or world view in which communion can be seen as either a stimulus to wider circles of love and justice, or it can be seen as a more exclusive experience for persons who believe similarly, etc. The person with a Stage IV faith is seeking to get behind the symbols of bread and wine to the "real" meaning. Some more systematic, overall way of thinking about communion will be sought. This will not be done merely at an abstract "thinking" level! A Stage IV faith is concerned about relationships, intimacy, and how persons care about one another. At this point communion will need to be a personal, joyous, honest, sharing experience with others, with God, and with the great figures who have gone before but whose spirits still live on.

Stage V Conjunctive faith pushes a step deeper in honesty and willingness to look beyond the system worked out as a young adult. The contradictory, the paradoxical matters concerning the eucharist, for instance, might well be discerned. For instance, persons come to the table celebrating God's love and Christ's sacrificial life which revealed this love in the breaking of his body, but act as though God loves only their small circle or even their nation—and not the entire world and all persons of diverse commitments. A person perceiving this paradox would begin to seek something of the wider, more fundamental meaning of communion. Stage V faith begins to see the relativity of our various beliefs concerning communion which separate us from one another. Such a quality of faith could grow to the point of wanting to get past seeing communion as only a symbol. Rather, such a person would see that the symbol has a fresh power to help him or her actually *experience* the living presence of Christ in the meal. This new experience would begin to have both conscious and powerful unconscious meanings which would become unified within the self. Moreover, the quest for a universal meaning for communion would begin in seriousness and anguish—not as an interesting intellectual possibility.

A Stage VI Universalizing faith, as rare as we are led to believe it is, would truly break through to a universal meaning for communion, and a set of actions which genuinely reveal a perspective in which Christ's gift of himself was for all persons of whatever condition, race, belief system, personal situation, or religious conviction. Such a sense of universal community with God and others employing different symbols, would be lived out in some "high risk" way—in a setting which called forth genuine entering into the suffering of others for purposes of universal justice or love. No one would perceive communion in a Stage VI way as an exercise or as a synthetic intellectual stance. It is either a response of the whole self in a particular situation of need or it is not authentic. In Stage VI faith, it is likely that the relationships of self-giving love and trust acted out in the eucharistic meal are also acted out in reality, not in a perfect way but in a way that really communicates God's universal love through Christ (as this love has been incarnated in the behavior of a person with a Stage VI faith). When this is actually done, people are often offended. Stage VI faith is risky. Also, of course, such growth is not neat and progressive. It is dynamic and irregular. It is not an intellectual matter alone. It involves the whole person—mind, emotions, will, and actions. It is not a faith stance which judges others. It recognizes that children can love intuitively in ways that humble the seasoned spirit. It is open to the love of God, coming through other faith communities, but rejoices in the identified mystery made known in Christ's self-giving, celebrated in the eucharist.

We have sketched the possible path of faith development as it could be related to communion. This will not be done with each sacrament we discuss, but it could be. Something at the heart of each sacrament is also alive and at work at each stage of life and at each of the stages of faith development. With this picture of possible development around communion as a backdrop, admittedly colored by our Protestant, academic backgrounds, we shall move on to a discussion of religious education and liturgy.

Religious Education and Communion

Religious education is much more than nurture into the life of love, trust, and righteousness made visible around the communion table, but it is certainly consistent with that life.

We are sympathetic to some degree with the notion put forth by John Westerhoff and William Willimon that communion is the center of Christian nurture. They see the service of the word and the service of the table as the central communicators of the life of faith revealed in Christ's gift of himself to the world. The liturgy, then, is crucial for Christian nurture. What happens in the family, within specific graded or intergenerational learning experiences can be communicated and celebrated in the common meal of the Lord. This central faith story is repeated and related to the great themes of the Christian year and the great issues of life in an ongoing, honest, earthy (not spiritualized or phony) way. All of learning is integrated in the lectionary readings from scripture, (the preaching, the sacramental focus, the education in family and church). Such a unity of forces, correlated as it is with the church year and with the festivals and celebrations that are a part of that annual pilgrimage, is the primary nurturing center for young children, older children, youth, and adults. All are learning and sharing together. But, each is approaching these great incarnated truths in relation to his or her own abilities, needs, and perceptions.[20]

While the centering of Christian nurture in communion is integrative and constructive the task of religious education is broader than that. There needs to be a creative tension present which will stimulate participants increasingly to assess what our praxis means. The nature of the life of faith and the meaning of communion itself need to be interrelated and evaluated. Young children, youth, and adults can become aware increasingly of the questions of truth and justice which are implied in the way we celebrate the sacred meal. For instance, who is involved in celebrating and serving the meal, and who is invited to the table? The answers to those two questions are quite revelatory. What ages (from children to the elderly, persons who are handicapped or persons who are physically mobile), races, sexes, persons with or without power are present or absent as leaders or participants at the table? Especially with youth and adults, we can ask the deeper questions about the core meanings behind communion (the biblical, theological, historical, and ethical concerns implied). This probing need not be some intellectual exercise for the elite. It should be an attempt to identify the attitudes and actions that people themselves have expressed through the celebration. Attitudes of inclusiveness or exclusiveness, actions which are self-serving or oriented toward others can be decoded by sensitive participants with a view to refinement and more authentic understandings and expressions of sacramental life.

The Eucharist As the Heart of Education for Peace and Justice

Relating the sacrament of the open table of the Lord to the nurture and growth of children and youth is self-evident. The relationship of the broken body and spilled blood of Christ to the needs of persons in a profound struggle for the very survival of humankind is not as self-evident. The open table speaks radically to the issues which divide us as a human family. How can we talk about the unity of all humanity and the sacredness of all living persons around the table when some are in poverty and misery and others are jaded by affluence? Deep religious concerns are at the root of the human issues of hunger, racism, and the just distribution of wealth, education, medical care, shelter, and other basic human services. The integration of the sacrament of the eucharist with religious education for peace and justice can be engaging, authentic, and theologically significant. The *Doing the Word* resources, one of four tracks of the Shared Approaches Curriculum of fifteen cooperating denominations, is especially rich in regard to religious education for peace and justice. The manual, *How to Use Resources in Doing the Word* by Manford and Nancy Wright-Saunders (United Methodist Press, 1980) is helpful in suggesting how an awareness-analysis-action-reflection model of religious education can be applied to issues of our time. Also, designs for intergenerational, youth and adult studies are presented along with ideas for integrating education and celebration. Some of the issues for which resource materials are available are race (a unit for younger children entitled *Journeys to a Dream*, by Kathryn Elmes Parker, opens up the contribution of Martin Luther King); violence (a unit for children, ages eight to twelve, on *Why People Fight*, by James E. Baler; or for adults, *What Americans Should Do About Crime*, by L. Harold DeWolf); peace (*Biblical Reflections on Shalom, Living Toward A Vision*, by Walter Brueggemann—excellent for adults); hunger and poverty (Julio De Santa Ana, *Good Views to the Poor*—for adults); justice (Thomas Fenton, ed., *Education for Justice*—especially for youth and adults); etc. We have mentioned only sample units. Many other units are available. The important learning from this effort to deal with such issues is this: Be sure to study in the context of an attempt to increase *awareness* of an issue, to *analyze* it carefully, to take some concrete *action*, and to do theological *reflection* about the issue in direct relation to the human needs being met. Celebration of these meanings and discoveries in the eucharist can bring a depth to the experience which is difficult to measure but of great significance.

The *religious education of parents* is a high responsibility within the model we have presented. If children are to be baptized, confirmed, and be given communion as infants, then parents need to understand ways to help young children not only experience communion but to be able to talk about its meaning in informal and very human ways. Occasional workshops for parents concerning the eucharist can be most helpful. Some of the material prepared for parents to interpret First Communion to their children, while not in line with our model precisely, is very well written and can be adapted and become fine resources. For instance, the Canadian book for catechists and parents, *On the Way to Their First Communion* (translated by James McGhee, Paulist Press, 1976), is a sensitive piece which describes conversations and prayers parents may use with small children. The thesis is that children are in communion with God all of the time in their families where love is shared, in nature, and in other relationships. Communion is being celebrated all of the time in preparation for the great celebration, communion with God at Christ's table.

Another resource to be used with parents to help them prepare their children for the eucharist is a fine book which details how children can participate fully in the eucharist. Again, while it is a book written for Catholics in response to the changes made possible in the Second Vatican Council, it is very adaptable to Protestant or Orthodox settings. It is Edward Matthews' *Celebrating Mass With Children* (Paulist Press, 1975). The book assumes infant baptism and the participation of children at the table. Calling for unity at the table, Matthews says, "The greatest sign of such unity is the gathering around the Lord's table which is really a family banquet. Everybody has a place at that banquet, and everybody must feel that he (she) is welcome. Hence the church's concern for the instruction and participation of children in the eucharist."[21] While this book is centered on preparation for an early first communion (ages five plus) it has many suggestions for the adaptation of the eucharistic liturgy to include younger children and many suggestions for parents and teachers to help children experience the core meaning of communion. Activities are suggested, such as children creating prayers and simple creeds to be used in the liturgy as well as making bread to be used in the service.

Several resources to help parents, teachers, educators, and pastors to interpret the Christian story follow the lectionary readings or adapt scriptures to the Christian year. Many of these resources have children participating in imaginatively designed eucharistic celebrations. Increasingly, parents and educational and liturgical leaders can find support and guidance in fulfilling their responsibilities to enable children to experience the depth of God's love through participation in the Lord's supper.[22]

Another powerful experience is the *Family Cluster approach to religious education and liturgy*. In this pattern several families agree to meet together for intergenerational education, worship, and action during which they plan and share the leadership for religious education and liturgical experiences in order to be strengthened for mutual ministry and outreach. Intergenerational curriculum resources are available from several denominations or through Shared Approaches. Margaret Sawin has researched and developed the Family Cluster model and has presented varying options. One of the deepest dimensions of such intergenerational and interfamily sharing, of course, can be the eucharist. Some of the options which Dr. Sawin presents are also ecumenical. In one design which took place in Nova Scotia, Canada (with Roman Catholics, Disciples of Christ, and United Church of Canada communities involved), the Family Cluster experience ended with a celebration in which the children, youth, parents, and other adults made bread together and reflected on the meaning of bread and honey in the lives of the participants. Then each person participated in the ritual of planting a hyacinth bulb which was taken home to nurture. Finally, all participated in the breaking and sharing of the bread they had baked and the prayer of Thanksgiving.[23] The depth of communication and communion which took place in this ecumenical setting was symbolized in this quasi-eucharistic celebration. It will be a great day when such ecumenical family experiences can be celebrated with holy communion, with the blessing of all cooperating faith communities. Of course, in many family cluster groups communion is an integrating and joyous celebration of the good news of God's love made manifest in Christ's gift of himself and also in the giving of the members of the cluster to one another and beyond.

In terms of the education of persons to fulfill the ministry into which they have been baptized, it is important to link communion with confirmation, not only in infant baptism, but also in adolescence and adulthood when persons are reworking their understanding of themselves in relation to their understanding and attitudes about the Christian faith. Communion is a sacrament which points to our essential oneness—a oneness which is deep enough to allow and encourage rigorous questioning and testing of the nature of faith in confirmation education and liturgical celebrations or in education of laity or clergy for ordination or consecration for service in the universal priesthood of all believers. At each of these stages of human and faith development parents and families have crucial roles to play. Moreover, they can be strengthened through communication and communion to have the courage to help children, youth, and young adults work out their faith in honesty and integrity. The creative tension between religious education and liturgy can remain while at the same time being integrated and wholistic.

The Liturgy

If we want to make the eschatological motif a real part of our eucharist we usually will discover that the character of our rites is an obstacle. It is hard to celebrate resurrection-presence-community, with joy, when what we say and how we act sets forth crucifixion-memorial-privacy, with solemnity. To find our way to a kingdom-awareness in our eucharists we need texts which express kingdom joy and festivity, ways of celebrating which catch us up in the genuine gladness of thanksgiving, and ways of being together which in fact bring us together, seeing one another, sensing one another, enjoying and sharing real presence together.

In the matter of texts we Christians live in radically different situations. Some of us worship using texts which are prescribed and which may be substituted only in special situations with special permission. Others of us have prescribed texts for our worship which are not mandatory and which may be freely substituted. And some of us are provided with no fixed texts at all and use whatever texts, written or improvised, which ministers and congregations find appropriate. So no universally helpful suggestions can be made.

Even situations where most of the liturgy is prescribed offer some opportunities for the exercise of choice and these are points where an "eschatological option" might be exercised. Some obvious choices are: the time of gathering, the singing of hymns and anthems, the prayers of the people, the manner of receiving the holy food, and blessing at the close of the liturgy.

The gathering of the congregation is an opportunity for festivity: in the music played or perhaps sung, the manner of greeting, the passing out of flowers or small decorations (sometimes to be worn), the reading of special texts as people assemble, festal processions—sometimes of the whole people from a gathering point to the place of worship. Clearly music has a great deal to do with the spirit of liturgy. What we hear played, what we enter into as song establishes a great deal of our "sense" of what is happening. It is the tradition in many churches for soft and grave music to be played during the people's communion.

Obviously, this will not support a spirit of festivity. The music will need to be lively, and the congregation can participate in singing during this time. The singing should not be continuous, though, because it can become exhausting.

Most liturgies allow considerable freedom in the common prayers. Mainly these take the form of intercession, but they can sometimes be expressions primarily of thanksgiving and be outpouring of our joy. This is a special opportunity for kingdom exuberance.

Eating and Drinking

In a great many churches the manner of receiving the elements of communion is itself a very solemn affair; the slow and quiet procession guided by sober ushers culminating in humble kneeling, or the reverent wait, with the people seated and quietly contemplative. A festive communion needs some holy hustle. We need to interact naturally, meet one another eye to eye. It is proper to stand, and "stations" where we receive the bread and wine may be anywhere in the room where there is space, and people need not be led there. They can be free to go where they want. The fact of procession, human movement, is itself a festive dimension. Seated, waiting passively for communion seems hardly the manner of participation appropriate for a festival eucharist. And elements should be *given*, not offered for the taking. We go to *receive*, and the rhythm of exertion to go and humility to receive is the natural movement of our communion together in Christ.

There was for some time an ambiguity between meal and eucharistic rite in the early church. The reintroduction of some element of this ambiguity can help our eucharist to have some of the human interaction necessary to the success of a festive meal. Even after the eucharistic rite was no longer a meal, other elements of food were brought to worship to be blessed, such as oil, cheese, and olives (cf. Hippolytus, *Apostolic Tradition*). The consecrated bread and wine were considered the first fruits of God's consecration of all creation, and the other food was blessed as a kind of extended action of the thanksgiving that had transformed bread and wine.[24] One assumes that they were not eaten as part of the liturgy; their possible use in the worship is unknown. But they were consecrated and eaten or used (in the case of oil) at some time by those who brought them. We might well return to this practice of blessing additional food at the eucharist which could then be eaten as part of the sacramental occasion. Sharing together in pieces of fruit, cheese, nuts, or other foods in small amounts can, on certain festive occasions, add a meal quality to our liturgy which heightens our celebration and encourages our attention to one another.

The blessing at the conclusion of worship has opportunities to underline kingdom rejoicing analogous to those of gathering; joyful music, personal leavetaking, giving of flowers or small decorations, a procession in good weather to a lawn or other suitable place, where a benediction might be sung together.

The Great Thanksgiving

In the matter of the basic texts of the liturgy most Christians are now speaking words which more than ever express the eschatological theme. Especially this is the case regarding the great thanksgiving, the prayer which blesses bread and wine. The titles used and not used indicate this. We once called it the prayer of consecration or the canon—indeed we still do—but more and more it is commonly called the great thanksgiving or the prayer of thanksgiving. Thanks is the opening note of this prayer in the many varieties of it which are in use today. Where allowed, this element can be exaggerated when the character of the liturgy as a whole dictates a eucharistic prayer where the quality of thanks needs to be dominant. And our thanks need not be limited to the opening of the prayer.

There are good studies available to instruct us in the tradition and character of the great thanksgiving,[25] and numerous collections of prayers from the tradition and from contemporary liturgies.[26] Especially in the so-called free churches where presiders at the eucharist are at liberty to frame the text of this prayer as they wish, it is imperative that those who preside and select and/or compose the great thanksgiving do so with understanding and skill. Great freedom imposes great responsibility. There are compelling reasons for the tradition of this prayer. They involve not only tradition as historical precedent, but also the logic of faith itself. Knowing what to do and why is the secure foundation of freedom.

Traditions

The emphasis we place upon the eschatological meaning of our eucharist, we wish to repeat, is not toward the exclusion or the neglect of the meanings provided us by the solemnities surrounding the upper room: the tragedies of misunderstanding, betrayal, arrest, denial, trial, crucifixion, and death. Our emphasis is toward a better balance in our holy meal between the necessary meanings provided us by both cross and resurrection. Bread and wine are our most universal symbols. They speak to us of Christ, our world in its elements and its manufacture, and our own personal selves. The symbols are potent of all Christian meanings. What has been forgotten, ignored, one might say even betrayed, is the eschatological meaning. Because of the nature of the message and mission of Jesus, we think this is the foundational and fundamental meaning.

Word

In denominations where eucharist is not the regular Sunday worship it is sometimes the case that the liturgy, being basically different from the usual Sunday service, is an exercise of a great deal of reading. This can be deadly and a cause of alienation from the eucharist itself. This is particularly the case in those churches which have prescribed texts for the Lord's supper and whose worship otherwise is mostly free from authorized texts. What the people usually have before them as a service on Sunday is an outline of events, but not a script. People used to worshiping as a sequence of events are usually bored and uninspired by a text which one follows, even when someone else is speaking. The great thanksgiving, for instance, ought to be a human happening, an inspiring prayer which we experience as words, a person, gestures, our neighbors, the table and its vessels, and bread and wine. What a travisty it is when this prayer becomes an exercise of "read-along" with the pastor. There is no reason for this dull foolishness. The printed text as a whole does not need to be before the congregation. They *cannot* attend to the event when it is. Of course there are churches where these texts are before everyone in books, but in these situations the liturgy is usually done every Sunday and the people do not attend to the text in the book because they more or less know it by heart. They attend to what is happening. The congregation needs only its spoken part and the invitation or brief text which precedes that part. In fact, in the eucharist they do not even need that, because the responses and acclamations, including the *sanctus,* can easily be learned and remembered, that is, in churches where the eucharist is celebrated as often as once a month or so and the peoples' spoken parts remain constant.

The role of the presider also needs careful consideration. If the people are to pray the great thanksgiving with the presider, they must be encouraged to do so by the way the presider prays. Careful reading—or well-considered free composition—with "including" and prayerful gestures, is essential. The thanksgiving fails if the minister and people are not together in the prayer. In some of the great thanksgivings of the early church, intercessions were a common part of the prayer. The inclusion of intercessions, some of which may come from the people, can give this moment more of a realistic quality of prayer in some churches.

Receiving

There are other "mechanical" matters which inhibit the effectiveness of our eucharist. The mechanics of receiving the elements of the supper are often so carefully managed that they inhibit natural participation in the event. It is hard to be spontaneous and in the Spirit while herded by ushers and overattentive to the proprieties of when to kneel and when to stand and when to leave, etc. We need to make the time of communion a time of relaxation, of free movement. One by-product of our overmanagement of communion is that it takes too long for people to commune. If we free this situation we will not only allow the spontaneity needed for communion to succeed spiritually, but we will usually cut more than in half the time that it takes. These two things can usually be accomplished easily. Eliminate management. Establish a pattern of movement to and from the table or chancel and allow people to move in that pattern freely. If some stand and wait as others kneel, or some stand behind others who are standing and receiving the elements, it doesn't matter. What matters is that we are unhampered by directions and unnecessary choreography. If we get in one another's way some, that is truly human. If we help one another, that is good. Eliminate also the practice of having communion in "tables." This takes a great deal of time and keeps people waiting on instructions. Let people come and go as they are moved to come and go. Some wish to extend the time of prayer at the table. Let them. The introduction of this freedom can greatly enhance the quality of this climactic moment of our worship.

Questions of hygiene intrude upon our sharing bread and wine. The problem, of course, is drinking from a common cup. The amount of alcohol in wine will kill some germs, not all. A common solution where people commune with both elements is what is called intinction, dipping the bread in the cup. This is hygienically acceptable to most people. It presents, at least, an aesthetic problem for many where ordinary American "air bread" is used. The bread crumbles into the cup by bits and presents, progressively, an unappealing sight to the worshipers. This can be avoided by using flat loaves of unleavened bread which will not crumble when dipped into the cup. This bread can be scored before baking so that it can be easily broken into individual pieces. A popular recipe for such bread is:

2½ cups whole wheat flour
1   cup regular white flour
2   tablespoons butter or margarine
2   teaspoons of salt

1½ teaspoons baking powder
3   tablespoons or more of honey
1½ cups of milk
2   teaspoons of sugar

Mix flour together and stir in salt, sugar, and baking powder. Mix honey and milk completely; add butter to this mixture and mix well (this works best when liquids are heated). Add liquid mixture to the flour and knead a few minutes; dough should still be sticky. Cut into four portions, roll out, and score. (Dough should have cookie-dough consistency.) Place bread on greased baking sheet, sprinkle lightly with flour and coat thinly with oil. Bake at 350° for 15-20 minutes.

This now widely-used recipe was first circulated out of St. Meinrad's archabbey and seminary in southern Indiana.

Churches which use grape juice for communion often use small individual cups which are carried on large aluminum trays. The substitution of a stack of these trays for the chalice is symbol diffusion and confusion enough, but the final difficulty is the obvious problem of the many filled glasses and the symbol this presents of our separateness and individuality. This can be partially relieved with the introduction of the kind of chalice designed for pouring. Such vessels are available from standard supply houses and work very well. The use of such a chalice eliminates the need for trays and prefilling the glasses. The glasses can be placed in small racks in the pews or on the backs of chairs and brought forward to be filled from the chalice. This keeps before us the simple signs of our union in Christ.

Offering and Transforming

Increasingly, we see the reintroduction of offering as a procession in which bread and wine are placed upon the Lord's table. Long before "offering" in the liturgy had to do with money, it concerned the bringing forward of bread and wine. It is the practice in some churches for the elements to be readied and placed on the table before the service and covered with a white cloth. How much more appropriate than this secret entrance is the return to the ancient practice of offering the bread and wine as the people's gifts. Presented in this way they appear as symbols of our life and work, given to be blessed and returned to us transformed as the gift of Christ. This transformation is not a special doctrine of some groups of Christians; it is the heart of the action of eucharist. *Metanoia*, conversion, which is symbolized for us in the ritual action of our great thanksgiving and spoken in the intention of its texts, is a sign before us of all that is meant by our affirmation of

Jesus Christ as a new creation in the world. This newness God introduces is nothing which happens hiddenly and abstractly "up there" on the table for the benefit of our souls somewhere, sometime; it is newness God introduces into our lives in this world. We are people changing, in that we are Christ's people, "from glory to glory" (2 Cor. 3:18) and into "his likeness." And we are a people speaking our own transforming word of blessing in the world, seeing what anyone sees, but regarding "no one from a human point of view," (2 Cor. 5:16) generating in our prayer and our life the kingdom values of Christ's new creation.

Behind such an understanding, which we think is common to all Christians, lie centuries of discussion and debate about transformation and the whole matter of the presence of Christ in the eucharist. We have already addressed this subject in several contexts, and will not develop it here, except to point out that anyone approaching this subject today from the standpoint of past stereotypical attitudes about what constitutes a Catholic or a Protestant point of view is going to have little understanding of what is being talked about.[27]

We have made reference and provided resources in footnotes concerning liturgical texts for the eucharist. There is also help available for the thoughtful minister seeking ideas about the doing of eucharist.[28]

Frequency

The question of the frequency of the eucharist has long been a question among Protestants, and is often the focus of debate. Some of us would like to see the eucharist celebrated weekly as our main and normal worship. This desire runs against the grain of the primacy of preaching in Protestantism. These need not be in conflict but they often are. First, because methods of receiving communion often and unnecessarily, as we have pointed out, take too much time, and second, because of philosophical differences which concern matters of communication and participation. This latter issue gets down to a question of what is eloquent and how do people become involved? It is accurate to say that, while things are changing, much of Protestantism still basically trusts explaining and exhorting and mistrusts the action parable which is sacrament. Sacrament is probably too much beyond the need of most ministers to control. Some of us see this as a great value of sacrament. Probably many ministers oppose more frequent eucharists because their experience of the service has not been vital, in contrast to other moving and personally involving worship. When the sacrament is primarily a text, with concluding somber and lengthy ritual participation or the quicker but often deadly, uninvolving seated reception, it is tolerable only as a mercifully occasional response to a command of Christ. This is, of course, a gross distortion of eucharist, which we ought never to approach as a text but as action. The supper needs to be conceived as something we are *doing* together. It must be planned, that is, thoroughly thought out, and then done as a sequence of involving events climaxing in the peoples' commitment (and participation needs underlining as commitment) in sharing together in the gifts of the meal. If the parable does not work as an involving action which compels our spiritual and physical response in commitment we probably ought not to blame the sacrament. We need to enlarge our vision. Some good resources to begin with are Patrick W. Collins' study of liturgy and imagination, *More Than Meets the Eye* (Paulist Press, 1983); *Sacraments As God's Self-Giving*, by James F. White, is a fine basic introduction to sacraments, with many practical considerations (Abingdon Press, 1983), and Tad Guzie's *The Book of Sacramental Basics* (Paulist Press, 1981). And for the passionate prophet who may demean sacraments as "priestcraft" more or less irrelevant to real life in the real world, we would recommend reading *Real Presence*, by Regis Duffy (Harper & Row, 1982).

Notes

1. Hans Lietzmann, *Messe und Herrenmahl* (Berlin: Walter de Gruyter, 1926). The publication of successive fascicules of an English translation began in 1953 and was completed "with introduction and further inquiry" in 1979. *Mass and Lord's Supper* (Leiden: E. J. Brill, 1979).

2. Oscar Cullmann, "La signification de la Sainte-Ane dans le Christianisme primitif," in *Revue de Histoire et de Philosophie religieuses*, Strasbourg, 1936. This was translated into English as "The Meaning of the Lord's Supper in Primitive Christianity," and published with F. J. Leenhardt's "This Is My Body" under the title, *Essays on the Lord's Supper* (London: Lutterworth Press, 1958).

3. Cullmann, in *Essays on the Lord's Supper*, p. 23.

4. Geoffrey Wainwright, *Eucharist and Eschatology* (London: Epworth Press, 1971).

5. Ibid., p. 131.

6. Ibid., p. 131f.

7. Ibid., p. 134.

8. Ibid.

9. Ibid., p. 141.

10. Jürgen Moltmann, *The Church in the Power of the Spirit* (New York: Harper & Row, 1975, 1977).

11. Ibid., p. 50ff.

12. Ibid., p. 57.

13. Ibid., p. 59.

14. Ibid.

15. Ibid.

16. Ibid., p. 62.

17. Ibid., p. 205.

18. Ibid., p. 245.

19. Ibid., p. 246.

20. John H. Westerhoff III and William H. Willimon, *Liturgy and Learning Through the Life Cycle* (New York: Seabury Press, 1980).

21. Edward Matthews, *Celebrating Mass with Children* (Ramsey, N. J.: Paulist Press, 1975), p. 25.

22. See John Behnke, *A Children's Lectionary,* Cycle A (New York: Paulist Press, 1974); Bernadette Kenny, ed., *Children's Liturgies:* Seventy-four Eucharistic Liturgies, Prayer Services, and Penance Services: Designed for Primary, Middle and Junior High Children (New York: Paulist Press, 1977); Jan Ihli, *Liturgy of the Word of Children* (New York: Paulist Press, 1979) (Cycle A & B).

23. Margaret M. Sawin, ed., *Hope For Families* (New York: Sadlier, 1982), p. 112.

24. Lucien Deiss, *Springtime of the Liturgy* (Collegeville, Minn.: The Liturgical Press, 1967), p. 123f.

25. Dennis C. Smolarshi, *Eucharistia: A Study of the Eucharistic Prayer* (New York: Paulist Press, 1982); John Barry Ryan, *The Eucharistic Prayer* (New York: Paulist Press, 1974); *Word and Table* (Nashville: Abingdon Press, 1976), pp. 44-46; Thomas Talley, "From Berakah to Eucharist: A Reopening Question," *Worship* 50 (1976), p. 115; Thomas Talley, "The Eucharistic Prayer: Directions for Development," *Worship* 51 (1977), p. 316.

26. Deiss, *Springtime of the Liturgy;* R. C. D. Jasper and G. J. Cuming, *Prayers of the Eucharist, Early and Reformed* (New York: Oxford University Press, 1980); John C. Kirby, ed., *Word and Action* (New York: Seabury Press, 1969); Robert F. Hoey, *The Experimental Liturgy Book* (New York: Herder and Herder, 1969); *At the Lord's Table* (Nashville: Abingdon, 1981); John Mossi, *Bread Blessed and Broken* (New York: Paulist Press, 1974). These are but a few of the historical and contemporary collections. One should compare also the official and in some cases "alternative" prayers of the several denominations as these are found in their hymnals and worship books.

27. For an introduction to the discussion, cf. Leenhardt, "This Is My Body," in *Essays on the Lord's Supper* (Richmond: John Knox Press, 1958), p. 24ff; Geoffrey Wainwright, *Eucharist and Eschatology* (New York: Oxford University Press, 1971), pp. 104-122; Peter Fink, "Perceiving the Presence of Christ," *Worship* 58 (1984), pp. 17-28; Regis Duffy, *Real Presence* (New York: Harper & Row, 1982), pp. 83-105; Joseph Powers, *Eucharistic Theology* (New York: Seabury Press, 1967), pp. 111-186; Tad Guzie, *Jesus and the Eucharist* (New York: Paulist Press, 1974), pp. 60-74.

28. Philip H. Pfatteicher, and Carlos R. Messerli, *Manual on the Liturgy: Lutheran Book of Worship* (Minneapolis: Augsburg, 1979), pp. 199ff; *From Ashes to Fire* (Nashville: Abingdon Press, 1979), see commentaries throughout; Marion Hatchett, *Commentary on the American Prayer Book* (New York: Seabury Press, 1980), pp. 289-423; Robert W. Jenson, *Visible Words* (Philadelphia: Fortress, 1978), pp. 115-123; Robert W. Hovda, *Strong, Loving, and Wise* (Washington, D.C.: The Liturgical Conference, 1976); Achille Triacca, ed., *Roles in the Liturgical Assembly* (New York: Pueblo Publishing Co., 1981).

Chapter 10

Confirmation: A Repeatable Sacrament

As has been indicated in our discussion of infant baptism, confirmation was originally a part of the baptismal act along with communion. The first centuries of the church found pastors baptizing children in remote areas, away from cities where bishops resided. Because of the substantialistic interpretation which soon developed concerning the power of the bishop to confirm (either through the laying on of hands or through chrism or both) several practical agreements were reached. Persons who had been baptized as infants by presbyters were confirmed later in life when they were in the presence either of a bishop or a chorepiscopus (a county bishop—one who had been empowered by the bishop to anoint persons in his absence), or in some cases by presbyters so empowered. Here we see the beginning of the separation of baptism and confirmation. Finally, in the Middle Ages confirmation emerged as a sacrament in its own right, detached essentially from baptism.

During the Reformation period confirmation started taking on the qualities which we now largely associate with it. The sixteenth-century reformers required that children be baptized as infants, be given catechetical instruction, and then be led to make a public confession before the congregation, after which they could be admitted to communion. As J. D. C. Fisher's excellent study[1] reveals, the reformers thought that they were returning to the authentic early church understanding of confirmation. Of course, they were mistaken. The reformers did add a dimension to the understanding of confirmation which later influenced Roman Catholic practice to some degree: the emphasis on the individual's honest decision to affirm a faith into which he or she had been baptized as an infant. Of course, a major fruit of the Protestant Reformation was the emphasis upon adult conversion and

191

baptism by immersion. This emphasis in several denominations has resulted in persons in late childhood or early adolescence deciding, often in a special series of evangelistic services, to surrender to God in faith and to be baptized. Sometimes this has been accompanied by special classes but often it has not. Sometimes communion has been received before baptism and sometimes it has been received only after baptism. Often infant dedication becomes a substitute for infant baptism. Church school experiences are often seen as the central context for preparing children to live the Christian life, but such nurture is perceived to be not enough and must be followed by a decision or an emotional experience of surrender or commitment. In both cases, the autonomous decision of the person is valued highly—whether in confirmation or in "adult" baptism. This element of honest personal decision and affirmation needs to be preserved but related to the original meaning of confirmation and also integrated with baptism and communion.

We have already developed the rationale for the integration of baptism, confirmation, and communion in chapter 8 in our discussion of infant baptism. The issue of the unity of initiation is further explicated in chapter 13 on adult baptism. While confirmation is a part of the initiation whether in infancy or adulthood, it is a *repeatable* sacrament just as is communion. Baptism is a one-time sacrament. Still, the need to renew one's commitments in relation to changes in self-understanding is sufficiently great that baptismal renewal or confirmation should be correlated with periods of struggle and redefinition throughout the life span. It is now quite clear that it is normal, not abnormal, for persons to change their ways of integrating the Christian life and world view into their actual self-understanding and faith stance. Therefore, confirmation education and sacramental celebrations can and should be repeated whenever the person has reached a new and clear level of commitment. This means that confirmation can take place in infancy, preserving its original meaning, in adolescence, and later in young adulthood or at various times in adulthood, thus preserving the Reformation emphasis upon honest wrestling with the meaning of the gospel and personal, public affirmation and confirmation by the faith community. However, the dimension most centrally associated with confirmation, the presence of the Holy Spirit to strengthen persons, must be reclaimed along with the autonomous decision to affirm the faith.

Max Thurian has done significant theological work on the reasons why confirmation can be repeated, even as communion is a regularly repeated sacrament. He believes that the church should encourage persons to be on such honest pilgrimages and that confirmation for adults especially should be related to decisions to be in ministry in certain specific ways—as consecrated lay ministers as well as ordained clergy. Adult education concerning possible ministries could precede or follow periods of reflection, decision, and rededication to particular ministries within the church and in the world of work, leisure, politics, and service.[2] If this perspective on confirmation is valid, as we believe it is, it is then possible to relate the sacrament of confirmation much more specifically to the stages of human and faith development, about which we are learning more and concerning which we need to find helpful educational and liturgical patterns.

In terms of human and faith development confirmation education and liturgical experiences are needed in early and late adolescence as well as at other times. Both Erikson and Fowler see the importance of educational and ritualistic experiences which help particular youth find a great fidelity, someone or something in which the youth can focus his or her faith and thereby find a center for the self. If the individual, as a child, has been engrafted into the body of Christ through baptism, confirmation, and communion, and has participated fully in the ministering community with increasing awareness of his or her unique place in the ministry, he or she will view confirmation, not so much as a "rite of passage," but as a "rite of intensification," as Urban Holmes reminds us.

Holmes questions whether or not confirmation as practiced in early adolescence is really a rite of passage. His fine study of the findings of social anthropologists such as Van Gennap concludes that a "rite of passage" should help the person define himself or herself in a new state of being in relation to the expectations of society—not just on a personal level. Since baptism is the primary sacrament of initiation, of engrafting the person fully into the body of Christ, confirmation does not define the person in any new way in relation to the expectations of the society. Rather, Holmes reasons that "the most consistent interpretation of whatever has gone under the name of confirmation is that it *strengthens* the recipient with the Holy Spirit that he (she) may grow in Christian faith and witness. Notions of status-change effected by the rite . . . have been most obscure."[3]

We agree. It is confusing rather than clarifying for a baptized, highly active and involved youth to prepare during confirmation education, to "join the church." Such a view denies the full membership which the youth has experienced for years and also fails to bring a genuine status change in respect to the way the community expects the person to function. Attempts to dramatize the new status of the youth after confirmation have been perceived to be perfunctory and largely "window dressing" by the youth themselves—such things as a youth representative on committees or being able to vote. The reality in most congregations is: Either children and youth have been accepted and treated as full members of the family for many years or they have not. The ritual of confirmation does not really change the quality or nature of that environment to any great extent.

We have been making a case for confirmation being a repeatable sacrament. If it is seen as a "rite of intensification" rather than a "rite of passage," if it is seen as a rite of maturity in Christ, it makes a lot of sense for it to be repeated when persons have matured to a new level of self-understanding and understanding and commitment to the Christian faith and life.

Theologically, it is clear that the sacrament was related to the laying on of hands which symbolized the empowerment of the person through the Holy Spirit. This empowerment took place in biblical accounts sometimes before, during, or after baptism. At the personal religious level there are countless reports of baptized persons having various subsequent experiences of insight, growth, surrender, conversion, or spiritual illumination which the person wanted to and needed to celebrate before the faith community. Therefore, pastorally at least, confirming kinds of responses have taken place on the part of clergy and laity. No status change was intended, but a new sense of the empowering of the Holy Spirit and a new vision of the self in relation to the ministry and mission of Christ in the world came about. Urban Holmes describes his response to a beautiful college student whose experience in an automobile accident left her disfigured but with a deepened faith. She asked Holmes to rebaptize her and he said no. "She then asked to be reconfirmed, which request seemed to me to make sense, but again I had to say no. Why?"[4]

Holmes is correct in wondering why we call the first or second of these maturing experiences, confirmation, and then have no clear way to respond to subsequent needs of persons to deepen or restate their faith in relation to the normal or abnormal periods of development in their lives.

Developmentally, it is clear that repeated experiences of education, decision making, and celebration are needed as persons continue their personal faith journeys. The church has sought to be responsive to this pervasive need by designing a myriad of pastoral and liturgical approaches. More often, the individuals on their own faith pilgrimages have demanded some response, including multiple baptisms or the more recent so-called "baptism of the Holy Spirit" common among charismatic groups. And, of course, to some extent, the emergence of the seven sacraments was in response to such genuine need for rituals which strengthened the sense of personal and corporate meaning and empowerment. The United Methodist alternate liturgy of initiation includes the possibility of baptismal renewal which can take place any time persons wish to celebrate a fresh vision, sense of commitment, or experience of rebirth. The response to this new service has been very positive.

Confirmation Related with Integrity to Human and Faith Development

In respect to studies of human or faith development it is very clear that the concept of confirmation as a repeatable sacrament is needed.

When we look more precisely at the adolescent and young adult years we find at least two and probably three periods of growth which require different educational and liturgical experiences. Erik Erikson found two clear stages of growth during these years. The first he called the period of identity vs. role diffusion during which time the youth is seeking to find his or her identity in relation to all of the conflicting values and norms flowing into his or her experience from the wider society. This is a period of search for a fidelity in the midst of diversity. Erikson believes that informal rituals, such as learning to drive and celebrating the occasion of passing the driver's test and getting one's license, and formal rituals, such as confirmation, have very great significance in helping a youth find a center of meaning, this vision of her or his place in society. The second step, according to Erikson, is for the young person to find a sense of intimacy with the opposite sex (or deal with one's identity sexually) and also to come to terms with what ideology, what philosophy of life or world view the person will embrace.[5] Erikson saw this second phase possibly lasting until twenty-eight to thirty years of age during which time society should declare a psychosocial moratorium in order for the young person to be able to experiment, to test and to refine his or her beliefs, and to seek to harmonize beliefs and actions with some consistent set of values by which he or she can live in community with others. It is not too difficult to see that particular educational experiences and unique informal and formal rituals are needed at both of these stages. Confirmation usually takes place in most churches at the beginning of these two stages (at thirteen or fourteen years) rather than at the end of the adolescent stage (eighteen or nineteen) or at the end of the young adult quest for a meaningful and workable philosophy of life which will hold up against the tests and threats which come from alternative philosophies of life or optional ways to deal with the profound need to give and receive love (Intimacy vs. Isolation Stage). Some theologians and religious educators have sought to postpone confirmation to one of these later times. These efforts have largely failed. Too much emphasis has been on confirmation as a time to "join the church." Programatically, if pastors and lay leaders waited beyond middle adolescence the youth had vanished from the congregation— making the question of confirmation as a time "to decide to join the church" largely academic!

James Fowler's research on the stages of faith development, as we have seen, calls for two stages during the adolescent and young adult periods. Both of these are crucial for finding a genuinely internalized Christian content for one's faith and a Christian world view which has again been tested, critiqued with some personal integrity and worked through with meaning. The first period Fowler calls Stage III faith (Synthetic-Conventional). It is appropriate for adolescents (twelve to nineteen years of age) but is the stage of faith many adults remain in all of their lives. The second period Fowler calls Individuative-Reflexive or Stage IV faith. This is appropriate for young adults but again is as far as many adults go on the pilgrimage of faith even though two more stages of growth remain.

Fowler's findings reveal rather clearly that confirmation which takes place in early adolescence is usually not what we think it is for the persons involved. Instead of coming to a clear decision to affirm the Christian faith after serious reflection, critique, and internalization, young adolescents do this to a very limited degree and come out with an important but conventional affirmation. Adolescents, especially person of thirteen to fifteen, ask critical questions but mostly at the personal or identity level. The "who am I?" questions are raised rather than, "Is the Christian faith as a system of belief and action really worthy of my total allegiance?" Fowler found no young or middle adolescents really critiquing the Christian faith as a system. He also found that adolescents still locate authority outside of the self and seldom genuinely get outside of themselves in an in-depth concern for justice or peace on a world scale. The result of their exploration in confirmation education is to bring together the ideas and feelings into which they have been introduced in a way which is very important, even emotion-packed, but limited appropriately to where they are in the pilgrimage of faith. Especially, Fowler finds adolescents not actually getting behind the symbols and myths of the faith, as Ronald Goldman thinks they can. Fowler found only a few late adolescents who were beginning to demythologize successfully, discovering the inner and deeper meaning coming through such stories. Most people are in their twenties or older before they critique the Christian faith as *a* system compared to other systems of belief.

In this sense Fowler seems to agree with Erikson that genuine decision making about a philosophy of life or an ideology which guides action tends to be the work of young adults. These findings reinforce the view held by several religious educators that the great time for confirmation is in adulthood, during which time a person genuinely searches and finally *owns* his or her faith. Certainly, some form of celebration of this Individuative-Reflective faith needs to take place. At the present time we have very limited educational approaches to these life issues for young adults, and we have almost no liturgical responses to these momentous decisions. Young adults can and do wish to get behind the symbols of the faith, to find a world view which provides a vision and purpose for decisions about vocation, sexual practice, marriage and family, and personal and social ethics. Therefore, confirmation as a repeatable sacrament may have very great potential for this period of life. Of course, Fowler's six stage theory implies that other reaffirmations need to follow. Stage V, Conjunctive Faith, and Stage VI, Universalizing Faith, need educational and liturgical experiences which nurture growth and celebrate new visions or dimensions of faithful living.

Urban Holmes reports the practice of Episcopal Bishop William Frey of Colorado who, "after confirmation," started inviting all persons who wished to reaffirm their commitments to come forward and receive the laying on of hands. Frey was amazed to see as many as three hundred persons come forward in a particular parish. Holmes rejoiced in the practice but urged advance notification, preparation in the form of "instruction and/or service." He wisely asserts that if we can get past the substantialistic idea of confirmation or reaffirmation there could be great value in such a practice. Moreover, he observes, "It would also reinforce the relationship between the process of theological education and the liturgical life of the parish."[6]

Education for Confirmation As a Repeatable Sacrament

While few theorists see confirmation as a repeatable sacrament, several see the importance of stages of growth along with educational and liturgical phases appropriate to the periods of self development. John Westerhoff III of Duke University has developed a six stage theory of religious development. These are the foundational (ages 0-3), the imitative (ages 3-6), the affiliative (ages 6-12), the individuating (ages 12-18), the consolidative (ages 18-25), and the universalizing (ages 25 up). It is his view that educational experiences and rites of passage are needed in relation to each of these stages: prior to the foundational, a parenting rite; prior to the imitative, infant baptism; prior to the affiliative, First Communion; before the individuating, a new rite called convenanting which affirms youth in their honest search to find an authentic Christian faith within the church family; prior to the consolidative, confirmation; before the universalizing stage, some form of reaffirmation.[7] As can be discovered rather quickly, Westerhoff has a developmental concept somewhat similar to Fowler's but quite different in several respects. Fowler sees the Individuative-Reflective period to be a late adolescent and young adult stage. He also finds little evidence to support consolidative and universalizing stages to be as early as Westerhoff maintains. However the concept of educational and liturgical experiences along the path of faith development is deemed to be important by both.

If we see confirmation as a repeatable sacrament, as communion is, then the strengthening and redefining of the content and quality of the Christian faith can take place at each of several periods of religious development.

The research of Ronald Goldman suggests that we should have quite high expectations for the quality of religious education of adolescents. He believes thirteen-year-olds and above can tackle some central problems in Christian understanding. These include the problem of literalism and authoritarianism, the problem of "Two Worlds" (breaking the perceived wall between the world of scientific thinking and the world of theological thinking), the problem of moving from an early Old Testament view of God as a war god, to a more universalistic God of Isaiah, Jeremiah, and, of course, Jesus, and the problem of biblical relevance (youth relegating the scriptures to a holy place, a holy people, or a holy period in history rather than to today).[8] While Fowler doubts that such study by adolescents will bring about the results Goldman desires, he would agree that sensitive stimulation of the thinking of youth with problems associated with the next stage of development (beyond where persons actually are) is helpful in bringing about such growth in faith.

With this growth in faith in direct relation to where youth are in their self-understanding one of the authors, Robert Browning, and his colleagues at North Broadway United Methodist Church in Columbus, Ohio, developed during the 1950s a three-stage program of confirmation education. Lance Webb, pastor, William Butterfield, minister with youth, and Dorothy Jones, director of children's ministry, joined Browning in designing a program which sought to recognize the need for persons in late childhood and early adolescence to start the quest to become "first-hand disciples" (the Disciples Program—for 6th and 7th graders), and for a more serious study of the types of problems Goldman identified, coupled with a program of action in respect to issues in the world which were in need of Christian reflection and service (The Crusaders Program—for 9th and 10th graders), and finally an attempt to help youth work through their own statements of faith and relate them to matters of ethical responsibility, to sexuality, to vocation and possible occupations, to college or continuing education, etc. (The Pilgrim Program—for seniors in high school). Each of these phases was integrated with the total life of the church in study, worship, and action and was related to the family in that parent education took place at each of the three levels in harmony with the content of the expanded confirmation program. Such a three-stage confirmation program was evaluated by parishes and youth to be significant for their growth in faith.[9]

A similar program is still functioning well at the First United Methodist Church, Winston-Salem, North Carolina.

While the program at North Broadway officially recognized confirmation as having taken place on the first level, there was great desire to extend confirmation to the senior year or to recognize the public celebrations at each of the three levels as confirmation—the beginning of a desire for confirmation to be seen as a repeatable sacrament.

Resources for confirmation education were designed and written for the North Broadway program by the professional staff. However, many confirmation resources, published by various denominations have genuine potential for being employed within our wide design. The major problem with such resources is not the biblical, theological, or educational relevance of the units; it is the basic understanding of confirmation itself that is problematic. Set in a wider interpretive frame, resources from several denominations could be used, especially for the work done with early to middle adolescents. For instance, the United Methodist Church has developed official confirmation resources for early adolescents, *Journey Into Faith* (Graded Press, 1983) and for late adolescents and adults, *The Way: Confirmation for Discipleship in the United Methodist Church* (Graded Press, 1981). A unique resource by Jo Morgan is *Church Membership for Persons Who Are Mentally Retarded* (Graded Press, 1981). Many Protestant denominations have similar listings of resources which have potential for use in this wider way. Catholic resources include *Spirit* (Benziger, 1980), *We Share the Spirit of Life* (Sadlier, 1983), and *We Celebrate Confirmation* (Silver Burdett, 1983)—aimed more at early adolescents. Programs for late adolescents include *Emmaus Road* (Our Sunday Visitor, 1982), using a shared praxis approach, *Water and Spirit* (Benziger, 1984), a two-year program similar to the Rite of Christian Initiation of Adults. These and other resources should be studied with a view to enriching the confirmation approach suggested in our model.

There is no reason, theologically or developmentally, why fresh educational and liturgical designs may not be projected and refined in relation to the best understandings coming from the continuing research on the stages of religious or faith development. In addition to confirmation for youth we shall be attentive to possibilities of adult faith development in relation to other classic sacraments or other "new" sacraments. For instance, James White is calling for a new sacrament related to the individual's sense of vocation. We agree about this possible focus but think the concern is related naturally to the sacrament of ordination and a widening of this sacrament to apply to the universal priesthood of all believers. More about this view later.

Liturgy: Confirmation As Baptismal Renewal

We have observed that the initiating signs of baptism and the sealing of the Holy Spirit are being rejoined in today's liturgical reform. This, of course, changes radically the situation of the rite we have called confirmation. In fact, the title may gradually fade. One notices in the new Lutheran liturgy, for instance, that it is called "affirmation of baptism." We can also expect that the renewal of the baptismal covenant will remain in our worship in the customary situations where we have usually "confirmed." Cynics will respond that we will continue as before under a new label. Some may, but the reform presents us with at least two clear differences: The affirmation of baptism is just that; it is not a "booster shot" which completes a somehow defective baptism. Second, the affirmation of baptism (or baptismal renewal) is not a one-time rite of church membership, taking place only at a certain "expected" time of life, it is a rite of intensification which we may join in with others during adolescence but which occurs in various ways and at different times, whenever it seems appropriate. These changes are substantial.

Continuities

There will certainly be continuity in most churches involving groups of young people making public commitment, although the new understandings will perhaps undercut some of the regularity of this procedure and encourage individual attention to the "right" time for baptismal renewal. A good case can be made for both the group and individual emphases. It is good for us to respond in faith in common; it reinforces the family aspect of our life as church. On the other hand, many people have been rushed, indeed pressured to Christian commitment before they were ready. Desire to "stay with the group" can be pressure. We must be careful at this point, and discerning.

Public renewal of baptismal covenant will also continue to be significant as people transfer membership within denominations (requirements differ here), from one denomination to another, or are restored into communion in a church after their membership has lapsed.

Reaffirmation of Vows

In most of the new liturgies, the reaffirmation of vows is at least an option in the forms of baptismal renewal. This involves the reciting of the Apostles' Creed in response to questions about belief in Father, Son, and Spirit, and certain other "reminders." The strongest of these, we believe, are the questions in the new *Book of Common Prayer* which are those put to the whole congregation in the *BCP* baptismal service (these were quoted in our discussion of baptism), and which are repeated to the ones who renew their covenant in the confirmation service. In the new Lutheran liturgy of affirmation of baptism, following the creed and prayers, there is this address to those making covenant renewal:

> You have made public profession of your faith. Do you intend to continue in the covenant God made with you in Holy Baptism:
> to live among God's faithful people,
> to hear his Word and share in his supper,
> to proclaim the good news of God in Christ
>   through word and deed,
> to serve all people, following the example
>   of our Lord Jesus,
> and to strive for justice and peace in all
>   the earth?

And the answer required is, "I do, and I ask God to help and guide me."[10]

Renewals whose texts of commitment set forth at least this much specificity in clear images seem to us to be preferred to the more general and ambiguous questions put in some liturgies.

First Communion?

Sometimes "first communion" is a consequent of confirmation. This will depend upon whether baptism or confirmation is understood as constitutive of church membership and whether participation in the eucharist is an exclusive right of church members. Our judgment is that baptism ought to be the mark of membership (we believe this on scriptural and traditional grounds). This means that acceptance at the table is an automatic right of the baptized, to be exercized whenever they wish. Of course, we go beyond that to believe that no one should be turned away from the Lord's table at any time for any reason, for it is the table of his grace, and an eschatological sign, the foretaste of the kingdom. It goes beyond us to include us.

Other relevant matters concerning baptismal renewal have already been considered in the section on liturgy in chapter 7.

Notes

1. J. D. C. Fisher, *Confirmation, Then and Now* (London: Alcuin Club, SPCK, 1978), p. 138.

2. See Max Thurian, *Consecration of the Layman* (Baltimore: Helicon, 1963), p. 84ff.

3. Urban T. Holmes III, *Confirmation: The Celebration of Maturity in Christ* (New York: Seabury Press, 1975), p. 50.

4. Ibid., p. 85.

5. Erik Erikson, *Identity: Youth and Crises* (New York: W. W. Norton, 1968).

6. Holmes, *Confirmation: The Celebration of Maturity in Christ,* pp. 94-95.

7. See John H. Westerhoff III, *Will Our Children Have Faith* (New York: Seabury Press, 1975), *The Sacraments and the Cycle of Life* (New York: Seabury Press, 1981).

8. Ronald Goldman, *Religious Thinking from Childhood to Adolescence* (New York: Seabury Press, 1964), pp. 241-246.

9. See Robert L. Browning, *Communicating with Junior Highs* (Nashville: Graded Press, 1968), pp. 192-206.

10. *Lutheran Book of Worship* (Minister's Desk Edition), p. 326.

Chapter 11

Marriage: The Sacrament of Love

Protestants are more open than ever before to the idea that marriage could be a sacrament; Catholics are radically changing their interpretation of the sacramental nature of marriage; and the Orthodox are relating their sacramental understanding much more to the human and faith issues married couples face in our contemporary world.

To Protestants, the marriage service has been privatized too often in the past, sometimes sentimentalized and cheapened by being made available to persons who have had little or no knowledge or commitment to the Christian faith, especially little sense of giving themselves to purposes for life in God's community of love and justice beyond the marriage. While Protestants have done more with premarital counseling and sometimes education and have been in touch with contemporary life issues of persons prior to and during marriage, there have not been many serious efforts to deepen the meaning of marriage or to explore seriously marriage as a sacrament. More recently, with the very high divorce rate and the open and highly visible experimentation with optional styles of life including living together, not marrying and not planning to marry, homosexuals wishing to marry, and individual males or females desiring to have families with the aid of the fruits of science and technology, Protestants are calling for, at least, a sacramental dimension in marriage. Often this desire is couched in a vague hope that some more profound understanding will give couples a deeper sense of commitment which will somehow help them remain stable and faithful in the midst of the countless threats to marriage which are a by-product of our high mobility, changes in the expectation of individual fulfillment on the part of both husbands and wives and the ravages of economic and ecological disorder. Some Protestant

203

thinkers are genuinely open to an ecumenical quest for a sacramental approach to marriage.

Changes in Roman Catholic understanding of the sacramental nature of marriage have greatly enhanced the possibility of an ecumenical consensus. For instance, earlier Catholic documents on marriage emphasized that the primary purpose of marriage was for the couple to become one flesh (Mt. 19:5, 6) in order to have children and to be faithful to each other as Christ is faithful to the church. Recent Catholic interpretations have looked much deeper. Marriage which is only valid if conducted in the Catholic church for baptized Christians who have objectively received the Holy Spirit and who have institutional blessing is not what Catholics since Vatican II are increasingly saying.

Walter Kasper, a German Catholic theologian, sees the objective and institutional understanding of the sacrament of marriage changing toward an interpersonal emphasis which highlights the mutual love and faithfulness of the couple. Catholics are discerning that the love and faith present in all authentic marriages have an essential religious dimension. Kasper says that in the bond of marriage

> a person commits himself or herself to an existence, the end of which cannot be foreseen, and which is something that is unconditional and cannot be called into question. One touches the ultimate mystery of his or her existence: this mystery concerns one deeply and yet remains hidden. People commit themselves, in other words, to something that they do not possess and that they will never fully possess. . . . Marital faithfulness, then, is both a symbol that points to a reality beyond itself and a participation in the faithfulness of God. In this definitive and unconditional way, two people can accept each other only because they have already been definitively and unconditionally accepted. *Faithfulness in marriage is therefore a place where transcendence can possibly be experienced.*"[1]

The sacramental nature of marriage is not grounded only in the power of the priest or the liturgy or the canons of the church, even though these are important elements in communication of the reality of God's love and kingdom to the persons. Rather, it is grounded in the reality of the mystery of God's love and the profound life-giving force of faithfulness which are potentially present in marriage.

It is the mystery of the good news of God's love which is freely given to all as an invitation to live now and forever in the community which we have called the kingdom of God. Kasper reveals just how revolutionary the change in Catholic thought is when he says that marriage is not an estate which is blessed only because the grace of God has been given to the couple by the church. Rather, he believes that marriage can be a means by which God's eternal love and faithfulness (revealed fully in Christ) are made historically present.

> The love and faithfulness existing between Christ and his church is therefore not simply an image or example of marriage, nor is the self-giving of man and wife in marriage an image and likeness of Christ's giving of himself to the church. The love that exists between man and wife is rather a sign that makes the reality present, in other words, an epiphany of the love and faithfulness of God that was given once and for all time in Jesus Christ and is made present in the Church.[2]

Kasper sees mystery as the central reality which points to and participates in God's eternal plan of salvation and wholeness for all humanity. While Christ is the sacrament of God and the church is the sacrament of Christ, all of life is profoundly filled with God's presence. The sacrament of marriage makes visible and celebrates that which *is* in the nature of things. Therefore "it is not the priest who bestows the sacrament of marriage, but rather the bride and bridegroom who give the sacrament to each other. Sacramental marriage, then, is founded on the personal act 'whereby the spouses mutually bestow and accept each other'—and their mutual consent constitutes the marriage."[3] The unity which is made possible because of the love between God and human beings, then, is present as a symbol in marriage.

The Vatican II Pastoral Constitution on the Church in the Modern World said that marital love is included in divine love and is guided and strengthened by Christ's redeeming power and the saving work of the church.

The sacrament of marriage celebrates the love and faithfulness to be revealed and made flesh in marriage. It does not supply the couple with love and faith not otherwise available to them. They were created out of love and faith by God. The liturgy nevertheless greatly points to and participates in that love and faithfulness and is therefore very important not only for the couple but for the surrounding community of persons. As Edward Schillebeeckx says in his monumental study of marriage, every marriage is connected with the promise of God to create the kingdom of God in our midst. In this sense every marriage contains a reference to Christ because Christ gave us a foretaste of the kingdom. "Every marriage, even civil marriage, is Christian—whether in the full sense, in the pre-Christian sense (marriage as having an orientation towards Christ), in the anonymously

Christian sense, or even in the negatively Christian sense (a deliberate denial of this Christian aspect of marriage)."[4] He concludes his biblical study by stating what is a major thesis of our work, namely, that the "primacy of the Kingdom of God, not only in regard to marriage, but actually in marriage, is a biblical fact which no dogmatic consideration of marriage can afford to ignore."[5]

Schillebeeckx performs a unique service as he distills the major forms that marriage has taken within the Western church especially. He reveals clearly that marriage was not seen as a sacrament until the eleventh or twelfth century. Starting with the Greek and Roman forms of marriage into which Christianity moved, Schillebeeckx traces the forms of marriage down through the centuries. He notes that marriage among the Greeks and Romans was not based on procreation or on the relational but rather on the 'religion of the hearth' and the gods of the household—the *manes, lares,* and *penates.* It was important to have a male heir because the household liturgy (with its own rites, prayers, hymns, and offerings) was conducted by the father and then the son. Barrenness, therefore, was a reason for dissolving a marriage.[6] Contrary to the perceptions of many Christians, marriage was introduced to people who already had a religious foundation for their marriages.

Building on the Hebrew view of marriage as a family affair, experienced in faith in Yahweh, early Christians, following Paul, saw marriage as a "worldly" event for baptized Christians. It was to be celebrated "in the Lord" and was seen as an image of the mystery of the unity of Christ and the church. For Tertullian and Clement of Alexandria, marriage was ecclesial any time it was contracted, following civil and family customs, between baptized Christians. Interestingly, a marriage of baptized Christians, following civil practices, was a "church marriage." Between the fourth and eleventh centuries in the West a marriage liturgy existed alongside the civil and family contract. Slowly these ceremonies were held in the church with the result that these ceremonies were given liturgical unity. By the eleventh century the civil ceremony had been taken over completely by the church and the idea of marriage as a sacrament arose, especially in relation to the priest's blessing of the marriage and not in relation to the partners' mutual consent. But if no marriage liturgy was involved a civil marriage between baptized Christians was still seen as a Christian marriage. After the Council of Trent the sacramental aspect was emphasized in substantialistic terms so that the validity of the marriage was completely related to the presence of a priest and the performance of the ecclesial liturgy. With rare exception a marriage in which the baptized partners mutually consented but without the presence of the priest was not only not a church wedding but not a marriage at all. The final result of these movements was that it is impossible in the Western church for baptized Christians to contract a valid marriage without it being performed by the priest with sacramental meaning. As Schillebeeckx underscores in his study, this trend has "led in our own time to many serious problems, in connection both with the cause of ecumenism and with the Christian's loyalty as a citizen to the state."[7] As we have already identified, a much more relational view of marriage as a sacrament has been the result of theological and pastoral reflection since Vatican II.

The Eastern church has for a much longer period of time made the liturgical celebration of marriage the heart of its sacramental understanding. Between the eighth and eleventh centuries the state itself made the church ceremony mandatory for validity. Today, the Orthodox church has the potential for greatly enriching the sacramental understanding of marriage and for heightening the sense of symbolism and drama in Christian marriages, ecumenically.

Orthodox thinker Alexander Schmemann has corroborated our emphasis on the need to overcome the sacred-secular split so common in our understanding of sacraments. He sees matrimony as sacramental, not because it gives a rel2gous sanction to marriage and family life or reinforces with "supernatural grace the natural family virtues. Its meaning is that by taking the 'natural' marriage into 'the great mystery of Christ and the Church,' the sacrament of matrimony gives marriage a new meaning, transforms, in fact, not only marriage as such, but all human love."[8]

The beauty and joy found in the Orthodox marriage ritual is indeed powerful. It consists of two services, the betrothal and the crowning. The betrothal service is performed in the vestibule and is a Christian recognition of the natural marriage. The priest, who is often a married person, takes the bridal pair into the church where in the crowning service the couple enters consciously and symbolically into the mystery of the kingdom of God. As persons they establish through the sacrament of marriage a small kingdom, a little church, "a sacrament of and a way to the kingdom." "Somewhere," Schmemann says, "even if it is only in a small room" there is an opportunity for each couple to be "king" and "queen" to each other in a way which proclaims that they are experiencing and living the love revealed by Christ to be at the center of God's kingdom.[9]

The concept of entering the kingdom of God's love takes marriage to a new level of meaning and purpose. Life in the kingdom carries with it crucifixion and suffering as well as joy. These deeper dimensions encourage the couple to be willing to "crucify" their own selfishness. The marriage in the mystery of the kingdom is led to die to itself in order for it to be resurrected in purposes greater than itself— but purposes in which the marriage can participate. Idolatry of marriage and family is a greater threat than are adultery, lack of adjustment, or mutual cruelty. When we make the family an idol and our quest for happiness the central motivation, marriage can cease to be a sacramental entrance into God's presence. In a Christian marriage there are three who are married, and "the united loyalty of the two toward the third, which is God, keeps the two in an active unity with each other as well as with God."[10]

Here we see a focus on love as the heart of the relationship between the husband and wife and God. Protestant Max Thurian agrees that the sacramental nature of marriage is revealed in the *mysterion* of the life of love in the kingdom. To Thurian, Christian marriage is a symbol of this relationship between Christ and the church in which a self-sacrificing quality of love is mysteriously present. In marriage which is a sacrament God's presence through the Spirit becomes evident and operative so that the couple will be empowered to live out what they "already are—united in God and a symbol of the mutual love of the church and Christ."[11]

The potential for an ecumenical dialogue around the sacramental nature of marriage appears to be very genuine. The need for such a sacramental understanding is exceedingly great in our technological, often impersonal world.

Marriage and the Stages of Ritualization and Faith

Marriage forces us to assess the content and quality of our commitments and the nature of our faith. Marriage is an opportunity to grow in faith, to focus on the internalization of our Christian commitments, the finding of a consistent set of values, after an honest critique of the beliefs and practices we somewhat conventionally have brought forward to young adulthood. The young adult can begin to see the external value of finding a Christian world view or ideology, of risking love for another person at the level of intimacy Erikson has identified, and of leaving room for growth by recognizing the honest mystery which is present even after our definitions and faith statements. Marriage is a time for education and counseling about the adult roles ahead, the opportunities to be ritualizers of the next generation, to be models of love and justice with the children couples may bring into the world. The major need in marriage is for a vision which the couple holds in common concerning the meaning or direction of life. This vision should have to do with not only the church, the family, work and leisure, but also concerning our total life as a people—a vision that is being tested and renewed so that it can be realized as life-giving rather than life-denying. Erikson believes, for instance, that religious visions (such as the realization of the kingdom of God on earth) deal powerfully with the major threat to persons in and out of marriage, the threat of nonexistence.

While marriage is the sacrament of unity with another person and God in love and faithfulness it creates a small faith community which finds fulfillment as it turns out to share love beyond itself. When it turns in on itself, seeking too intently for self-fulfillment, it begins to lose the vision which nurtures, not only married persons, but those who elect to be true to the vision by being single or those who are seeking new ways to live in community and find fresh rituals of meaning which renew and revitalize the vision.

Religious Education for Marriage

Education for marriage, of course, should start in childhood, not only within the family, but also in the church which is a larger intergenerational family with high potential for clarifying male/female roles and functions, for discerning couples and persons who have potential for revealing the inner sacramental meaning of an honest and growing marriage—or for modeling authentic ways to meet every person's need for intimacy and love. Education of youth concerning marriage is often overlooked in favor of sex-education or courses on relationships with the opposite sex. This can be corrected. More explicit premarital education for young adults or persons of any age preparing for marriage can be scheduled along with premarital counseling of couples more specifically in relation to that more personal preparation for the sacrament of marriage. Marriage enrichment experiences have already proven to be quite helpful in order to keep marriages growing, healthy, and honest. These should be extended to persons at each of the stages of life or the stages of faith development. Growth in biblical and theological understanding of the mystery of the kingdom of God (in which marriage finds its meaning and direction) can take place in educational or support groups. Education concerning the power of rituals, faith stories, the place of symbols in deepening religious commitments without "leaving the mind at home" can be scheduled prior to marriage. This timing has the potential of helping person find the essences of love and faithfulness basic to a sacramental approach to marriage.

Marriage Education in the Family Setting

Education for Christian marriage obviously starts with small children as they interact with their respective mothers and fathers or deal with the dynamics of a single-parent family or surrogate family. They are educated by the subtle attitude toward the opposite sex and the responses of trust or mistrust, affirmation or suppression which are evident in the family interaction. There is probably no more profound setting for marriage education than the family itself. For that reason alone, the sensitizing of parents or surrogates should be undertaken in order to show the high potential of the family for establishing positive or negative perceptions of the nature and purpose of marriage. Family life education, therefore, can focus on the family life cycle in which marriage, while deep running and consistent in purpose, is understood to need to grow and mature from stage to stage in order to fulfill the partners as persons and to strengthen the members of the family.

One of our most rewarding experiences has been in a course entitled *Ministering with Persons in their Strengths.* In this experience students and families at different places in the family life cycle (from beginning families to retirement families)[12] relate to one another in order to help the families identify their strengths and how those strengths can be channeled into creative forms of ministry within the family and beyond the family in the areas of work, community, leisure, and outreach through the church. The students and the families see one another each week to experience as well as discuss the families' gifts and opportunities for mutual love, support, and ministry in the world. It becomes clear rather soon that families which address the realistic issues and questions of the members of the family in *advance* of the time that these issues are critical strengthen all the members for effective relationships in respect to life with peers, issues of acceptance or rejection, male-female roles and functions, feelings of adequacy or inadequacy, sense of competence or incompetence at family tasks, school, or work, and positive or negative images of marriage and family as such. Families (whether nuclear or one-parent or surrogate) project positive images of marriage and family when they recognize and affirm the strengths of parents and children as they tackle the real-life issues openly and in advance of crises or deal with conflicts as opportunities for deeper self-knowledge and most profound commitment to one another. We have learned during several versions of the course that the most significant marriage preparation takes place for children and youth as they participate in families that are open in their communication concerning problems and opportunities in marriage and family in an honest way which is "on target" as the children and parents grow. They can reflect upon their learnings and celebrate their strengths together.[13] We have also discovered that marital partners are much stronger when they develop a *life plan* which is fulfilling to the individuals but also respectful of the needs of the whole family, has accountability in it but encourages change and growth. Also, marriages which have a clear foundation in a common faith at the level of daily decisions provide not only stability but the security needed for risk taking and a venturing faith. Such a common faith has to do with basic values shared, symbols affirmed, sense of direction felt. It does not mean agreement on every belief, or common denominational roots—although the finding of a meaningful and dynamic faith community is very important.

Students and families find that their views of themselves as persons of sacred worth and their views of the potential of marriage and family life in a technological world are enhanced. After several weeks together opening their lives to one another, they seek to agree upon an educational or pastoral design which will further strengthen the family for unique ministries.

Marriage Education within the Faith Community

Again, marriage education takes place within the body of Christ in many subtle ways. Children and youth get their views concerning the nature of Christian marriage and family life through the images projected in the roles and functions taken by husbands, wives, and children in the total life of the church. They learn that husbands and wives are partners in family, church, and community life or that husbands are dominant or (in the church context sometimes) that wives are dominant, in that religion is caricatured as being more important to women than to men. Images about mutuality in marriage and family can be projected in respect to the person with whom church leaders communicate (the husband, wife, or the children), or the way the sermons and curriculum address sexuality or male and female roles and functions within the family or within the church family. Church educational experiences for young children can picture men in caring roles and women in decision-making or vocational roles more traditionally taken by men. Children need to play out their images of marriage and have opportunities to face their secret fears about family disorientation as well as to celebrate the joys of marriage and family as gifts from God. Children in elementary years can be strengthened by units that help them deal with the new dynamics of family life where both mother and father are working or where death or divorce have set up new expectations. Children can amaze us by their sensitive perceptions and insights about marriage and family life in our contemporary situation. They know many children who have families different from their own. Differing marital and family patterns can be discussed in terms of their immediate experience rather than theoretically. Education concerning the sacramental nature of marriage can take place with children and youth but also in intergenerational settings or in family cluster groups. Fortunately, many denominational curriculum resources are designed to include positive yet realistic explanations of male and female roles and functions in marriage and family life, from nursery resources on through the life span to older adults. Credit must be given to curriculum designers, writers, and editors for this improvement.

Specific counseling and education for marriage should be planned for those preparing for marriage, regardless of the age of the couple, or the number of times they have been married before. Local congregations should discuss the need for counseling and education and develop specific policies concerning marriage and the guidelines appropriate for couples seeking to be married in the church. Several denominations have policy statements about marriage counseling and education and have produced materials for pastors and couples. Increasingly local congregations are agreeing upon policies and guidelines which strengthen the pastoral staff in interpreting the importance of counseling and education. In many of these congregations the expectation is for the pastor or pastors to have four or five counseling and/or educational sessions with the couple before the wedding and at least one after the marriage.

Some writers speak about *educative counseling* as compared to problem-centered counseling. Educative counseling, in this view, deals with issues such as how the couple understands and interprets money, sexuality, parenthood, developmental matters, common philosophy, or religious values. Antoinette and Leon Smith wisely say, "You may find it difficult to know when you are doing educative counseling and when you are doing problem-centered counseling since premarital counseling is such a mix of the two."[14] While the Smiths make this helpful distinction, it seems that they may need to see the educational dimension in even more critical and still constructive terms. Such education should raise the deeper questions concerning the adequacy of our current views and practices in respect to marriage in the light of the gospel. This deeper kind of educative counseling can raise presuppositional questions in a supportive environment but in a way that may start the couple on a pilgrimage to explore and expand their concepts of Christian marriage and to commit themselves in the pre-marital period to ongoing growth in marriage. This would mean that they could begin to see that the ceremony is a commitment to work together in subsequent supportive settings to refine their vision of Christian marriage and to set up patterns of communication with one another and other couples which will maximize the possibilities of increasing depth of relationship. Many churches now are relating couples preparing for marriage to such educational groups made up of married couples who have been trained to be the lay counseling teams with the pastor or pastors. Such couples are trained to be good listeners but also to share their own marital pilgrimages where appropriate in order to model honest communication and patterns of growth. Denominations have published official and unofficial resources for such counseling and educational approaches.[15]

Premarital educational designs are very important but seemingly more difficult to organize and lead. Couples are somewhat used to the idea of premarital counseling sessions but they are not very used to premarital educational experiences. The latter implies longer lead time in order to recruit couples who are interested in marriage during a similar time period. Moreover, church guidelines seldom present the importance of premarital education in favor of the strengthening of the expectation about longer and deeper premarital counseling. Nevertheless, premarital educational experiences have great potential for looking much more specifically at the sacramental nature of marriage along with the exploration of the issues commonly dealt with in educative counseling sessions such as sexual knowledge and attitudes, male and female roles and functions in a Christian marriage, the meaning of money and financial planning, communications problems and skills, parenthood, ways of dealing with conflict, and finding values and commitments in common. Such educational designs can be planned over several weeks of group sessions or can be planned in all-day or weekend retreat formats. Resources are available to pastors and teams of couples who can help plan and lead such experiences.[16]

Educational groups should study the deeper sacramental nature of marriage during such sessions. The resources in the manuals are not as rich at this point. One of the books that came out of group study around the sacraments is George McCauley's *The God of the Group*. It has a fine introduction concerning the nature of sacramental life as well as good chapters on each of the sacraments. The chapter that reports the work of the marriage group raises many very honest questions (two and one-half pages full) concerning marriage. These questions include: What are the actual reasons people marry? Is lifelong commitment desirable? Is marriage a failure of nerve? Does Christianity make sex better? What kind of God is envisioned in the sacrament of marriage? What of homosexual marriage? What are the impediments to a sacramental marriage? And many more. McCauley highlights the importance of dealing with such questions in a supportive group. He asserts, "People do not cope with such complicated issues . . . simply by thinking about them. Their very complexity warns us against that. Issues are resolved rather *by the company we keep* than by our prowess at logical assessment. What the sacrament of marriage provides a couple is the right company in which to work out problems connected with the issue of marriage."[17] McCauley goes on to help us see that Jesus' kind and quality of love can be a central model for sacramental marriage.

One of the best Orthodox resources is a book by Demetrios J. Constantelos, *Marriage, Sexuality and Celibacy: A Greek Orthodox Perspective.* Constantelos presents a very honest picture of the strengths of the Orthodox view of sacramental marriage but also raises the critical issues of the lack of intercommunion, the difficulty of intermarriage, the issue of married priests, and the norm of unmarried bishops. His interpretation of marriage is very sound and has the potential for helping us find an ecumenical sacramental approach to marriage. His chapters on the history of marriage are very helpful, not only for Orthodox couples, but also for couples in Catholic and Protestant groups.[18]

The expectation that marriage is not a constant state but a commitment to growth means that marriage groups should be available for persons at the various stages of development in life. The marriage enrichment movement has been a positive force in many of our churches. Resources and educational designs have been developed to enable couples to face the real issues which emerge in their marriages and to celebrate the strengths that each finds in the other. Many pastors and married couples have been trained to lead such groups. Many good resources are already written and tested.[19] Marriage education resources are available which deal with the first year of marriage,[20] the problem of the middle and older years of marriage,[21] the issues of mixed marriage,[22] and the two-career marriage.[23] A fine book to deal with incompatibility is Lance Webb's *Making Love Grow: Love That Can Make Incompatibility a Myth* (Nashville: Abingdon, 1983). Marriage education in respect to the sacramental nature of this basic relationship is a lifelong enterprise. It is an exciting venture which should be linked with liturgies of reaffirmation. It also must face the genuine problems in marriage and the failures of marriage such as divorce and long-term marital dysfunction. The basic issues must continue to be raised in the light of the Christian faith so that the concept of marriage can grow as well as the practice of marriage in our society. The dissolution of marriage must be faced openly and where appropriate symbolized in liturgies of meaning.[24]

Liturgy: Confusion

Anyone attending weddings with any frequency over the last two decades has experienced at least a measure of chaos and confusion concerning the wedding liturgy. In some situations where considerable latitude of practice is normal, there has almost ceased to be any "normal" in the marriage service. The wedding becomes a kind of liturgical do-it-yourself kit where couples write their own vows and import into the service whatever appeals as a celebration of their union. This situation is attributable to our cultural insecurity about marriage and the basis of marriage. But it is also attributable to the fact that ministers are *pro tempore* officers of the state serving to authenticate the legality of marriages. In our culture a church wedding is a first-class wedding. The processional, the flowers, the music, the minister, vows and reverent words are all *proper*. Being married by a judge or justice of the peace is, in the eyes of many, just not quite a respectable thing. It is entirely legal, but it lacks the proprieties. So it is that the joining of a man and a woman before a minister in a place intended for worship often has nothing at all to do with marriage as a sacrament of the kingdom of God.

Would that pastors were free of obligations of state and that weddings were in some way civil and legal events, and ceremonies of faith, separately and independently. There seems to be no reason to suppose that this soon will be the case. The best, therefore, that Christian churches can do is to so define *what* and *how* they intend in liturgies of marriage that couples who do not see their wedding ceremonies as celebrations of faith will choose some other situation for their wedding.

A Sacrament

The wedding ceremony of a church is a service of prayer and praise which celebrates commitment in love—the choice of a partner in life and love in the context of a people who exist to witness to specific qualities of living and loving. It is appropriately understood as a sacrament. The dismissal and blessing at the end of the new United Methodist liturgy makes this faith dimension of the wedding commitment of Christians very plain:

God the Eternal keep you in love with each other,
so that the peace of Christ may abide in your home.
Go to serve God and your neighbor in all that you do.
Bear witness to the love of God in this world
    so that those to whom love is a stranger
    will find in you generous friends.
The grace of the Lord Jesus Christ
    and the love of God
    and the communion of the Holy Spirit
    be with you all.[25]

The Ceremony

The customary entrances of the bride and groom in the wedding are being challenged broadly today, primarily on two grounds. Some couples who understand their commitment to one another as a sacrament wish to have the brief wedding ceremony set in a larger frame of Christian worship in which they wish to be present. Many choose to enter unceremoniously with their families and friends and simply sit together in the front row of the church. Some reject the traditional entrance because they see it as a symbol of a false social order: A woman "handed over" from the keep of one man to that of another.

There is validity to both of these attitudes. Still, many prefer the traditional wedding procession for strictly ceremonial and familial reasons even when they wish their wedding to have a wider context of worship, or when they reject the social order which it seems to symbolize. It is powerful tradition in the culture, after all, and means can be found to provide a fuller liturgy or to articulate social relationships. At any rate, the entrance is one of the elements of the rite most easily and properly adapted to the wishes of those being married and their families. It may be grand and lengthy or it may be as simple as any other entrance into worship.

The greeting with which the wedding liturgy usually opens in this country is generally something strained and superfluous. It is superfluous in that it tells us what we already know and strained because the traditional reference to the fact that Jesus "graced" a wedding in Cana of Galilee is just utterly irrelevant. This text was much used in the past to "prooftext" the sacramental character of marriage. The opening of the wedding ceremony in the *Lutheran Book of Worship* avoids the greeting and is a simple blessing directed to everyone: "The grace of our Lord Jesus Christ, the love of God, and the communion of the Holy Spirit be with you all,"[26] which is followed by prayer for the couple. It seems the most fitting beginning.

Following the declaration of intention there usually is a moment in the order for what used to be called "the giving away of the bride." This was the responsibility of the father of the bride; it became common for both parents to join in this act. Now it is frequently omitted from the service or done in a manner which recognizes the new family relationships created in a marriage. In the new United Methodist liturgy, for instance, the minister declares to the congregation, "The marriage of (name) and (name) unites two families and creates a new one. They ask your blessing." Parents and other representatives of the families are to respond: "We rejoice in your union, and pray God's blessing upon you."[27] All of the people are then asked, as they are in the wedding liturgy in the Episcopal *BCP*, if they will "do everything in your power to uphold and care for these two persons in their marriage?" All answer, "We will." This response of the people is an important innovation in new wedding liturgies. It, in essence, asks the people's consent. In so doing it widens the circle of commitment. It would make the nature of the event clearer as sacrament if this expression of commitment went further and asked not only for our willingness to uphold the marriage but for our own commitment to love as a primary quality of the kingdom of God.

In most liturgies a period of scripture and prayer, with perhaps a sermon, follows. This section is an option in many traditions. The heart of the ceremony, the vows, comes next, with the blessing and exchange of rings usually following immediately.

The marriage is accomplished, in fact, by those who are being married. Their consent, their expressed mutual commitment is what seals a marriage, not the declaration or blessing of a minister or a civil authority. So the vows are the heart of the ceremony. What comes before builds toward them. What follows evolves from them. This ought to be clear in the way the liturgy happens. It is appropriate, for instance, for the couple to move to a higher step to say the vows, to join hands and to turn from facing the minister to face one another, and a suitable moment of silence many precede and follow this central action.

The rest of the service is really blessing. It is becoming increasingly common for the service then to transit to the eucharist. If the eucharist is celebrated, it should be served to all present who wish it and not exclusively to the wedding couple, because the thanksgiving in this event is general.

For a thorough study of the history and variety of Christian marriage liturgies, see *Nuptial Blessing: A Study of Christian Marriage Rites*, by Kenneth Stevenson (Oxford University Press, 1983).

Notes

1. Walter Kasper, *Theology of Marriage* (New York: Seabury Press, 1980), p. 23.

2. Ibid., p. 30.

3. Ibid., p. 40.

4. Edward Schillebeeckx, *Marriage: Human Reality and Saving Mystery*, Volumes I and II (New York: Sheed and Ward, 1965), p. 386.

5. Ibid., p. 386.

6. Ibid., p. 234.

7. Ibid., pp. 378-380.

8. Alexander Schmemann, *For the Life of the World* (Crestwood, N.Y.: St. Vladimir's Seminary Press, 1973), p. 88.

9. Ibid., p. 89.

10. Ibid., p. 90.

11. Max Thurian, *Our Faith* (Les Presses of Taize, 1978), p. 142.

12. See Evelyn M. Duvall, *Marriage and Family Development* (Philadelphia: J. B. Lippincott, 1977).

13. See Robert Browning and Paul Nicely, "Ministry with Persons in their Strengths: Design for Strengthening Families for Ministry in Work, Leisure and Community Contexts," in *Seminary and Congregation: Integrating Learning, Ministry, and Mission,* ed. LeRoy H. Aden, (The Association of Professional Education for Ministry, Duquesne University, Pittsburgh, 1982), pp. 47-54.

14. Antoinette Smith and Leon Smith, *Growing Love in Christian Marriage: Pastor's Manual* (Nashville: The United Methodist Publishing House, 1981), p. 71.

15. See Joan and Richard Hunt, *Growing Love in Christian Marriage: The Official Marriage Manual of the United Methodist Church* (Nashville: Abingdon Press, 1982). Originally published as Pastor's Manual for *Growing Love in Christian Marriage.* Other denominations have similar resources.

16. See David J. Rolfe, *Marriage Preparation Manual* (New York: Paulist Press, 1975). This is a guide for host couples and facilitators organizing marriage preparation and pre-Cana programs for groups of engaged couples. The United Methodist manual for couples by Joan and Richard Hunt, *Growing Love in Christian Marriage*, can also be used as a resource for educational groups of engaged couples.

17. George McCauley, *The God of the Group* (Niles, Ill.: Argus Communications, 1975), p. 98.

18. Demetrios J. Constantelos, *Marriage, Sexuality, and Celibacy: A Greek Orthodox Perspective* (Minneapolis: Light and Life Publishing Co., 1975).

19. See Larry Hof and William Miller, *Marriage Enrichment: Philosophy, Process and Program* (Bowie, Md.: R. J. Brady Co., 1981); Howard Clinebell, *Growth Counseling for Marriage Enrichment, Pre-Marriage and the Early Years* (Philadelphia: Fortress, 1975); David Mace, *Marriage Enrichment in the Church* (Nashville: Broadman Press, 1977).

20. David and Vera Mace, *How to Have a Happy Marriage* (Nashville: Abingdon Press, 1979).

21. Clayton C. Barbeau, *Creative Marriage: The Middle Years* (New York: Seabury Press, 1976); James A. Peterson and Barbara Payne, *Love in the Later Years* (New York: Association Press, 1975).

22. Evelyn Kaye, *Crosscurrents: Children, Families and Religion* (New York: C. N. Potter, 1980); Barbara D. Schiappa, *Mixing: Catholic-Protestant Marriages in the 1980's: A Guidebook* (New York: Paulist Press, 1982).

23. Wade Rowatt, *The Two Career Marriage* (Philadelphia: Westminster, 1980).

24. See John H. Westerhoff III and William H. Willimon, "The Recognition of Divorce," in *Liturgy and Learning Through the Life Cycle* (New York: Seabury Press, 1980), p. 121ff.

25. *We Gather Together,* p. 23.

26. *Lutheran Book of Worship,* (Minister's Desk Edition), p. 328.

27. *We Gather Together,* p. 19.

Chapter 12

The Sacraments of Vocation: The Ordination of Clergy and the Consecration of the Laity for Ministry

The revolutionary nature of the concept of the universal priesthood of all believers is quietly but significantly breaking through in Catholic and Orthodox as well as Protestant views of ministry. The emphasis upon the centrality of the general ministry of all Christians, in their varying understandings of their vocations in life is increasingly present in the literature concerning ordination. In fact, this emphasis on the ministry of all "the people of God" is being discerned to be somewhat threatening to the self-images of some priests and ministers who were drawn to ordination by a desire to be distinctively engaged in ministries in ways lay persons could not be.

The revolution is incomplete in most churches, however, because laity have little preparation, educationally, and no high moment of decision, liturgically, which publicly celebrates the unique focus of their universal priesthood in a particular occupational or voluntary expression. James White's suggestion that a new sacrament of vocation could be instituted is a clear recognition of this omission in our approach to the ministry of laity. We should like to discuss the sacramental nature of vocation for all believers with an emphasis upon the education of all the people for ministries through their sense of vocation and in their varying occupations. All are in need of nurture into a clear understanding of commitment to their Christian vocation which is the universal priesthood of all believers. Each, then, is in need of education and counseling concerning decisions about specific ways this sense of vocation will find concrete expression through occupation, family, leisure, community life, and service through social and political avenues.

The issue of whether a person wishes to be ordained a priest/minister *or* consecrated as a lay minister in some other occupation is

220

related to his or her self-understanding, particular sense of call, and the call of the church. Both public celebrations (ordination or consecration) of these mutually supported decisions are sacramental. Both are celebrations of the decisions of individuals and the congregation to make visible Christ's ministry in specific ways in the world. Presently, for the most part only ordained clergy have specific education for their ministries and only ordained clergy are given the public liturgical affirmation of the congregation for such ministries. That is, such is the case in most churches. Happily, there are a few exceptions, such as the Church of the Saviour, in Washington, D. C., where laity are educated and consecrated for ministries through their occupations, individually or through various corporate approaches to systemic change in health care, education, or governmental structures or programs.[1] The goal of these ministries, of course, is the liberation and humanization of all of life through these extensions of the ministry of Christ through the Body of Christ, the church. We shall return to the discussion of the specific program of the Church of the Saviour later in this chapter.

The Emergence of the Concept of Consecration of the Laity

Ordination has a long history, but consecration of laity to ministry, of course, is new and somewhat problematic.

We are grateful for the creative thinking of Max Thurian in respect to the concept of the consecration of the laity for ministry. As we mentioned in our discussion of confirmation, Thurian has influenced many of us concerning the possibility of confirmation as a repeatable sacrament. Thurian developed his view of consecration in direct relation to his understanding that confirmation can be repeated when persons have been prepared by life's experiences and by specific forms of ministry as laity. Thurian defended the unity of baptism by water and confirmation in the spirit as a full engrafting of the person into the body of Christ. Confirmation–consecration, then, could never be a completion of baptism. Rather, confirmation, or as he preferred to say, consecration of the laity, was a strengthening and a focusing of an earlier "ordination" to ministry in baptism. Grounding his view of consecration on the fact that all Christians are called to be members of the people of God in a ministry of the royal priesthood (1 Peter 2:5), Thurian saw baptism as a first "ordination" to the universal priesthood of the church in the world and consecration as a second "ordination" of laics to the service of the church.[2]

Thurian clarifies this idea, stating that "consecration to the royal priesthood does accompany entrance into the church by baptism; but the laying on of hands can be repeated when one's service or ministry becomes more specific, or is modified. . . . There is no theological objection to keeping the imposition of hands, consecrating to a service, from being repeatedly given with different intentions on the part of the church. Thus, there may be laying on of hands to confer the divers gifts of the Holy Spirit: at baptism in the Spirit, at confirmation, at the ordination of a deacon, a pastor, a bishop . . . each time with a different intention on the part of the church, in view of a different situation or different service in the church."[3]

Thurian sought an ecumenical agreement on the unity of baptism and confirmation in infancy (but not of communion) so that confirmation could be repeated as a consecration of lay persons to ministries in the church at any time new commitments arose or new self-understandings emerged.

While we understand why Thurian emphasized consecration as a commitment to ministries *in the church* (assuming all baptized Christians are already "ordained" to ministries in the world), we believe that the consecration of the laity should include commitment to ministries within the church but especially commitment to ministries in the world through clarity about vocation and occupation. This is the only major difference in our thinking. Thurian does recognize that the unique emphasis of consecrated lay ministers should be a public witnessing and praying "for the world." He proposed a day-long consecration festival in which all people could be involved in liturgy, sermon, communion, consecration, and "a lecture revealing some urgent aspect of the Church's work and stimulating the vocation of everyone there."[4] While our difference with Thurian may be one of emphasis, we believe the focus on consecration to ministries "in the church" can be interpreted too narrowly. We prefer to emphasize consecration to ministries of members of the body of Christ both within and especially beyond the church into the world.

The Sacramental Nature of Ordination and Consecration

In the motion picture, *Dinner with Andre*, two men enter a dialogue about their lives in such depth and intensity that the audience remains engaged, with excitement and satisfaction, in this interaction for an entire evening. Amazing, in view of the nature of film. Supposedly, motion pictures engage us because of movement and action. The camera captures the details of the ritual of eating and the expression in the eyes and faces of the playwright and former director who converse about their hunger for meaning in life. Andre, the director, after a period of disengagement from directing and several years of soul-searching, finally reveals his desire for all humanity to recover or discover the sacramental nature of all of life. He sees himself and others taking roles in life which kept them from perceiving reality. People, he thinks, are protecting themselves from the fact that they are finite, from the fact of their death. They fill their lives with activities which are designed to hide their fear and emptiness. They are afraid to *be*. They are afraid to trust themselves, others, and the goodness of God's universe. The implication is that all work and all leisure are sacramental ways to point to and participate in God's grace and love which fill the universe when we genuinely perceive what reality is all about.

This reality, which is the sacramental nature of all of life, is the foundation for all specific sacraments, whether of baptism, which is the "ordination" of all persons to the universal priesthood, or communion, which is the thanksgiving of all for the gift of Christ as the paradigm for our common ministries, or ordination and consecration, which are specific concrete expressions of our common ministry extending and making alive and visible the love and grace of God which is always present but often hidden from us by our inability to see.

Ordination and consecration are sacraments because they are an epiphany of grace which transcends our liturgies, an illumination of God's grace and a focusing of that grace in particular forms of ministry which more fully realize the love, joy, and justice implied in our membership in the kingdom of God.[5]

The Sacraments of Ordination and Consecration Symbolize the Congregation's Call to Embrace Ministries which Participate in the Mystery of the Kingdom of God.

Orthodox thinker Alexander Schmemann, writing about ordination, says that it is through ordination that the mystery of God's love of life is revealed in a unique way. Agreeing that all people are created as priests before God, as persons who "offer the world to God in a sacrifice of love and praise and who, through their eternal eucharist, bestow the divine love upon the world," Schmemann urges us not to split clergy from laity in ministry. Pointing to Christ he says,

Christ revealed the essence of priesthood to be love and, therefore, priesthood to be the essence of life. He died, the last victim of the priestly religion, and in his death the priestly religion died and the priestly life was inaugurated. He was killed by the priests, by the "clergy," but his sacrifice abolished them as it abolished religion because it destroyed that wall of separation between the "natural" and the "supernatural," the "profane" and the "sacred," the "this-worldly" and the "other worldly"—which was the only justification and raison de'etre of religion. He revealed that all things, all nature have their end, their fulfillment in the Kingdom, that all things are to be made new by love.[6]

The purpose of ordination, then, is to make specific the call to ministry which is the vocation of all. Priests are ordained precisely in order to reveal to each vocation its priestly essence, "to make the whole life of all persons the liturgy of the Kingdom, to reveal the church as the royal priesthood of the redeemed world."[7] Ordination is not a substantialistic giving of powers to priests or ministers that all other members of the ministering community do not possess. Ordained persons sacramentally make visible what is in the nature of things. Consecrated lay ministers make visible in unique and profound ways the love, justice, and service needed in the total society. The Spirit of God moves in and through the lives of those in ministry. Ordained persons are called to ministries of word, sacrament, and order (or unity, as Thurian proposes). These ministries are of equal value. Each is a high calling, a part of the royal priesthood which is powerful when it is authentic and self-giving rather than regal and self-seeking.

Ordination and Consecration Are United As Ministries of the Sacrament of Christ, the Church

The body of Christ is one body. We are individually members of it—with no distinctions of greater or lesser worth or greater or lesser inherent power. Ordination makes possible certain crucially important functions to be performed by the priest or minister for the whole body. Consecrated lay ministers likewise perform ministries in the world for the whole body. Both are, in this sense, representative ministries of the people of God. Both serve as extensions of the community and at the pleasure of the community of faith.

Ordination and Consecration Are Community Acts

Each of these sacramental acts establishes specific roles and functions for the leadership of the ministering community. Ordained clergy are those who have been called by inner conviction and an outer call from the church to provide leadership in preaching and teaching the word, in preparing persons for and taking initiative in celebrating the sacraments throughout the life span, and in providing administrative structures and caring relationships which result in decisions which free the whole people for ministries to the wider world. The faith community helps persons recognize and accept their gifts of leadership, assists persons in preparation, (biblically, theologically, ethically, etc.) to take up their ministries with integrity. The community gives each person authority to minister in agreed upon ways.

George McCauley sees the ordained priest as a necessity. The priest or minister is a "reminder" to the community of the sacrament of God's love which Christ, in fact, was. The community needs to be reminded of God's love at the center of life. It is not Christ's need; nor is it only the priests personal need. Hence priests are made, as it were, by public demand. (This is perhaps why people get just about the kind of priests they deserve.)[8] Likewise, the extensions of Christ's ministry in family, community, business and industry, technology and ecology, government, etc., are primarily ministries of consecrated laity who know who they are and what they are called to become as persons; but also, they are called by a discerning congregation to tackle special needs which have been corporately identified. Such identification of ministries mandates high involvement in the world and careful assessment of problem areas and major strengths and weaknesses so that the ministries of the ordained will be fully in touch with life as it is (to be reflected in preaching, teaching, liturgy, administration, pastoral care, and leadership in outreach). The ministries of the consecrated will be more precisely focused through occupations or voluntary service.

Ordination Is a Call to Office and Consecration Is a Call to Service within and beyond the Church

There is a general recognition of the functional nature of ministry in respect to the roles and functions to be performed by clergy and laity. However, there appears to be a dissatisfaction with this organic view of the ministries of the church. Ordained, full-time clergy need clearer self-understandings and a stronger sense of identity mutually agreed upon in the faith community. Walter Burghardt asks us to accept the functional view but to get behind the functions to the concept of offices being assumed so that personal responsibilities can be agreed upon and fulfilled. The responsible lay officers of the church representing the community call the ordained person to represent the church in its official actions. The priest or minister then dedicates himself or herself publicly to a life of service in this office. The ordained person then becomes a public servant in a sense different but no better than a lay minister.

The concept of ordination to an office is in need of safeguards. It can sound like and *be* an institutional, bureaucratic image. It must be

understood symbolically and sacramentally as pointing to and participating in the gospel of God's liberating love and justice. As Burghardt
states,

> Understand me: when I say "officeholder," when I say "representa-
> tive," I am not saying "one who parrots the party line"! The priest
> may have to stand *over against* the community, over against bishop or
> pope. Not *outside* the community, not outside bishop or pope, but
> conceivably over against them, even as public servant, precisely as a
> public servant.[9]

The priest or minister, then, is to take his or her office seriously and
keep faithful to the central purpose and mission of the church, which
is the reconciliation of all persons with God and one another through
the mediator of God's love, Jesus Christ. The office of ordained minister includes, Burghardt thinks, the proclamation of the word, not only
in preaching, but dialogically; the building up of the faith community
through strong collegial leadership; service to humankind by being
involved in the world and by enabling the ministries of the whole
people. The liturgical leadership, including the administration of the
sacraments, can strengthen the unity of the congregation with all
Christians and with all humankind.

The concept of ordination to the office of minister or priest has
great symbolic as well as actual power. The office of pastor carries
great moral as well as spiritual and administrative weight in the actual
functioning of a congregation or in an outpost of specialized ministry,
to which many ordained persons are assigned.

Max Thurian reminds us that God is free and the Spirit blows
where it will and that Christ can and does move through many faithful
witnesses besides the clergy. However, he has a high view of the sacramental nature of ordination. He reminds us that ordination is "an
apostolic institution, an integral part of the sacred deposit of the faith,
since it endows the church with signs and instruments of the ministry
of Christ in the word and the sacraments." Ordination brings more
certainty to the church that the word of God will be communicated in
an authentic way.[10]

Hans Küng agrees that ordination to the office is the central issue
and that the apostolic nature of ordination into the office is crucial.
However, he maintains that it cannot be documented that bishops in a
direct and exclusive sense are the successors of the apostles but that it
is acceptable to speak of apostolic succession in a functional way as a
part of the leadership through the ages which founded the churches

and in the sense that these leaders were rooted in the gospel. Küng also emphasizes the public affirmation and authorization involved in ordination.

Küng's views are quite revolutionary if taken literally. He genuinely believes in the functional and flexible approach to ministry when he says,

> Any particular form which has come into existence historically must be changed if it no longer corresponds to the function of ministry in question. In the light of the particular tasks, circumstances and personal aptitude, offices in the church in each case can be exercised full time or part time for a period of a lifetime, by men and women, by married or unmarried people, by graduates or non-graduates. The present breakdown of the clerical "state" does not mean a breakdown of the church's ministry of leadership as a whole.[11]

All of these functional ministries will be tested by their authenticity in extending the mission of the church, in bringing about a world of love and justice. The vocation of every Christian is this *diakonia*, this active service in every form needed. Such a position implies a high view of the ministry of the laity as well as specialized ministries of lay professionals or committed deacons on a full-time or part-time basis.

There is much legitimate concern today to upgrade the office of ordained deacon or the office of consecrated diaconal ministers (lay professionals in education, music, administration, communications, etc). Again, the issue is to avoid the double standard between ordained and nonordained forms of ministry while, at the same time, recognizing functional differences and various matters of responsibility of those who are full-time and well-prepared persons within the life of the church. The improvement of the relationship between ordained elders, ordained deacons, certified lay professionals, and consecrated lay ministers is a concern which deserves much more discussion. An understanding of the sacramental nature of ministry needs to emerge which will undergird a high view of the integrity of each form of ministry. This must be done, however, in ways which respect various polities and deal honestly with the political realities having to do with placement and security. Placement of persons should reflect a matching of talent with needs. The way we resolve security matters (such as salary, tenure, etc.) must reveal our commitment to the whole ministry of the people of God and not the special interests of any one group.

The consecration of laity for ministries of love, justice, and service is an unfinished matter in the life of the church. It is more comfortable for both clergy and laity to keep things as they are. Clergy are sometimes threatened by active, knowledgeable, questioning laity. Often laity like to think they are paying the clergy to perform the ministry and mission of the church. The universal priesthood of all believers is a concept which is long overdue! The extension of Christ's ministry in a very complex technological society will be almost impossible without laity being prepared biblically and theologically to deal with the ethical issues before our world community. The education of older youth and young adults in our churches is typically weak and erratic. This is true not only because such persons are in transition from dependency to independence, from home to college or work arenas, from singleness to marriage or deliberate singleness, it is true also because the church has no clear sacramental understanding of lay ministry and no specific liturgy which celebrates the Christian vocation of laity.

Confirmation has sometimes been thought to be such a rite or sacrament. However, it is not timed in our churches to correlate with vocational preparation or decisions which relate to a particular occupation. If we conceive of confirmation as a repeatable sacrament, it is possible to invite young laity to prepare themselves for a public declaration of their ministry through their wider sense of Christian vocation in all relationships and through their particular occupational expressions.

It seems clear that the preparation of laity for consecration should have sound biblical, theological, historical, and ethical foundations but should come into focus on the nature of ministry through their sense of vocation generally and their occupations specifically. This preparation should follow engaging educational principles and be in dialogue with the psychological realities of lay ministers. The preparation should not be a mini-seminary course of study.

We have discovered in explorations with laity in various work contexts that they seldom automatically see the connections between lay ministry and the specific opportunities for ministry in the work situation. We are pleased when some lay persons not only see this connection but are deliberate and conscientious in their attempt to minister to co-workers, or in their willingness to tackle the ethical issues of honesty or genuine responsibility for clients, or matters of social responsibility associated with production, distribution, or sales. Each occupation has unique opportunities for ministry as well as specific threats and temptations. Education for consecration should explore these issues concretely, rather than generally. This means consecration education should have contextual elements in it. It should be action-reflection in mode so that it takes on a sense of realism and practicality while of course being grounded theologically in the nature and mission of the church and ministry.

In summary, we should admit to what is obvious in this discussion, that we do not have an ontological view of ordination. We do not think that ordination impresses an indelible "character" in the person in ministry. We also are critical of most strictly functional views of ordination because they underestimate the vital place of what we choose to call a special office of ministry in the church. So our concept is what might be called a "high" functional one. Ordination to the particular office of ministry which requires a person to take special responsibility for preaching and teaching the word of God and administering the sacraments and maintaining the good order of the church is a special office requiring a high degree of commitment and training. It is the key leadership role among Christians, and a role which represents and encourages all the other roles in ministry.

Stages of Ritualization and Faith Development

When we look at ordination and consecration from the perspective of Erikson's stages of ritualization and Fowler's stages of faith we can see exciting possibilities for education and liturgical renewal.

Erikson sees young adults normally working on identity issues especially in respect to the discovery of a world view or ideology which gives content to the faith the person is seeking to refine and develop. The young adult, and now older persons who are having to rethink their occupational identity, need something which Erikson likens to religion, ". . . a clear comprehension of life in the light of an intelligible theory. . . . this something between—a theory and a religion . . . an ideology."[12]

This ideology has the power to tie the loose ends of ego formation together and propel the self into the future with a consistency and identity which is both personal and social. By making public one's ideology, one's world view and its tangible references in society, the person may be given affirmation and support in his or her identity. What is needed is for the person to acquire "a conflict-free, habitual use of a dominant faculty, to be elaborated in an occupation, a limitless resource, a feedback, as it were, from the immediate exercise of this occupation, from the companionship it provides, and from its tradition."[13] The occupation, then, becomes a way for persons to express their ideology and to reveal and witness to their fidelity, the virtue which accompanies their quest to organize the self around someone or something to which they give themselves in an ultimate way.

This approach is similar to James Fowler's concept of human faith as an underlying structure of the mind, affection, and will which brings together the essential meaning and direction of a person's life. This faith structure, which each person has, is given richness and content by the Christian or some other world view with particular master faith stories, symbols, rituals, and moral practices which accompany the faith commitment. Whether a person commits himself or herself to ordained or lay ministry or some variation, such as a certified lay professional within the organized church, is finally a matter of his or her sense of Christian vocation. The conflict-free requirement means that the occupation is conflict free *enough* to become a channel of ministry which maximizes the person's talents, interests, self-understanding, sense of social responsibility, and sense of Christian vocation. For some persons, this conflict-free commitment may be ordination to word, sacrament, and order; for others this commitment may be consecration to particular ministries through occupations or service as lay persons; for still others this commitment may take the form of ordination as deacons or consecration or certification as lay professional educators, business administrators, communications experts, church and community workers, or various occupations in the mission field. With each of these commitments goes specific orientations into the traditions, stories, symbols, and rites associated with the particular occupation. These traditions should be lifted up and dramatically celebrated as a part of the liturgy related to the ordination or consecration. Continuing renewal or reform of the occupation to keep it faithful to the Christian vision is, of course, the exciting challenge for the persons involved.

The faith community's recognition is crucial in order for the identity of the person being ordained or consecrated to have external as well as internal confirmation. The ordained person's decision is celebrated as a public declaration of this internal and external identity and call. He or she is affirmed in an occupation in which his or her faith may be channeled in a way which is a genuine sacramental extension of Christ's ministry but in a way no better than the ministry of laity. Likewise, the consecration of lay ministers or lay professionals can have this same public affirmation and become a sacrament of Christ's ministry through the church as it moves out to the worlds of family, work, friendships, leisure, politics, and government.

What is important in ordination and consecration as sacraments of Christian vocation is the clarity of the understanding and identity of both laity and clergy concerning the Christian world view and vision which propels each into specific, agreed-upon forms of ministry, with particular roles and functions being performed with integrity and mutuality.

Education for Consecration and Ordination

The education of such persons can be enhanced by being aware of where the persons are in respect to the stages of faith development or the stages of ritualization. For instance, most young adults who are preparing for ordained ministry are working through Stage III or IV issues in terms of Fowler's research. Certainly they need to be challenged to critique the nature and quality of the faith they have developed. They also need to penetrate closer to the core understandings of Christian beliefs and the Christian world view. The biblical foundations of the Christian belief systems must be wrestled with, demythologized where necessary, or remythologized in terms of contemporary issues and categories. The other elements in Fowler's Stage IV (Individuative-Reflective faith) grid such as perspective taking, moral decision making, conception of authority, use of symbols, world perspective, etc., can be important guides to the questions raised and processed theologically, ethically, and in terms of the ministry and mission of the church.

Those preparing for lay consecration in some form are working on similar issues. The questions of lay contexts and self-understanding need to guide the educational designs. Matters of biblical and theological understanding of the nature and mission of the church will probably become organizing life issues for the learning experiences designed. Unique issues related to the balancing of family developmental tasks, work, leisure, community, and church involvements will no doubt arise as central questions. Erikson's understandings concerning the power of family and community rituals can be important to the educational and spiritual formation of laity. Adults are the ritualizers of the next generation. They have profound ministries to perform in their roles in the priesthood of parenthood if they elect to have children. With or without children they are the numinous models for those who follow. They communicate values and reveal the content and quality of their faith in everything they do. Educational designs for those preparing for lay ministry should especially focus on the Christian vision of love and justice in all the arenas of life, how the sacramental nature of life in all its richness can be experienced and celebrated. When the rituals of parenting, teaching, producing, sharing resources, caring or curing lose touch with the liberating and humanizing vision revealed by Christ, lay ministers have the responsibility to critique, change, and reritualize their practices.

As persons grow from one faith stage to another new opportunities come to the church to help both clergy and laity understand and process these changes. Then, of course, we can help all persons celebrate fresh visions and decisions about new forms of ministry. The liturgical life, then, can be rich, flexible, and clearly related to the personal pilgrimages of all members of the body of Christ and to those beyond the community who may be influenced directly and indirectly.

Specific Expressions of Education for Consecration and Ordination

The pioneering work of the Church of the Saviour in Washington, D. C., was mentioned early in this chapter. The pastor, Gordon Cosby, and his associates have developed a congregation with high expectations for lay ministries both within and beyond the church. Designing a strong School of Christian Living with a two-year curriculum to prepare lay persons to be ordained as lay ministers, the leaders of the church raised the expectations of all concerning the meaning of "full-time ministry." We often think that the ordained pastor is in full-time ministry and that the laity are in ministry but not on a full-time basis. The Church of the Saviour sees all Christians in full-time ministry wherever they are—in family, work, community, or worldwide ministry settings. As Elizabeth O'Connor says in her description of this emphasis, "The ordination of a lay person to ministry in the world is much more than recognition of significant activity. It means that the person knows himself (herself) to be grasped by God for a task that only he (she) can do and which the church must have done. This awareness of God's call has grown out of searching and prayer and participation in various areas of the world's life."[14]

The service of ordination for lay ministers reveals the essential focus and the basic meaning of the commitment. The ordaining minister says to the person being ordained. "Your work and your worship are intimately interwoven. In fact, they are not separate at all. Your work grows out of your worship and your worship grows out of your work. (Name), do you come today to acknowledge that the place where you work is as holy as the place where you worship?"

"I do." (Kneels) "Enabled by Christ's love for me, I shall endeavor to make each day's work a sacrament."[15]

The ordination of lay ministers continues with great strength at the Church of the Saviour. At present, the church is functioning in seven different worshiping communities specifically related to ministries in the world. The issues around which these ministries are formed include health care, housing, refugees, vocations, spiritual renewal, etc.

The religious education of lay ministers include counseling, liturgical life, community action, retreats, coffee house dialogue, and specific courses. The latter include Old and New Testament studies, Christian doctrine, Christian ethics, and stewardship. There is a strong emphasis on spiritual growth as a basic resource for ministries in the world.[16]

While we see the value of using the word *ordination* for the public celebration of the commissioning of lay persons for ministry, it appears to be somewhat confusing to do so. The ordination of clergy is a high need with clear reference to the distinctive ministries of word, sacrament, and order. The language of consecration (to the universal priesthood of all believers) is symbolic of this full ministry without getting us into the somewhat awkward language of the Church of the Saviour ("professional and nonprofessional ministers").

The main concern we have is for the up-grading of the expectations of laity for full-time ministry wherever they serve. And, we need a great increase in our expectations about education for consecration along with the institution of various times for the liturgical celebration of consecration in the church year and in the life span of individual members.

Several churches have sought to raise these expectations but have encountered difficulties in respect to denominational norms or other issues. Various attempts to up-grade the preparation of laity for ministry are extant, nevertheless.

We strongly urge that experimental educational efforts be inaugurated and that existing programs be more widely accepted.

One such experimental program is called Affirmation Training and has been written and employed widely by John and Adrianne Carr of the Candler School of Theology at Emory University. The program is built clearly on the premise that confirmation is a repeatable experience and that "each of us needs new confirmations of faith as he or she moves into new stages in their personal pilgrimages."[17] The program assumes that persons who are seeking to deepen their commitment or who are wanting to focus their ministries in new and specific ways will enroll. The topics dealt with in the study include the following: (1) You Are Believed In; (2) You Are the Church; (3) You Are Free; (4) You Are a Minister; (5) You Are a Disciple; (6) You Are a Steward; (7) You Are an Actor; (8) You Are Chosen; (9) You Are Commissioned. The educational and counseling program ends with a commissioning service which features a charge written specifically for each person, the laying on of hands, and the prayer of affirmation. The service can take place before the entire congregation or at a special time. Persons do serious study; take assignments which include biblical research and concrete efforts to live out what is being learned in their daily lives.

While the Carrs use the concept of commissioning it is clear that they are moving in a similar direction to the concept of consecration.

The issues of the kind and quality of education for the ordination of clergy or the consecration of lay professionals are under study today in fresh ways. These matters are far-reaching and are exceedingly important. The issues are being addressed by both denominational and ecumenical studies. The most recent ecumenical manifestation of this concern to refine our understandings and practices in respect to ordained ministry is the World Council of Churches' document, *Baptism, Eucharist and Ministry,* It is interesting to note that this study calls for a movement toward the mutual recognition of all ordained ministries (both men and women) and a strengthening of the conception of ordained ministry without undermining the ministry of the whole people. Ordination is seen as a consecration as well.

> Because Jesus came as one who serves (Mark 10:45; Luke 22:27), to be set apart means to be consecrated to service. Since ordination is essentially a setting apart with prayer for the gift of the Holy Spirit, the authority of the ordained ministry is not to be understood as the possession of the ordained person but as a gift for the continuing edification of the body in and for which the minister has been ordained. Authority has the character of responsibility before God and is exercised with the cooperation of the whole community.
>
> Therefore, ordained ministers must not be autocrats or impersonal functionaries. Although, called to exercise wise and loving leadership on the basis of the Word of God, they are bound to the faithful in interdependence and reciprocity.[18]

Little attention is given to the specific educational preparation of ordained ministers. The assumption is that such preparation will be substantial in respect to scripture, theology, prayer, and spirituality and that it will deal with social and human realities in the contemporary world. Denominational studies are inclined to be much more comprehensive and critical.

The striking thing about the World Council positions on ministry is that there is no discussion of the specific forms of ministry lay persons can assume and no discussion of any educational or liturgical ways to extend and celebrate such ministries. While other studies sponsored by the World Council have emphasized strongly the ministry of the laity, this most recent study focuses almost exclusively on ordination of clergy. A much wider stance is needed in which the ordination of clergy is balanced with the consecration of laity for specific ministries within and beyond the church in the world.

Liturgy: Lay Consecration

In addition to the liturgies referred to above, described by Elizabeth O'Connor at Church of the Saviour and by John and Adrianne Carr of Candler seminary, there are other options for services of consecration with lay people. Probably the primary liturgy we should consider is the service of baptismal renewal (confirmation) we have described already in discussing baptism and confirmation. If baptism is, in fact, the ordaining sacrament of every Christian, then it follows that baptismal renewal is bound to be some specification of the baptismal commitment. This will be so even when no specific ministry is indicated because the renewal of a basic faith affirmed in the past is necessarily undertaken in relation to new, present-life situations. When a service of baptismal renewal becomes the occasion for commitment of an individual or group to specific ministries in the church or the world, then there needs to be added to the liturgy a simple commissioning section which will contain a description of the ministry, a charge to the person to be faithful to it, and a response of commitment. This part of the service is directly analogous to the baptismal vows themselves. The renewal would follow immediately, with the individual consecrated receiving the sign of the cross on the forehead with water with the words, "Remember your baptism and be thankful," or with the laying on of hands with a "confirming" formula such as, "(Name), the power of the Holy Spirit work within you, that, having been born through water and the Spirit, you may continue to be a faithful witness of Jesus Christ. Amen."[19]

There are other possibilities in the lexicon of available liturgies for services of consecration of lay persons to specific ministries. There is in the Episcopal *BCP* a brief liturgy, titled, *A Form of Commitment to Christian Service*.[20] It is specifically intended for someone wishing to make or renew a commitment "to the service of Christ in the world." It is understood as a reaffirmation of baptismal promises and the rubrics suggest that questions and answers from the baptismal liturgy be used.

The Lutheran book of *Occasional Services* contains liturgies for the "Recognition of Ministries in the Congregation" and "Affirmation of the Vocation of Christians in the World."[21] Both services should be considered forms of baptismal renewal and begin with the words, "Dear Christian friends: Baptized into the priesthood of Christ we all are called to offer ourselves to the Lord of the Church in thanksgiving for what he has done and continues to do for us." In the service for ministry in the congregation, after a pledge to "follow our Lord's example of humble service," the rite prescribes specific prayers for ministries of worship, education, witness, service, and stewardship. In the service affirming a vocation in the world the candidate is asked, "Having determined to live out your baptismal covenant as _____, will you endeavor to pattern your life and service after our Lord, Jesus Christ?" The person responds, "Yes, with God's help." The liturgy concludes with this eloquent prayer: "Almighty God, look with favor upon these persons in their commitment to serve in Christ's name. Give them courage, patience, and vision; and strengthen us all in our Christian vocation of witness to the world and of service to others; through Jesus Christ our Lord. Amen." An alternate concluding prayer echoes St. Paul's appreciation for the manifold gifts of the people of God.

The United Methodist book of occasional services, *Blessings and Consecrations*,[22] contains an order for commitment to Christian service, which is an "edition" of the form found in the *BCP*. The volume also contains liturgies for recognition of leaders in the church, for church school workers, and for those engaged in music ministries.

The *Abingdon Manual of Installation Services*[23] contains many consecration services which are of widely uneven quality, some excellent, some excessively wordy and colloquial.

We need in our life together in the church these recurring small dramas which articulate and celebrate the many forms of lay commitment. They help focus on the necessary work which we Christians are called to do; they demonstrate to us our mission's great variety and they help us to rethink the ways we may be in ministry in the life of the church and in our occupations throughout the cycles of our personal lives. These occasions of affirmation should not be forced on people. The liturgical and educational program involving such services needs to be flexibly administered. Personal sense of need for renewal and public commitment must be a critical concern. No pressure should be applied to people to do something they are not ready to do. The focus needs to be on the pilgrimage of a personal life *within* the pilgrimage of the whole people of God.

According to the logic of our argument in this chapter, ordination is one of the forms of baptismal renewal, since baptism is the fundamental "ordaining" sacrament of every Christian. This point is a least implied in some of the new ordinals. At the beginning of the "examination" in the United Methodist ordinal the bishop says:

> My brothers and sisters,
> you are to be ordained to the ministry of elders
> in the church of Jesus Christ.
> All baptized Christians
> are called to share Christ's ministry
> of love and service in the world,
> to the glory of God
> and for the redemption of the human family.
> As an elder in the church,
> you are called to share in the ministry of Christ
> and of the whole church:
> by preaching the Word of God. . . .[24]

This is a clear affirmation of the universal ministry. Would that this point were as clearly made in all ordinals and that they all had, in an unambiguous way, the character of baptismal renewal. In general, though, our churches are excellently served by the well-formed new ordinals which have recently appeared.[25]

In addition to liturgies of ordination many denominations now have services for receiving new pastors into local churches.[26]

Notes

1. Elizabeth O'Connor, *Call to Commitment: The Story of the Church of the Saviour* (New York: Harper & Row, 1963).

2. Max Thurian, *Consecration of the Layman* (Baltimore: Helicon, 1963), p. 90.

3. Ibid., p. 84.

4. Ibid., p. 99.

5. See Ralph A. Keifer, "Response: The RCIA and Sacramental Efficiency" in *Worship* 56, 4 (July, 1982), p. 335. Keifer rejoices in the epiphany notion of sacraments in the Roman Church but decries certain recent magisterial documents which return to a narrow view of sacraments as the sole way of bestowing grace.

6. Alexander Schmemann, *For the Life of the World* (Crestwood, N.Y.: St. Vlademir's Seminary Press, 1973), p. 93.

7. Ibid.

8. George McCauley, "The Priest: A Simple Reminder," in *Sacraments for Secular Man* (New York: Herder and Herder, 1969).

9. Walter J. Burghardt, "What is a Priest?" in *The Sacraments*, ed. Michael Taylor (New York: Alba House, 1981), p. 167.

10. Thurian, *Consecration of the Layman*, p. 149.

11. Hans Küng, *On Being a Christian* (New York: Doubleday and Co., 1976), p. 439.

12. Erik Erikson, "Identity and the Life Cycle," in *Psychological Issues* 1, 1 (New York: International University Press, 1959), p. 142.

13. Ibid., p. 110.

14. O'Connor, *Call to Commitment*, p. 104.

15. Ibid., p. 105.

16. See Elizabeth O'Connor, *The New Community* (New York: Harper & Row, 1980).

17. John and Adrianne Carr, *Affirmation Training*. An unpublished manuscript, p. 1.

18. *Baptism, Eucharist and Ministry*, Faith and Order Paper No. 111 (Geneva: World Council of Churches, 1982), pp. 22-23.

19. *We Gather Together*, p. 16.

20. *Book of Common Prayer*, p. 420f.

21. *Occasional Services*, p. 143ff and p. 147ff.

22. *Blessings and Consecrations*, Supplemental Worship Resources 14 (Nashville: Abingdon Press, 1984).

23. E. Jane Mall, *Abingdon Manual of Installation Services* (Nashville: Abingdon Press, 1983).

24. *An Ordinal: The United Methodist Church* (Nashville: The United Methodist Publishing House, 1979), p. 39.

25. See note 24 above; *BCP*, p. 510ff; *The Rites V. II*, p. 25ff; *Occasional Services*, pp. 192ff.

26. *BCP*, p. 559ff; *Occasional Services*, p. 218ff; *Blessings and Consecrations*, p. 28ff.

Chapter 13

Adult Baptism: The Sacrament of Evangelization

Everyone agrees that there is one baptism, but there is disagreement about when it should be received.[1] While infants and children were probably baptized along with their parents in the New Testament church, the primary emphasis was on the evangelization of adults who had heard the good news of the gospel and were baptized into new life in Christ. The apostles and members of the early church were in a minority situation. Adult baptism was a dramatic and profound symbol of dying and rising with Christ—dying to the old life and its values and practices and rising in total commitment to the new life in Christ within the close-knit body of Christ, the church.

At great personal risk the faithful reached out to Jews and Gentiles alike in affirmation of Jesus' admonition, recorded in Matthew 28:18-20, to "go therefore and make disciples of all nations, baptizing them in the name of the Father, and of the Son and of the Holy Spirit, teaching them to observe all that I have commanded you; and lo, I am with you always, to the close of the age." Here we see evangelism, education, liturgy, and the ethical commandments integrated in Jesus' words. These words no doubt reflect the reality of the life of those who, like Paul, preached the good news that to live fully was to be in Christ both now and in the life to come.

During the first four centuries the pattern that developed increasingly was one in which those seeking this new life were asked to commit themselves to become learners (disciples) of the way, to become catechumens (hearers). After one to three years of participation in study, ethical reflection and testing, worship and service, they were elected to prepare for the Paschal experience at Easter, where they would "passover" into their new life through baptism by immersion, confirmation by the laying on of hands, and communion.

239

Exorcisms and scrutinies were important parts of the process, aiding the candidates to put away or renounce evil (the Devil, in these liturgies) and give allegiance to Christ. The wearing of the sign of the cross and the cutting of the hair, the tonsure, were ways that announced to the world that the person was radically different in his or her commitments than before.

We get a picture of this change in Colossians 3. "If then you have been raised with Christ, seek the things that are above. . . . Put to death therefore . . . immorality, impurity, passion, evil desire, and covetousness which is idolatry . . . and put on . . . compassion, kindness, lowliness, meekness and patience, forbearing one another. . . . The new nature is after the image of God, the creator. In this estate the divisions of the past die. Here there cannot be Greek or Jew, circumcised and uncircumcised, barbarian, Scythian, slave, free man, but Christ is all, and in all" (Col. 3:1-11). Baptism was a radical step which moved persons toward a universal justice and equality. Of course, such a radical justice is very much needed today. At its deepest levels baptism is the symbol of our unity as God's family.

While infant baptism carries these same meanings in that the child is engrafted into the body of Christ in which the life of love, trust, and justice is incarnate, it is a fact that today great numbers of persons are not baptized as infants and nurtured into this quality of life. They grow to adulthood with values that are oriented toward self-protection or commitment to power, position, possessions, or political entities which become idols they worship instead of the true God.

We are now living in a post-Christendom period of history in which an honest, nonmanipulative evangelization is required. This implies announcing and living the good news of Christ's abundant life that will have integrity and will be seen as authentic by those who are experiencing the despair and alienation.

There is a need for a process of evangelization which integrates the proclamation of the gospel with genuine opportunities to learn (including an honest education which encourages examination of the claims of the gospel as well as the quality of life possible), with the liturgical celebrations of the community, along with the corporate witnessing to the validity of Christ's life in the ethical decisions we make in personal and social arenas.

The culminating action parable for this spiritual pilgrimage for adults is baptism. This is a baptism which includes several important steps which reveal genuine concern for the persons preparing for the sacrament. These steps include (1) careful listening to the deep needs of persons involved, (2) joyous invitations are given, (3) thoughtful dialogues are made possible, (4) free decisions to explore in more depth are made, (5) careful and honest education concerning the great central beliefs and practices progress at the rate each person can proceed, (6) warmth of caring and love are experienced with sponsors and the church family in the worship and actions of the community (including participation in open communion if desired), (7) after a decision to give wholehearted commitment to become a member of Christ's body in ministry to the world, there is final preparation for dying and rising with Christ through baptism, confirmation, and communion. This total process buttresses the strong action parable of baptism.

Of course, in a nonmanipulative process, the person can ask for more time to reflect, or decide not to be baptized without being rejected or made to feel that he or she is totally outside of God's grace.

This process should focus on the lifelong nature of the baptismal commitment—one which implies commitment to continue to grow in faith. The resurrected life of Christ can come to earth in every baptized person. As the joint statement of the Lutheran-United Methodist bilateral team on baptism says, "By this growth, baptized believers should manifest to the world the new race of a redeemed humanity, which puts an end to all human estrangement based, for example, on race, sex, age, class, nationality, and disabling conditions."[2] Now, such growth in living out our baptisms into Christ's ministering body will not be easy. This quality of new life will call for repeated dying and rising as we see and experience the forces in society arrayed against such love and justice. A new life in Christ calls for radical justice, inclusiveness, and a forgiving and reconciling spirit. Moreover, such a life prompts us to *risk*, to leap out beyond our neat and tidy securities. This style of life can lead to many small crucifixions and resurrections—but all in confidence that Christ will live in and through such risks.

The Sacrament of Evangelization

Baptism, so interpreted, can be seen in our time as the sacrament of evangelization. This evangelization must avoid the demonic forms of manipulation and deception which sometimes accompany the concept. We need a rebirth of open communication concerning the good news in Christ which does not put down all other religions, which does not boast about the achievements of the church or seek to hide her failures. We need to recover the joyous sharing of the nature of the grace of God which is in the very fabric of life but which Christ lived fully and clearly so that we can perceive its truth and discover its power to renew us over and over throughout life. Such a life inspires us and also calls us to die to loyalties not as full of grace. Such an evangelism cannot pit one group against another, cannot split preaching from teaching or liturgy from ethical living, cannot call persons to close their minds and quit probing the truth of Christ's way of life in comparison to optional claims. It is also an evangelization which realizes that we hear the good news in many ways—through interaction with those who proclaim and witness in words, but more powerfully through relationships of caring, trust, searching, and honest confrontation of differences. We can help persons discover for themselves the power of the gospel of love as they share meals with us—and respond to the power of Christ's self-giving in the celebration of the meal that has become sacred to us. The power of the eucharist to unify persons in loving relationships through Christ's gift of himself cannot be underestimated. Also, of course, the eucharist cannot be misused as a more subtle form of manipulation. It must be an open meal, and it must have those present who have responded freely and honestly. More crucial, of course, is the necessity to communicate with those with whom we have taken communion about the meaning of the Christian life and invite them to consider honest preparation to become a committed member of the body of Christ in baptism. Here again is where education and evangelism, liturgy and ethical living proceed hand in hand.

Baptism and God's Grace

Since God's grace is profoundly built into the very fabric of life itself, baptism does not provide grace in some substantialistic way. Baptism is grace because it is the symbol of new relationships of love and trust with God and others—relationships which, in fact, create an environment of grace, acceptance, forgiveness, and reconciliation. Baptism of adults symbolizes their total affirmation of the ultimate reality of God's grace and their entry into the body of Christ, the community committed to celebrating and making visible the grace of God which has been freely given to every child of God.

Alexander Schmemann, the Orthodox thinker, traces how the Western church contributed to making baptism into a magical rite in the minds of so many. By separating the essence of baptism from the form, the Western church made baptism into a "means of grace" which could be given or taken away as an entrance to eternal life. In this way baptism was used as a means of conquering original sin and giving grace as a substance distinct from the relationships of love, acceptance, and renewal which were and are the real grace. Schme-

mann believes that this pattern was the "original sin" of all postpatris-
tic Western theology. In this approach to all of the sacraments and
baptism in particular "the form is no longer the 'epiphany,' but only
the external sign and thus the guarantee that a particular 'essense' has
been duly bestowed and communicated." Strangely the battles over
the validity of baptism took place around the issue of which form was
most correct—immersion, sprinkling, pouring.

Baptism should not contribute to such divisions. Schmemann admits
that the Eastern church also fell into such legalistic approaches to the
sacraments, but at base the Eastern view of the sacraments is grounded in creation theology which is more wholistic. Schmemann believes
that in the early church

> grace meant above all that very victory over all dichotomies—
> "form" and "essence," "spirit" and "matter," "sign" and "reality"—
> which is made manifest in the sacrament and, indeed, in the whole
> life of the church and which ultimately is the victory of Christ
> Himself, in whom and by whom the "forms" of this world can truly
> be, truly communicate, truly fulfill, that which they represent: the
> epiphany in "this world" of the Kingdom of God and of its "new
> life." Thus the grace of Baptism was the very event: a man dying
> and rising again "in the likeness" and "after the pattern" of Christ's
> Death and Resurrection; it was the gift to him not of "something"
> resulting from these events, but of that unique and totally new
> possibility: truly to die with Christ, truly to rise again with Him so
> that he may walk in newness of life.[3]

This *is* grace.

Schmemann makes a profound contribution when he marks the
meaning of a new view of sacramental life. The revolutionary nature
of this thinking means an end to the dichotomy of life and religion. He
maintains that "Christ did not come to give us a new religion, even if
He is the trusted one. Christ didn't come to add to the existing
religions another one which would synthesize them. . . . He has come
to give new life to us and, through us, to the world. . . . The new life is
in the Kingdom, and the Church is the presence of the power and
glory of the Kingdom in this world."[4]

Baptism is a powerful symbol of the grace of God which was made
brilliantly and powerfully visible in Christ and in which the baptized
participates joyously, accepting the responsibility to continue making
visible such grace throughout his or her life in varying ministries
within and beyond the body of Christ.

Baptism is an ordination of those who are engrafted into the body of

Christ. The church is called to continue making visible God's grace, love, and radical justice in the world. The vocation of every member of the body is *ministry*—the universal priesthood of all believers. For adults who are deciding to enter this community of faith the issue of their life's vocation is usually uppermost. This is true even if they have embraced one or more occupations during their pilgrimage. When they respond affirmatively to the good news in Christ they are seriously rethinking the purpose of their life and to what they should give themselves until the end of their earthly life. Baptism makes us equal members of Christ's church as clergy and laity. We must then have opportunity to experience this acceptance and to understand the meaning of such a ministry in a world such as ours. This need is one which must be met in any approach to preparation for adult baptism. It is also crucial for infant baptism in relation to the education of the parents, sponsors, and the total congregation. Children can minister unto others in subtle but penetrating ways. In a sense, adults are becoming little children again in order to learn of Christ's way and to be open to and aware of God's grace in every facet of life. However, adults are also able and ready to critique the faith with rigor. Therefore, preparation of adults for baptism must include solid food and not just milk.

The Emerging Consensus about the Threefold Nature of Adult Initiation

This emerging consensus is based on a renewed interest in research on the rituals of initiation in the early church and throughout history, the liturgical movement of our time, and a recognition in biblical and theological studies that catechetical and liturgical praxis has been the seedbed for the theologizing which has taken place, especially up through the patristic period.[5]

These studies, ecumenically done, have revealed a pattern of initiation which unified baptism, confirmation by chrism or the laying on of hands, and the celebration of the eucharist. This pattern has been normative for the Orthodox community throughout history. The Roman Catholic Church revised its rite of initiation during the Second Vatican Council and returned to the catechumenate of the second to fourth centuries with its steps leading to full initiation by baptism, confirmation, and communion, usually celebrated at Easter, with post-baptismal catechesis until Pentecost. Increasing numbers of Protestant study groups are coming to a similar conclusion.

The Episcopal study on holy baptism is a case in point. As we indicated in our discussion on infant baptism "the unified rite of baptism, consignation, and eucharist was set forth as the standard." This unified rite is not only redemptive in meaning but it is also a "commissioning for ministry," a strengthening of persons for combat against evil, and an ordination of the laity for creative ministries. "It sets one within the people of God, the holy priesthood; it brings one into the eucharistic fellowship. There is nothing left over that must be said at a later stage because it was not said at Baptism."[6]

Protestant theological scholars such as James White, William Willimon, John Westerhoff, and others agree with this trend.[7] The most perceptive and knowledgeable Catholic interpreter of the new position in respect to the new rite of adult initiation is probably Aidan Kavanagh. He affirms the focus on adult initiation as the norm but states that "whenever it is deemed advisable to initiate a Christian, regardless of age, that Christian should be initiated fully and completely by water baptism, the 'sealing' of confirmation, and the first eucharistic communion."[8]

This unified rite is especially powerful for adults who have decided to turn from one way of life to the Christ-centered life. Some think that the essential matter is a subjective turning toward Christ, a conversion experience, and think such an experience must take place before adult baptism. The catechumenate process recognizes the importance of the conversion of the person but sees this more as a process than as a single experience.

Let us now look more carefully at the process of evangelization of adults envisaged in the new Roman Catholic catechumenate, visually and physically enriched by the Orthodox rites, and projected somewhat tentatively by interested Protestant groups.

The Potential Integration of Evangelism, Education, Liturgy, and Ethics in the Catechumenate

Since the publication of the new rite of initiation of adults many Roman Catholic parishes have inaugurated the catechumenate pattern with four distinct but interrelated periods.[9] These periods take place within a one to three year span or more and include:

(1) *The Precatechumenate*—where members and clergy form parish teams for outreach to inquirers, through visitation, announcements, posters, radio spots, and most importantly, through the integrity of the life and witness of the faith community. Those who respond meet with the team to discuss the hard questions, to listen to the hurts and needs of the inquirers, to nurture the inquirers to the

point of deciding to become catechumens. During this time the good news is preached and celebrated in the congregation to which the inquirers are invited. Sponsors for inquirers are selected and relationships of care and trust are developed. Sometimes inquirers have professed personal subjective experiences of release or conversion during this period. Others do not, but wish to become catechumens and commit themselves to worship, education or catechesis, and action in ethical living in relation to the church's witness in the world of tough personal and social issues. If the inquirers freely decide to become catechumens they are invited to participate in a congregational celebration of the Rite of Becoming Catechumens. Here, it is clear that they are a genuine part of the community but are free to decide not to be initiated into the body of Christ—without pressure or judgment.

(2) *The Catechumenate*—the learners become students in catechetical classes, participate fully in the community's life, receive love and support from their sponsors, seek to explore the radical nature of the changes called for in the new life in Christ (in attitude, beliefs, in actions), test and critique these experiences, worship with the congregation, but are dismissed for further catechetical work during the eucharist. (Here is where our model differs significantly in that we see open communion as a part of the nurture of those wanting to relate deeply to Christ. Therefore such catechumens would participate in the life of dying and rising, of celebration and thanksgiving inherent in the eucharist, if they so wish.) After study, participation, and individual counseling the catechumen decides to give himself or herself fully to become a member of the body of Christ and to enter the period of specific preparation for initiation. This second period of the catechumenate is where honest education will encourage full discussion of problem areas, doubts, fears, possible formulation of belief which fit with the person's honest self-understanding, possible conceptions and feelings about the nature of commitment to Christ and the embracing of specific forms of ministry in the future. If this period is done with integrity, it will move at the pace appropriate for each person in his or her life situation. Some may move through this period in a few weeks or months; others may need a few years; others may decide to delay or drop out. Christian acceptance and love must guide the relationships in order that pressure and manipulation will not be the ethos out of which decisions for the Christian life come. Decisions to prepare for full initiation in baptism, confirmation, and communion are celebrated in the Rite of Election and the enrollment of the names of catechumens before the congregation.

(3) *The Lenten Period of Illumination*—during these weeks the candidate is assigned a spiritual director with whom he or she prepares

for the final step of commitment before the congregation at Easter. Stories of personal pilgrimages are shared; motivations are examined; prayers and fasting deepen the quest; the rites of exorcism and scrutiny are conducted in order to push the candidate to face the realities of personal and corporate evil and dehumanization ever-present and to turn solidly toward Christ's new life of love and humanization. The candidates are prepared to understand baptism, the laying-on-of-hands, and the eucharist before the Easter vigil and the final celebration but also after the celebration during the period between Easter and Pentecost known as the mystagogia. The Eastern church employs the sacramental rites with less cognitive preparation *before* in the view that the rites themselves are such powerful educators and communicators of the gospel that they should be experienced first and then understood cognitively later. Some of both approaches seems advisable, if persons are not to fall into the experience of initiation without conscious decision. This period of illumination is climaxed by the Easter all night vigil and the high celebration of baptism, increasingly by immersion, the laying on of hands and the sealing of the Holy Spirit, and the procession to the eucharist.

(4) *The Period of Mystagogia*—this period ends with Pentecost and is a joyous time of parties and the enjoyment of the new relationships in Christ coupled with meditations on the deeper meaning of the gospel, sharing the eucharistic celebration and deciding on and preparing to be in specific ministries, and doing simple works of charity.

In some parishes the person who has been the catechist helps the neophytes unpack the meaning of their experience of the gospel, a spiritual director helps them to listen to the Lord "in order to discern their gifts and to offer them in service," and the priest celebrates the eucharist and other sacraments with them and counsels them about wider ministries of the church in the world, and the sponsors help them share their stories with the congregation and with persons who may be entering the precatechumen period—as the cycle of evangelization, education, liturgy, and personal and corporate ethical living starts over again with new participants. Mystagogia means to learn about the mysteries experienced in the great sacraments of initiation.

Variations and creative refinements of this process of adult initiation can be found in several fine books by persons who have designed and experienced differing approaches to the catechumenate. We have found James B. Dunning's *New Wine, New Wine Skins: Pastoral Implications of the Rite of Initiation of Adults* (Sadler, 1981) to be exceptionally innovative and sensitive to the necessity for non-manipulative planning and administering of the catechumenate process. Dunning recommends designing the process for the unique life situations and needs of each person. In order not to rush people he suggests a pattern which continues over a two-year period of time for most potential members. The *Precatechumenate* will start after Easter with the visitations, conversations, social gatherings with parishioners during the summer, the personal interviews and formal sessions from September through November. The *Catechumenate period* will go from January of one year to January of the next with catechetical sessions four times each month (once a month in the summer). The *Election* or decision time is January of the second year. The *Illumination* is from the first Sunday of Lent until Holy Week climaxing in the initiation at Easter. The *Mystagogia* is from Easter to Pentecost of the second year.

Several parishes have found a one-year schedule quite workable, starting in June with the formation of a core group of lay leaders and the precatechumenate and ending with the mystagogia from Easter to Pentecost.[10] Various Protestant approaches to evangelism reveal a similar sensitivity to the open communication needed in authentic evangelism, education, liturgy, and ethical life. Some of these integrate study of the Christian life with careful listening to those to be evangelized, with vigorous critiquing of the Christian claims and styles of life, with attention to sacramental understandings, with concern for ministry and service being central. One of the more engaging of these approaches is called service evangelism.[11] The service evangelism approach, developed by Richard Armstrong, focuses on the deeper needs of those being visited, with attention to relationships, rigorous exploration of the essentials of the gospel, involvement in efforts to serve those visited at the points of mutually identified need. This service is with no strings attached. Persons who respond positively to this incarnational approach are then nurtured and educated within the worshiping congregation toward commitment and baptism. Open communication and a non-mechanistic spirit come through as major strengths of this Protestant expression. There are many other Protestant approaches to evangelism, but few genuinely integrate evangelism, education, liturgy and real engagement with the ethical dimensions of the faith—within the context of a sacramental understanding of life.

Adult Initiation and the Stages of Faith

Adults at each of the stages of ritualization of faith can be motivated deeply to find a new integration for the self, an orientation of the total being to someone or something of ultimate value. This is a profound need young adults begin to sense as they move out beyond the securities of home, family, the nurturing institutions of school and community. There is a need for discovery of an honestly tested spiritual center for the self. This need has intellectual dimensions, in that the young adult is seeking to form a world view and an ideology or philosophy of life to which to give the self. This is a crucial need. Without such a centering the self will not find a sense of direction and purpose so greatly needed in order to step out firmly if not boldly into the future. The young adult also needs to find intimate relationships which have care and fidelity in them. Love is sought and found by many in various levels of significance. However, sexual fidelity and love need to be supported by a community of loving and trusting relationships. The church can become such a community when authentically embraced by the young adult.

Young adults who have been baptized as infants or children and who have been conventionally related to the church are often ripe for a deeper probing of the nature of their actual loyalties and sense of commitment. A program similar to that of the catechumenate (which is not repetitive but builds on past preparation and experience) could be exceedingly powerful for young adults and lead to the celebration of consecration for lay ministries through vocation or to confirmation as a repeatable sacrament. The need to hammer out a Stage IV faith is real—a faith in which the person internalizes the Christian system of beliefs and practices, critiques the system "as a system" in relation to all other experiences the young adult is having and the widening knowledge of optional beliefs, styles of life, attitudes toward self, others, and God which he or she has grasped.

This searching is normative for lively and honest young adults. However, some fear to move out in faith. They may wish to remain in the meaningful orientation of a conventional faith which became the organizing center for the self in the adolescent years. Personal equilibrium was found there and, for some, the young-adult years can remain relatively secure and cause little disequilibrium. Usually, however, if such persons are allowed to reveal to themselves and others their actual concerns, anxieties, fears, or areas of confusion or lack of understanding, they will admit to enough disequilibrium to motivate them to search more deeply and honestly for a more adequate and growing faith. Each of the structures of faith may be explored with such persons—how they think about the faith, how they deal with moral and ethical decisions in light of the Christian story, how they relate to persons and groups with very different values and practices, how they deal with Christian symbols, what they make authoritative in their lives, etc.

Great numbers of young adults have not taken the church seriously and are out of communication with those who live and share the good news. These persons, however, may be profoundly in need of the good news and are very real candidates for sensitive and authentic evangelization. We need core groups of adults, including growing young adults, who will identify and seek to listen to and communicate with such persons. The catechumenate approach has the advantage of a precatechumate period of inquiry and testing as well as stages of development within the process, during which time the individual may agree to continue, go "on hold," or discontinue. The other positive factor is the opportunity to experience the accepting, loving community while at the same time critiquing the Christian faith "as a system" with openness. The emotional power of this process of intellectual probing, personal reflection of actual values revealed in behavior, participation in the small group and corporate celebrations is great. The full commitment to the new life in Christ in baptism, confirmation, and communion at Easter or some other significant time in the church year can amount either to reorganization of the self at a deeper level or a genuine conversion during which the person leaves one style of life and set of values and turns wholeheartedly to Christ's life of love, trust, and justice.

Fowler has found that persons can have conversion experiences within a particular stage or as they move from one stage to another. When searching for a new grounding or equilibrium for the self they recapitulate the issues and concerns of previous stages of faith through which they have moved.[12] This means that earlier problems, fixations, fears are worked through in the process of conversion—if in fact, the individual is freed up to grow to a new level of commitment and integration.

This process, of course, is true for middle or older adults. In terms of Erikson's insights, middle adults are normally working on the matter of their significance in terms of what they have or have not been able to generate that is important to their children, others, themselves. The recognition of the inadequacies of their lives comes crashing in on them. Feelings of guilt are mixed with feelings of meaning and well-being. Middle adults are often open for a recapitulation of their earlier experiences in terms of the dynamics of their actual faith. Fowler finds middle adults to be the most likely candidates for the struggles of a Stage V or VI faith. The paradoxical nature of life and the sense of incompleteness in respect to previous faith images become the disequilibrating forces which open middle adults to new growth. This is true for those within the Christian community in certain ways, but much more so for middle adults who have organized their lives around less adequate values. Again, older adults, while searching for integrity and simplicity in their lives, are also open to the quest for a universal faith which can bring genuine unity to a world in strife and suspicion. In other words, adults of every age and state of need can become men and women with a profound inner ache for spiritual wholeness, integration, and sense of ultimate meaning. The evangelization of such persons beyond the faith community and the awakening of those within the community can be a part of our understanding of baptism. It is in baptism that we recognize God's grace and love at the heart of all of life—now and then. Such an awareness can become a joyous, integrating first experience for many adults who have not known it, and it can be a lifelong process of fulfillment and renewal for those who have been engrafted into this community of life-in-its-fullness.

Religious Education for Adult Baptism

In this model of adult initiation it is clear that the catechumenate process as a whole is powerfully educative. The listening and dialogues, the friendships created, the rich liturgies and preaching, the exposures to the great beliefs, the sharing of the stories of faith, traditions and informal rituals of the community—all become part of the learning that takes place. Religious education, however, should be more than socialization into the community. It should preserve the integrity of the freedom of the individual to question, reconstruct, and internalize the learnings. It should involve the whole person—not only the mind but the emotions, the behavior, and the will. The catechumenate process, when conducted with openness and yet conviction can bring about a fine balance. The warmth of relationships created, the opportunity for sharing personal faith pilgrimages and hearing those of others, the participation in the high drama of the liturgies of election and decision, especially the sacraments with the use of the earthly elements of water, oil, touching—all can penetrate deeply into the psyche of the persons involved. The attention to the ethical behavior of the catechumens in the interaction with the congregation, especially through the sponsors, can penetrate the consciousness and conscience of the candidate and bring about changes in behavior in an environment which is supportive of significant changes in lifestyle and values. The preaching concerning the gospel and the nature of the mysteries being celebrated can be powerfully educative of mind and heart. Of course, the classes or learning groups are directly related to honest explorations of the nature of the Christian gospel. While these interactions should guarantee freedom of belief and integrity of thought, they should also be genuine communities of love and care in which the honest reservations of persons are seen as signs of growth and not as signs of spiritual resistance. The process followed by the catechist or educational leadership team should be sensitive to the unique experiences brought by each learner and to the contributions each can make as the questions are raised and the faith pilgrimages shared. The catechumens can be active in leadership roles in the learning group and not be "hearers" only as earlier catechumens no doubt tended to be.

The context of the education is crucial. Certainly it must center around the central issues of the nature of the new life in Christ, with special attention to the nature of the church as the body of Christ, extending Christ's ministries into the world. The nature of the universal priesthood of all believers and the fact that the catechumens can become active ministers in their every day lives are important issues with which to deal. A sound biblical, theological, and historical grounding should be sought in sensitive relationship to the actual life issues the learners bring with them. Here is where individualization is essential as different persons bring different backgrounds and unique questions and perceptions. There should be maximum "testing" and checking with the learners concerning the areas of major concern as well as the previous readings and studies already done. Individual learning tracks can be encouraged while at the same time keeping a strong sense of commitment to one another in the learning group.

In each church, of course, there should be the sharing of the life history of the faith community, the great stories and personalities of the past being very important to the identification of the members-to-be with the community. The great statements of faith of the past can be studied appreciatively but also analytically for what they say not only about the Christian faith but also about the people who created them. Then, opportunity can be given for the candidates to develop their own contemporary statements of faith or credos.

One approach has three major sections to it. They are: (1) *The History of Salvation*—in which contemporary biblical interpretation is opened up in reference to the central themes and stories of the Bible but always in dialogue with "our stories"; moving on then to the continuing history of salvation in the church until the present day. (2) *The Names of Jesus*—in which the names used in Old Testament times on through the New Testament are explored in terms of their original meanings but also in terms of existential meanings for the learners today. (3) *The Ultimate Questions*—in which the crucial questions of faith and life are raised and grouped so that honest analysis and discussion can take place, using the resources of the faith community and the biblical, theological, ethical, and historical resources already studied.[13]

Liturgy

The commentary on the liturgies of initiation found at the end of chapter 8 is applicable to the baptism of persons of all ages.

Notes

1. The Anabaptist emphasis on adult conversion and personal rebirth as a subjective experience required before baptism is very much alive, however (sometimes leading to re-baptism). See Donald Bridge and David Phypers, *The Water That Divides: The Baptism Debate* (Downers Grove, Ill.: Intervarsity Press, 1967).

2. "A Lutheran-United Methodist Statement on Baptism," *Perkins Journal* XXXIV, 2 (Winter, 1981), p. 3.

3. Alexander Schmemann, *Of Water and the Spirit: A Liturgical Study of Baptism* (London: SPCK, 1974), p. 58.

4. Alexander Schmemann, "The Eastern Church," in *Initiation Theology*, ed. James Schmeiser (Toronto: The Anglican Book Centre, 1978), p. 56.

5. See Edward Yarnold, *The Awe-Inspiring Rites of Initiation: Baptismal Homilies of the Fourth Century* (Slough, England: St. Paul Publication, 1971).

6. Daniel B. Stevick, *Holy Baptism.* Together with a form of affirmation of baptismal vows with the laying on of hands by the Bishop (also called confirmation) (New York: Church Hymnal Press, 1973), pp. 88-89.

7. See James White, *Sacraments as God's Self-Giving* (Nashville: Abingdon Press, 1983), William H. Willimon, *Remember Who You Are: Baptism, a Model for Christian Life* (Nashville: The Upper Room, 1980), and John Westerhoff III and William H. Willimon, *Liturgy and Learning Through the Life Cycle* (New York: Seabury Press, 1980).

8. Aidan Kavanagh, *The Shape of Baptism: The Rite of Christian Initiation* (New York: Pueblo Publishing Co., 1978), p. 174.

9. See *The Rites of the Catholic Church* (New York: Pueblo Publishing Co., 1976).

10. Kenneth Bayack, *A Parish Guide to Adult Initiation* (New York: Paulist Press, 1979).

11. Richard Armstrong, *Service Evangelism* (Philadelphia: Westminister Press, 1979).

12. James W. Fowler, *Stages of Faith*, pp. 289-290.

13. James B. Dunning, *New Wine: New Wine Skins* (New York: Sadlier, 1981).

Chapter 14

Penance: The Sacrament of Confession and Reconciliation

The historic sacrament of penance has probably been the most controversial of the sacraments. Protestants correctly resisted the misuse of the sacrament by rejecting the power of priests to stand between the confessing person and God to judge what acts would make satisfaction and to grant forgiveness and absolution. The substantialistic view was rejected by Luther and the reformers. Due to considerable frustration with the way the sacrament has been administered and due to the marked decline of the practice of individual confession within the Roman Catholic Church today there has been a movement to reform the understanding of the sacrament of penance within Catholicism. The direction and tenor of the reforms auger well for fresh communication between the major faith groups concerning authentic ways to deal with the pervasive human need to confess and be reconciled with God, self, and others. Honest attempts to move penance away from legalism and substantialism toward relational and personal/corporate interpretations have led Roman Catholics to change the name from the sacrament of penance to the sacrament of reconciliation.

Protestants have come to admit that their almost exclusive emphasis on the general confession within corporate worship, while deeply significant, has not dealt adequately with the dynamics of guilt within individuals and with their need for liturgical forms which point to and make possible relationships with God, self, and the corporate body which are healing, renewing, and reconciling. Also, while a legalistic interpretation of "doing penance" is rejected, it is generally acknowledged that decisions to make restitution to those harmed through attitudes and acts of caring or service can be powerful fruits of a new life which comes from forgiveness. In short, Protestants are not as

254

rigidly opposed to some form of individual confession and renewal within the faith community as they once were. The pastoral counseling movement which was strong within Protestantism and which was an answer to the need for individual opening of the self in honesty before God has been broadened to various approaches which now are identified as pastoral care. Moreover, the moral dimensions of pastoral care are being reclaimed in fresh ways.[1] Many of these approaches now include liturgical and sacramental aspects as well as individual or group experiences which are more clearly related to counseling. Still, Protestants lack a clear understanding of the sacramental nature of reconciliation and also lack liturgies and educational experiences which enhance specific forms to help persons deal with moral or ethical failure, individual or corporate behaviors which dehumanize persons or distort community.

It is our view that the ecumenical church is in need of a deepened understanding of the sacrament of reconciliation and of liturgical and educational expressions which will help persons deal with their sense of personal and corporate alienation from God, themselves, and others.

Some of the characteristics of the sacrament of reconciliation should be as follows:

(1) The sacrament can be seen as another way of participating in the mystery of the reality which is called the kingdom of God. The community is both a present reality and an eschatological hope. The minister who administers the sacrament represents the community of faith and helps persons renew their vision of the kingdom.

As Tad Guzie says, the new approach to the sacrament of reconciliation is based, not on a judgment model, but on the celebration of the nature of God as loving and merciful. This is a celebration within the community of the faithful (who acknowledge nevertheless their tendency to separate themselves from God and the vision of the kingdom). The celebration is led by the priest who represents the other members of the church. The priest is ordained so to represent the people, but the priest (minister) does not have power to forgive any more than the other members of the church can forgive. Commenting on the new rite of penance or reconciliation in the Catholic church, Guzie says that the encounter with the minister is horizontal rather than vertical. In the liturgy the church sacramentally "proclaims its faith and gives thanks to God for the freedom with which Christ has made us free."[2] The new rite makes it clear, says Guzie, that "it is only the Lord who forgives sin; the priest declares that forgiveness in the name of the Lord and his Church. Throughout the rite, the confessor appears as a kind of 'transparency,' revealing to the penitent and leading him or her to see and proclaim the love of God. The ministry of the confessor is a ministry within and on behalf of the community of faith, not over it."[3]

If this change in understanding of confession and the absolution of the priest can genuinely take root and be communicated to Protestants and Orthodox, it is possible that there can emerge a climate in which an ecumenical approach to confession can be developed.

(2) The sacrament of reconcilation should be understood to deal with the reality of sin and not with the listing of sins which we have committed. For so long Protestants have not only resisted the idea that the priest forgives sin (rather than God through Christ in direct prayer) they have rejected the confession of small "sins" such as drinking or lying as well as the saying of "Hail Marys" or making satisfaction in some other seemingly perfunctory way. Such criticisms are being faced within Roman Catholicism, often in response to expressions of frustration with the old forms of penance. Ralph Keifer, also commenting upon the effort to reform the sacraments in the new rite, says that many Catholics have given up the sacrament "because it is not meeting the need for a more profound assessment of life. . . . This may be interpreted as a silent plea to improve pastoral practice both within and outside the moment of confession. The introduction (to the new rite) views contrition in the light of the New Testament understanding of *metanoia* (change of mind and heart): a 'profound change of the whole person by which one begins to consider, judge, and arrange' his whole life (no. 6)."[4] Such a statement moves in the direction that many Protestants could find meaningful if not exciting.

Contemporary psychotherapy is recognizing the therapeutic power of confession and making restitution for ways in which persons have injured their relationships of trust and love with others. Hobart Mowrer has emphasized the health-giving power of confession of wrongs done (according to the norms of the individual as developed over the years in his or her particular cultural setting). His definition of sin, then, relates to actions which violate the standards of moral behavior the particular person has internalized and made a part of his or her conscience. Mowrer's view of sin is not profound enough in that it does not deal with the total orientation of the person, or with the matter of transcendent unity with God, others, and self. His clinical experience, nevertheless, points to the extreme need of persons in our society to confess in a community of trust, to be forgiven by others, and to deal with guilt by taking some concrete steps to rectify the hurts of the past.[5] He believes that this state of affairs exists in society at least partly because churches have ceased to deal honestly with the sin of persons and have failed to find ways to help them find forgiveness, renewal, and mental health. Other psychotherapists have taken a somewhat similar position.[6] It seems clear that the Christian church is not communicating the whole gospel unless it is helping persons face their sense of sin (seen relationally and not legalistically), find forgiveness within the community of faith, and discover creative ways to respond in concrete forms of love and servanthood.

(3) The sacrament of reconciliation should be seen as a part of the ministry of the whole church.

The call to repentance is central to the prophetic ministry. Repentance and renewal are never to be associated only with the particular liturgy of reconciliation. There are basic realities being addressed in the proclamation of the good news, with baptism, (which symbolizes the cleansed and renewed life), with the eucharist (which gives thanks for the gift of Christ's body and blood "for the remission of sin"), in the ongoing call to "growth in grace" and the recognition of our need for honest accountability before God. The whole of life is, in fact, a process of ongoing reconciliation. This theme is also present in the attempts to reform the sacrament of penance and turn it in the direction of a process of reconciliation, not only of individuals, but of the life of the church itself.

The corporate nature of the sacrament is crucial. Protestants have made an important contribution in their strong emphasis on the church as a community of repentance, mutual forgiveness, and increasing responsibility to extend Christ's love and justice into every aspect of the social fabric.

The new Catholic rites have recognized the importance of the corporate dimensions of reconciliation while at the same time protecting the need and right of persons to experience individual confession, forgiveness and absolution. The new rite includes three liturgies which reflect this change of emphasis. They are: (a) a communal celebration with opportunity for individual confessions after or during the corporate worship, (b) a rite for the reconciliation of the individual penitent in which the priest ministers to the person as a representative of the church and the bishop (the absolution stresses the role of the church's total ministry in the church and to the world), (c) communal reconciliation without individual confession. (This liturgy recognizes the fact that general confession and absolution have been a part of the history of the early church but is an innovation today and to be employed carefully in certain circumstances where it is "lawful and even necessary to give general absolution to a number of penitents without their previous individual confession.")

These changes are stimulating ecumenical dialogue and beginning to open doors for fresh thinking about the importance of confession and reconciliation in the human pilgrimage.

(4) There is a movement away from legalism in the understanding and administration of the sacrament of penance or reconciliation. For many years the Orthodox approach to the sacrament of penance has been personal and nonlegalistic. In the Orthodox liturgy the priest and the penitent stand before an icon often representing Christ's ministry of reconciliation. The priest and the penitent are, in this sense, both in the same human situation. The priest bends toward the penitent to hear him or her confess. The priest, then, may give some counsel, may or may not suggest actions leading to satisfaction. The priest puts his stole on the head of the penitent and gives the prayer of absolution. While there are various penitential services during the year no form of general penance appears to be in operation. The Orthodox view of penance, as in other sacraments, emphasizes the personal relationship and understanding of the priest and penitent while also keeping the priest as a representative of the mystery of the kingdom.

The Orthodox emphasize the importance of direct communication with God as foundational to the development of God-centeredness. There is a tendency for Orthodox Christians to celebrate the mystery of God's revelation and to be happier with ambiguity than some other Christians. There is a stronger emphasis on art, music, and liturgical forms as symbols which point to God's revelation in Christ but do not capture or define God's actions precisely. The Orthodox value the principle of apophaticism. This principle guards the church from ever proclaiming too much, too rigidly. Anyone who claims in a moment that he or she knows what God is—in some ultimate way—or what God demands is a person with a depraved mind.[7] Such a principle helps keep legalistic interpretations of the sacraments from gaining as much credence as has sometimes been the case in the Western church.

Getting past legalism is probably the greatest issue in the further refinement and development of healthy approaches to reconciliation. We all want an atmosphere of openness, where the community will let us be ourselves in our strengths and in our sin. George McCauley hits the nail squarely when he says,

> The thirst for openness is especially present in the matter of our sinful selves. We long for some means of identifying ourselves to the world as sinners. Like Oedipus, we have a faint realization that the sickness of the city comes back in part to ourselves. We have carried

the plague into our town. We would like to say so, but we fear the consequences. The laugh, the sneer, the I-told-you-so, the vengeance, the tag of unreliability—these make us recoil back on ourselves, where we remain closed.

The Christian community wants things to be otherwise. It is convinced that Jesus wanted to create an atmosphere in which sin can be expressed *because* a favorable hearing can be preserved. The burden on the community is to create this atmosphere for forgiving.[8]

There seems to be an atmosphere in the ecumenical church so to do!

The Stages of Ritualization and Faith Development

In relation to issues of human and faith development, when should the sacrament of reconciliation be celebrated? Probably the most critical period in the human pilgrimage is middle life, because we are often painfully conscious of our failure to realize the hopes we have had for ourselves in our family life, occupation, wider social relationships, etc. This awareness of unrealized goals calls us to face our need to confess the reasons for our failures. In so doing we can be helped to accept the forgiveness of God and others, and to forgive ourselves and be renewed. Fowler's Stage V faith points to a quality of faith which sees the paradoxical nature of life—both the good and bad, the amazing and renewing human ability to give selflessly coupled with surprising and depressing moments of selfishness and self-deception in the lives even of the seemingly mature. In the moral arena, middle age is a time when we have lived enough to be able to discern more clearly that conventional morality is often not enough. We feel guilty for hurting people, for breaking the laws of society or going against the norms of those in our work settings. We can begin to realize that many social conventions are really hurtful to people of various racial, sexual, or social groups. We can see ourselves being silent when others are being hurt. Such growing awareness can produce guilt and an inner sense of shame for our sin of separation from genuine engagement with those being hurt. We recognize that a more radical faithfulness to justice for all is needed, even to the point of appearing to be "fools" for calling attention to the persons being hurt or by seeking to change poor or hurtful laws.

Stage V faith pushes those in middle years to have the courage to disobey laws (civil disobedience) which cannot be changed for the better by dialogue or the ballot box. Such struggles often have unfortunate by-products which cause alienation between family members, marriage partners, colleagues, friends or associates in church or community groups. The opportunity to come to terms with such alienation and guilt in liturgical and educational experiences related to the sacrament of reconciliation can be especially powerful for such individuals and the total community. Stage V faith moves us to raise questions about our too neat integrations of Christian beliefs with our larger orientation to life. We have lived long enough and some of us have struggled enough to discover that people from other world religions or even from no announced faith have "put us to shame" by their concern for mercy and justice. We feel guilty not only because the Jewish friend appears more Christ-like in her actions than we, but also because we had indirectly marked off this person because of her faith community. The struggle for an openness to others (and how God can work through the rejected or unaffirmed) is appropriate for Stage V faith. The desire for a unifying quality of faith is high in the midst of our awareness of how we split people into "good guys and bad guys." At a deeper level we seek to look at the meaning of the symbols we use, and especially at the authority we project as the basis for believing one thing or another. Not only does this struggle result in fresh insights and greater affirmations of God's presence in all of life, but it can result in confession, anxiety, and guilt. These factors make it easier to see why maturing adults need to confess their sense of separation and sin, hear the good news of the forgiveness of God through Christ, and to do so in a community of other honest, searching people who confess not only to God but to each other and find support from one another.

However, Erikson's work on the stages of ritualization as well as the research on moral development by Kohlberg, Bull, Peters, and others have made it clear that the sense of moral failure starts early in life, not just in adulthood. Moral education can take place not only in families and schools but especially in church education and liturgy. The personification of Christ's love and justice in the lives of members of the body of Christ can have profound influence on the moral development of children and youth.

Erikson sees the second year of life as the time for early feelings of being a "good" or "bad" person. When the child starts separating himself or herself from parental influence by saying "no" when we want a "yes," the child gets immediate messages of acceptance or rejection, freedom or control, goodness or badness. While two-year-old children do not have the power to decenter from themselves enough to make judgments about themselves in a way which makes guilt the problem it will become later, they are getting early intuitive feelings which are the preconditions for a sense of justice to develop later. Erikson believes that the ritualization of goodness or badness between parents and children are the very early foundations for our morality as a people, our laws, and our images of justice or injustice. As was noted in our analysis of this stage Erikson believes that every child has a need for new experiences of moral discrimination in the everyday rituals of the family. These rituals center around the rituals of elimination in the second year of life, around early sexual identification in the third to fifth years, around successes and failures in academic work, social relationships and sports in school age period, etc. Therefore, the need to deal with standards of moral and ethical life, with acceptance and rejection by others and self, with forgiveness and renewal is evident in some form at each of the stages of personal development. Not only do parents and children develop these qualities in the informal ritualizations of life, they can be helped by creative but more "formal" liturgies of reconciliation.

Religious Education and Reconciliation

Several educational resources have been designed, for instance, for young Christians and their parents by Roman Catholic leaders, seeking to interrelate the new rite of penance/reconciliation with the stages of personal and moral development of young children through adolescence.

In *Come, Be Reconciled! Penance Celebrations for Young Christians* the authors make an effort to take a positive approach to penance for children and parents in primary grades, middle grades, and high school. These liturgies include periods of discussion with children, catechists, and parents about behavior or attitudes taken which have separated them from one another.[9] While the approach seeks to define sin in terms of separation from God, others, and self, the liturgies become concrete for younger children concerning requests for forgiveness "for times we have taken things that did not belong to us," or "for times we have left others out," or "for times we have kept ourselves out of trouble by lying," etc. Scripture, music, and creative activities make these liturgies significant learning experiences as well. Care is given to keeping the focus on God's loving presence and openness to honest communication with all of the human family rather than on failures or punishment. As children and parents wish for individual confession and absolution this is possible within the liturgical format. Several other resources have been written to serve children and youth at the various stages of their moral and faith development, especially by Roman Catholics.

The entire matter of confession has become problematic within the

Roman Catholic Church. Large numbers of Catholics have ceased going to individual confession. Catholic leaders are the first to recognize that this decline is related, without much doubt, to the legalism and paternalism which often accompanied the administration of the sacrament. Therefore, it is with considerable relief and a sense of renewal that Catholic Christians have received the new Rite of Penance with its nonlegalistic tone.

Cora Dubitsky and Nathan Mitchell analyze the new rite's value for religious education and conclude that the answer is both yes and no. They are pleased about the fact that the new rite is much more sensitive to human dynamics and communication. The structure of the new rite "has the advantage of permitting dialogue between ministers and people, and it also permits the celebration to be 'shaped' according to practical factors like the size of the community, the architectural space, the age of the participants, and the number of ministers available." The disadvantages, however, have to do with the too abstract nature of the language of the document, the fact that research on moral development indicates that penance is much more a process than a "sacramental moment" as implied in the concept of absolution still in the rite, that the language and style of the new rite does little to help persons create their own stories of sin and sorrow, conversion and reconciliation—something needed for the sacrament to penetrate into the psyches of the participants.[10]

It is our judgment, nevertheless, that the new rite has set in motion some quite healthy and responsible attempts to deal with the separation between what we are, at times, and what we want to become. Moreover, the new rite and the three approaches to reconciliation recommended (individual, communal, and corporate with a general absolution) provide enough flexibility and sensitivity to make it possible to recommend for serious consideration the resources for children, youth, and adults which are being generated in response to the rite.

In general agreement with Tad Guzie's caution concerning the nondiscriminating marching of seven- and eight-year-olds to confession,[11] we believe that many of the resources for children and youth are worthy of review by Protestants and Orthodox pastors and laity. For instance, the series by Christiane Brusselmans and Brian A. Haggerty, entitled *We Celebrate Reconciliation* has been prepared in a way which reveals awareness of where children are in their personal and moral development, what the deeper biblical and theological dimensions of penance/reconciliation are, and how parents, program directors, pastors, and the children themselves can be involved in honest communication concerning a sense of sin and separation from God, others, and self, along with creative and imaginative ways to share and celebrate the good news of God's forgiving love. The nine celebrations included in this catechetical/liturgical series employ a participative approach with children interacting with parents and others through dialogue, dramatization, music, readings, prayers, stories, homilies, processions, banner making, communal confession and forgiveness followed by opportunities for individual confession and forgiveness. There is recognition of the right of parents and children to decide at what age they feel the child is ready for participation. Also, there are resources for sessions with parents and catechists in advance of the child's participation. The series is grounded in an effort to reinterpret the nature of sin and transformation as well as findings about moral development coming especially from studies by Lawrence Kohlberg.[12]

While many of the issues concerning moral development and faith development are still somewhat controversial, we believe the efforts of Catholic interpreters and religious educators should be taken seriously by the wider Christian community. We particularly like the emphasis upon the family as the context for moral growth and an environment of acceptance, forgiveness, and renewal. Suggestions and additional resources for home and church settings can be found in Elizabeth Jeep's book on implementing the rite,[13] not only for children but also for adolescents and adults.

Finally, it must be reiterated that the primary audience for these educational and liturgical programs are adults, who are most aware of what is unreconciled within their lives and who need most to exteriorize the guilt within themselves at the same time that they are being interpreters and sensitive guides for children and youth. Protestants have included units in church education on moral development and have designed liturgical experiences in church school or homes. However, recognition of the meaning of the sacrament of reconciliation for persons at each of the stages of life has not been well articulated in Protestantism nor have rich resources been designed. The Orthodox have written in ways that illustrate an excellent sensitivity to the normal stages of growth of persons in their pilgrimages of faith.[14] The possibility for finding common understandings of educational and liturgical life in relation to personal reconciliation seems to be real.

Liturgy

In addition to the three forms of the rite which were referred to above—reconciliation now used by Roman Catholics for individual penitents, for several penitents yet with individual confession and absolution, and for several penitents with general confession and absolution[15]—there are other new liturgies for repentance and reconciliation available.

The *Lutheran Book of Worship* contains services for corporate confession and forgiveness and individual confession and forgiveness. In both services there are provisions which make the event personally involving. In the individual service the penitent must become specific about "the sins of which you are aware and the sins which trouble you," and confess "before God that I am guilty of many sins. Especially I confess that . . ."[16] And in the corporate service where people do not make individual confession, but confess in prayer together, there is provision after the words of forgiveness for the penitents to come forward and kneel at the altar. The minister lays both hands on each person's head and says: "In obedience to the command of our Lord Jesus Christ, I forgive you all your sins."[17]

In addition to these two services there is a brief order for confession and forgiveness which is intended as an optional prelude to the liturgy of eucharist. In many other denominations, this penitent beginning to the eucharist is a fixed part of the liturgy (e.g., United Methodist, Presbyterian, United Church of Christ, Episcopal).

Forgiveness is also a primary motif of another sacrament: baptism. We discussed this dimension of baptism above and return to it here simply as a reminder that the baptismal liturgy should be a situation in which all present have opportunity to celebrate their own re-creation in the assurance of the forgiveness of sins.

The *Book of Common Prayer* of the Episcopal Church contains two forms for the reconciliation of a penitent. Both are services for private confession. The longer form makes provision for the penitent also to be a forgiver. The question is asked: "Do you, then, forgive those who have sinned against you?" and the penitent answers, "I forgive them."[18]

Penitence is one of the traditional themes of Lent, and Ash Wednesday is a particular time in the church year for the expression of our mortality and our human weakness. The Ash Wednesday liturgy of the United Methodist in *From Ashes to Fire*[19] contains a penitential section which begins with an invitation to Lenten discipline and proceeds to thanksgiving over the ashes, the imposition of ashes and corporate confession in the words of Psalm 52, verses 1-17; this is followed by a declaration of forgiveness and culminates in the prayers of the people (a response, but no text, is given; spontaneous participation is expected) and the exchange of the peace.

Most pastors discover that a great deal of what they do under the heading of pastoral care is the hearing of confession. Too often we manage this encounter entirely in terms of acceptable psychological techniques. The tools of psychology are indeed helpful and relevant, but they do not substitute for the divine word of forgiveness which needs to be heard and which it is the pastoral responsibility to express. It can be a great help in pastoral work to have a means—an objective, liturgical means—to let guilt get articulated and faced and also to respond to this human acknowledgement with the divine word of reconciliation, and with the encouragement of the amendment of life. Counseling, in the human situation of faith and unfaith, needs sometimes to transit to prayer.

Notes

1. See Don S. Browning, *The Moral Context of Pastoral Care* (Philadelphia: Westminster Press, 1976), and *Religious Ethics and Pastoral Care* (Philadelphia: Fortress Press, 1983).

2. Tad Guzie, "Comments on the New Form of Confession," in *The Sacraments,* ed. Michael J. Taylor (New York: Alba House, 1982), p. 210.

3. Ibid., p. 212.

4. Ralph Keifer, "The Mystery of Reconciliation," in Ralph Keifer and Frederick McManus, *The Rite of Penance Commentaries* (Washington, D. C.: The Liturgical Conference, 1975), p. 31.

5. O. Hobart Mowrer, *The Crisis in Psychiatry and Religion* (Princeton, N. J.: Van Nostrand, 1961).

6. Karl Menninger, *Whatever Became of Sin?* (New York: Hawthorn Books, 1973).

7. Lee A. M. Allchin, *The Kingdom of Love and Knowledge: The Encounter Between Orthodoxy and the West* (London: Darton, Longman and Todd, 1979), pp. 15-16.

8. George McCauley, *The God of the Group* (Niles, Ill.: Argus Communications, 1975), p. 59.

9. See Howard Hale, Maria Rabalais, and David Varasseur, *Come, Be Reconciled,* Youth Penance Resources (New York: Paulist Press, 1975).

10. Cora M. Dubitsky and Nathan Mitchell, "The New Rite of Penance: Its Value for Religious Education" in *The Rite of Penance: Commentaries,* Background and Directions, ed. Nathan Mitchell (Washington, D. C.: The Liturgical Conference, 1978), pp. 92-103.

11. Tad Guzie, *Confession for Today's Catholics* (Chicago: Claretian Publications, 1976), pp. 20-21.

12 Christiane Brusselmans, and Brian Haggerty, *We Celebrate Reconciliation,* Program Director's Manual and Participant's book (Morristown, N. J.: Silver Burdett Co., 1976).

13. Elizabeth McMahan Jeep, ed., *The Rite of Penance: Commentaries: Implementing the Rite* (Washington, D. C.: The Liturgical Conference, 1976).

14. Sophie Koulomzin, *Our Church and Our Children* (Crestwood, N. Y.: St. Vladimir's Seminary Press, 1975).

15. *The Rites* (New York: Pueblo Publishing Co., 1976), pp. 361-379.

16. *Lutheran Book of Worship,* Ministers Desk Edition, p. 322.
17. Ibid., p. 319.
18. *Book of Common Prayer,* p. 451.
19. *From Ashes to Fire* (Nashville: Abingdon Press, 1976), pp. 34-45.

Chapter 15

Sacraments of Healing and Wholeness in Life and Death

Growing Consensus

There is some ambiguity among Christians today concerning rites for healing and dying. They are linked to one another in the history of the evolution of liturgy, but they are achieving separate identities.

Unction, the anointing with oil which was originally part of the prayer liturgy for healing, was used by some Christians for hundreds of years as a "last rite," and it is still regarded by many as the liturgy of the time of dying. This common understanding of the sacrament of unction as "extreme" unction is widely challenged by the revival of healing ministries which identify unction as the sacrament of anointing and laying on of hands for healing and the renewal of life. And, in addition to the rite of unction as a "sacrament" with the dying, the Christian funeral rites are now appearing for discussion in volumes which consider sacraments.[1] There is no clear agreement here about character, number, or sign of sacrament, but there is a practical consensus emerging. Healing is standing out as a sacrament in its own right, distinguished from a rite with the dying, and liturgies with the dying and funeral liturgies are coming gradually to have a sacramental standing. What has been understood as one sacrament is coming to be understood as three: (1) a sacrament of healing and wholeness for those who are ill, (2) a sacrament to strengthen persons and affirm the meaning of their death (last rite), and (3) a sacrament for the celebration of the passage from death to life beyond death (funeral). Each is a parable of the kingdom of God in its own way. *Healing* is the renewing reversal of evil which is a continuing ministry of Jesus; the *last rite* is a reassurance of God's faithfulness in a final caring which is an inevitable upholding ministry among that unique people of Christ who tend with love "those who were about him" (Mk. 4:10); and the *funeral* is a proclamation of the eternity of the kingdom, a word about the transendence of *eternal life* over death which tells us that "death is real, but God's self-giving in love is even more real."[2]

All of the crises of life represented in these three "times" logically call for sacramental ministries.

Healing

Nothing is more logical than that healing should achieve its own status as a sacrament. The sacrament of healing is one of our action parables which most straightforwardly continues a ministry of Jesus clearly documented in the gospels. Healing will occur to many Christians as something outside our main concerns and activities. A single reading of one of the gospels reveals healing to have been a central concern and activity of Jesus. The many stories of Jesus healing show this work as a natural expression of his compassion and as symbols of his authority and of the coming kingdom. This is still the rationale of a Christian healing ministry. In the fullness of his grace, Christ cared for the bodies of people as well as their spirits. Concern for physical healing is a natural expression of the Christ-compassion which is the Christian reality. The hurt of the world is the business of God, and nothing is a more important business of Jesus' disciples. In fact, Jesus specifically sent disciples out to heal (Mt. 10, Mk. 6, Lk. 10). We who speak for Christ's authority and continue to announce the coming time of God have the healing work placed in our hands. If we shrink from this ministry it probably is because it has been much exploited by religious hucksters and opportunists preying on human desperation and/or because we doubt our own share in the powerful divine grace which can radically reverse human fortunes. There is much here we do not understand, but we can believe in the healing authority of Christ, in the reality of this gift in the church, and in the power of the laying on of hands and of prayer. This confidence bestows on us no power to play God, but lets us give God opportunity and lets us rejoice in success, in illness overcome, and lets us support the sick with our loving care in those situations where the evil of sickness will not be reversed.

Emergence of "Last Rites"

Apparently, before the ninth century in the church there was no indication that the anointing with oil was seen as a rite preparatory for death.[3] Motives for the sacrament of unction lie in images of ministry such as one finds in James 5:14-15: "If one of you is ill, he should send for the elders of the church and they must anoint him with oil in the name of the Lord and pray over him. The prayer of faith will save the sick man and the Lord will raise him up again; and if he has committed any sin he will be forgiven." There was in this early ministry an involvement of the whole congregation through the elders and a focus upon the healing presence and power of Christ rather than the charisma of the elders.

In the Carolingian era a trend was established away from ministry to "ordinary" illness and toward unction as a last rite to prepare Christians for death. Unction gradually became a ministry limited to priests. As lay anointing was discontinued, pastoral anointing and laying on of hands became increasingly interrelated with confession and reconciliation so that the final absolution by the priest could prepare the soul of the dying for judgment. This solution continued in the Latin church in various forms until Vatican II. The new solution in this tradition separates unction as a sacrament for the sick from viaticum and last rites as a commendation of the dying, with anointing as a possibility in either liturgy.

The Funeral

This resolution in the Catholic tradition makes sense historically and pastorally, but it does not grant the funeral the status of a sacrament. Would it not make more sense if as sacrament we included not only healing and wholeness but last rites and the funeral, celebrating the life-giving power of God's love within the faith community in the hope of health, but beyond it in the acceptance of the transcendent meaning of life even if death comes? James F. White argues for the funeral as a sacrament in *Sacrament as God's Self-Giving,* calling it "a witness to an enduring love that surrounds us on earth and the beloved one in God's keeping."[4] In an earlier work he stressed the rite as establishing a new relation: "It could be a sacrament of establishment, for through death the Christian moves to a new relationship within the community. Separation is obvious, but the beginning of a new relationship of love within the community of saints needs to be underscored. One does not leave the body of Christ by death but passes into a new relationship to its members, just as at other stages of life."[5]

The funeral as a sacrament of life transcendent over death is an understanding we need. Too often in our culture funeral services are rites of popular religiosity utterly unable to celebrate the good news of God's gift and the eternity of the kingdom of God's love. The funeral is regularly lost in various forms of denial of death and cultural sentimentalities.

Unction and the Stages of Ritualization and Faith

While Erikson depicts the many rituals within the family and community and describes their power to communicate the numinous quality of life—a quality which points to ultimate meanings—he does not discuss the rituals related to illness and death. Also, James Fowler's study of the stages of faith development only indirectly deals with the reality of illness and death. The various stages, of course, symbolize the meaning of death in characteristic intuitive, concrete (literal), or abstract ways. It would be very informative to study the rituals around illness and death as well as the image of health or well-being throughout the life span in different cultures.

Countless rituals take place throughout life concerning illness, health, and death. Small children soon encounter illness, their own or someone in the immediate family. Also, they encounter death—all the way from insects, plants, birds, animals to humans. Parents and friends develop characteristic expressions on their faces, say things in certain tones of voice, or remain awkwardly silent in the face of illness or death which reveal death is to be feared and illness avoided. Also, these rituals reveal the vision of the meaning of life and death which these important persons have internalized. In other words, the content and symbolic power of the rituals in the family and community concerning the profound threats to life brought about by illness and death are of great importance. The quality of these responses is of essential sacramental power. The content of our messages, our master stories (which interpret the ultimate meaning of health, illness, and death), and our liturgies communicate either that life is holy and sacramental or that it is finally meaningless.

The co-director of our Early Childhood Center at the Methodist Theological School in Ohio and a colleague made an excellent phenomenological study of the perceptions of young children concerning death. The study took place around the experience of finding a dead bird, of talking with three- and four-year-old children about the bird, of burying the bird with ceremony, of having the children want to dig up the dead bird, of agreeing to do so with explanation of reasons for wanting to do so, and finally burying the bird again. The issues of life, death, health, and illness all came roaring out in the midst of this episode. One of the authors studied preschool children's attitudes at Riverside Church in New York City and also found life, death, and resurrection themes in the group stories the children created.

The children in our Early Childhood Center seemed to be interested in concrete issues. They asked, "Who killed the bird?" or "Who shot him?" The researchers noted that the children associated death with stillness or lack of motion. One child talked about sleep and wondered whether the bird was asleep. Death had to come about because of something outside of the bird. Another child said the reason flowers die is the removal of water or the separation of the flower from the ground. The concept of death was not something that was intrinsic to life. Also, death appeared to them to be accidental rather than inevitable. If we get "runned over," we are dead. To the children they would not die inevitably—sooner or later—but only if an accident happened. In fact, the children did not see themselves becoming ill, old, or dying. Digging up the bird was desired by the children in order to see "where the bird is," or to see "if the bird can fly again," or "where the bird went after he died."

Expressions of fear of separation were found on a tape recording of the experience in several places. Carey's comment that "my mommy never died," seemed to appear out of nowhere. These fears and anxieties were also present as the children talked about the funeral (back in the Center). Scott was concerned, "How will the bird fly up to God?" "How will God find him?" "If we didn't have the flowers on the grave, then God wouldn't be able to find the bird." As can be seen from these questions the children revealed the concept of God they had learned from their parents. God is "up there." The researchers found not only a rich range of images, concerns, and incipient fears they also found clues for the education of the children in the normal cycle of life and death as well as appreciation for the mystery of both life and death.[6]

The above vignette is representative of many which take place throughout the pilgrimage of life. At each period of our lives rituals related to illness, restored health, or death take place in unique ways. In a secularized culture we have rituals which seek to hide death's reality, rituals which deny death as a waste of life or a bad joke, and rituals which point to secular forms of "eternal life" such as wealth, power, family, or even the individual's contribution which will go on forever. In a secularized society we still find rituals of a popular religiosity which, however shallow, do have great significance for persons. Dionisco Borobio describes what he conceives to be the four sacraments of popular religiosity. They are birth, growing up, marriage, and death. Every culture must find some rituals which help people deal with these crises of life in some way. Some of these popular rites are not very profound in respect to the sacramental nature of life, but they can only retain their vigor and meaning, according to Borobio, when they "combine the freshness of creativity with the original strength of the archetype." He believes that there is something in the nature of being human and finite that demands the presence of "the supreme archetype" and "an opening out to mystery, a self-offering and consecratory desire, a wish for communication between the divine and the human; all these are hard to repress at the decisive moments of life."[7]

There appears to be a very rich potential for educational and liturgical experimentation in relation to these normal rituals. Many denominations which have previously been very cautious about liturgies or education concerning healing or death are now embarking on rites of healing, extensive efforts in death education, and rethinking seriously the liturgies around death.

The psychological and theological literature concerning a wholistic approach to health and illness is rich and varied. The literature concerning death and dying is almost a part of our popular religiosity. What is needed is the integration of these sources with a sacramental understanding of wholeness in both illness and death. Such should be done in a way which speaks to the everyday but universal anxieties and concerns of persons of all races and cultures—not reflecting the distortions and taboos which have become so much part of our experience.

Religious Education for Healing and Death

Education concerning illness and health should start with the parents of children and with the children in very early years. Also the participation of children in the liturgies of life and death needs to be made possible in the family and in the faith community. The stages of development discussed by Erikson, Fowler, and others must be honored so that persons will not be manipulated or involved in the discussions or symbolizations beyond their ability to perceive realistically what is going on. Yet, we must not be too timid about exposing children naturally to the realities of illness or death. The issues of illness and death are pervasive. Adolescents are experiencing not only the natural illness and death of their friends, they are experiencing an increasing rate of teenager suicides. Can we prepare youth to deal with their own or other's illness or death in a society which is seeking to push off the day of death with organ transplantations, open-heart surgery, artificial organs, etc.? We are in a day of computer/mind hook-ups and pacemakers which begin to raise the most basic questions concerning what it means to be human—and especially what it means to live, die, and live again. These matters could stimulate the church to do some of its most profound theologizing about the sacredness of all of life, or it could threaten the church to hide in formulas and rituals which do not reveal the essentials of the Christian vision. Erikson is correct. When the rituals we have developed become wooden, legalistic, or incapable of communicating the vision of the meaning of life we should have the courage to reritualize them. We appear to be at a time in our history as a Christian people where some reritualization is required in order for the rites to be life-affirming and authentic carriers of the Christian vision of life in God's ongoing kingdom of love and justice, of mercy and ultimate hope for all.

The ministry of the ordained and lay can be related with integrity to the sacrament of healing and the sacrament of life in death. Lay ministers are doing remarkable work today in the hospice movement with the terminally ill. Others may be educated to perform ministries with clergy in respect to the prevention of illness as well as the creative response to illness when it comes. The integration of the other sacraments, especially the eucharist and reconciliation, with the sacrament of healing has genuine potential and meaning. The preparation of children and youth to participate in visitation of the ill or the care of families which have experienced death has very rich possibilities. The warmth and spontaneity of children and youth can be so much appreciated by those who are ill or those who are grieving. Let us remember that all the sacraments are events which reveal God's love for all creation and are corporate events. They are also processes which involve persons in preparation, personally and corporately, to receive them. They also imply changes in action or attitude. They are significant when they nurture and strengthen people to be in ministry and to fulfill God's mission of love and justice in the world.

Fowler's sixth stage of Universalizing Faith provides an image of the wider goals of our pilgrimage. As we move toward the middle and end of life we can continue to risk, to grow, to seek to live more simply but also more radically the life of love for all of God's family of whatever race, nation, belief system—even our enemies. This quality of faith (which can see the sacramental nature of life revealed in a Gandhi as well as a Mother Teresa) can celebrate our Christian revelation in Christ and also see God's loving presence in the lives of non-Christians of integrity and ultimate concern. Probably in the back of most of our minds, we hope we may have the courage and the support within the faith community to move out adventurously in living the Christian vision in universal terms. More importantly, it is an implied goal of the faith community as a whole. All of us wish to sit down at the eschatological table and find, not only Christian brothers and sisters, but members of God's family who come to be faithful servants using master stories and symbols different than our own. Such an image can and should guide our education and liturgy throughout all of the stages of life.

Education for Healing Ministry

In order for persons to get beyond their resistances to ministries of healing or to deal with the overenthusiastic responses of those who have experienced or witnessed healing, we need to help persons wrestle with and develop a more wholistic concept of the relation of mind, body, and spirit. Such an enterprise can be tackled by a task group made up of persons from the worship and education committees of the church. The members can start by educating themselves and then move toward developing a policy statement about a healing ministry for the congregation along with educational, liturgical, and pastoral-care guidelines and resources. Many churches have done this study in advance of starting healing services or other forms of healing ministry. The result is largely positive.

Such studies should be well-balanced and draw upon medical, psychological, and religious resources. The latter can include analyses of healing ministries within various denominations as well as ecumenical studies.[8] Teams of hospital chaplains, physicians, and nurses have conducted scientific studies concerning the relationship of attitudes of acceptance and healing rates,[9] the relationship of meditation and healing,[10] and many other areas of concern.

One of the most engaging ways to study the wholistic approach to healing is to read the personal stories of those who were so ill that death seemed inevitable but who were healed spiritually and physically in ways that clearly identify the resources of faith. One of the most significant stories, written by a person who guards against any mentality of magic, is William Stringfellow's, *A Second Birthday*. Stringfellow, the brilliant attorney and theologian, tells his story of discovering new life in response to the mystery of healing which resulted from the risk-taking of a dedicated surgeon, the prayers and love of his friends, and the experience of the eucharist and the anointing by oil by his dear friend, Bishop James Pike. The book is exceedingly honest. Stringfellow raises the tough questions for himself and others. The meaning and power of the healing ministry comes through in a way that recognizes that healing and wholeness could well have been present even if he had died.[11]

Another personal story of one who studied healing quite critically at first is that of Emily Gardiner Neal in her *The Healing Ministry: A Personal Journal*. Ms. Neal has moved from being a news reporter to a lay ministry of healing within the Episcopal Church. Her journal again raises the fundamental questions but reports her own experiences of participation in the healing of others who have sought her help. While she reports many physical healings her most profound experience was with a friend, Sister Virginia, who was not healed physically and died at fifty-eight but was spiritually whole and victorious. While we cannot affirm all of her theological views, the integrity of her healing ministry is evident and inspiring.[12] Neal recognizes the relation of confession and forgiveness to the process of healing.

A similar recognition is found in many studies of the healing ministry. Peter S. Ford, a physician, identifies the issue of spiritual separation from others, God, and, finally, self as a source of many physical and psychological illnesses. Working on teams of physicians and chaplains he delineated some principles of healing which are continuing to be a stimulus to those who are seeking to develop authentic healing ministries. Ford found in his research that many people would not improve until they found the moral failure and guilt within their lives. The illness, he said, was spiritual at base rather than physical or psychological. His approach to healing was wholistic, however, in that he recognized the interaction of all of these aspects of illness and health. Citing clinical evidence for his views, Ford defines spiritual illness as "an emotional and cognitive failure that arises out of the human failure to respond to God's love."[13] He saw acceptance and love as the sources of healing. He calls for education of the congregation and others in society concerning a wholistic understanding of healing and the training of persons to assist in meeting this great need.

Starting a healing ministry in a local congregation is to be done with care. As we have said, those involved should do basic studies in the issues of illness and health with attention to the problem of the meaning of the suffering of those who are ill and the condition of those who do not become physically healed as a result of a cooperative approach of physicians, psychologists, and ministers, both clergy and lay. A good resource for this study is Paul Feider's *Arise and Walk: The Christian Search for Meaning in Suffering*. He also calls for a "healing trinity" in the attempt to interrelate mind, body, and spirit. He sees no dichotomy of natural and supernatural. "A look at the New Testament and the healings of Jesus indicates that it is within the very naturalness of relationships that Jesus healed. It is the natural event of an encounter with another person that he transformed into a healing encounter through the intensity with which his personality manifested the unselfish love of God."[14] Another resource for individuals or groups is George Leach's *Hope for Healing*. This is an imaginatively written book for use in private meditation and group experience and reflection. It is designed in a McLuhan-like style.[15]

Finally, local church pastors and study groups will be helped by James Wagner's *Blessed To Be a Blessing*. Wagner, a pastor in a mainline church, undertook a study of healing ministries in an attempt to develop a sacramental model of healing, "emphasizing God's grace, love, and power within the obedient community of faith." He takes a wholistic approach to healing and integrates healing services with the sacraments of communion and anointing. The book is sensitive to the need to study, discuss, and come to some consensus at the local church level concerning an approach to healing. Discussion questions are presented at the end of each chapter for that reason. Also, a survey of attitudes concerning the desirability of a healing ministry is included. While the short book could profit from more basic theological and psychological grounding it is worthy of study, especially by local church committees seeking to start thoughtful ministries of healing.[16]

Religious Education for Death and Dying

Curiously, religious education for death and dying has been greatly increased as a result of the strong emphasis on death education in society as a whole. Some of the early leaders were physicians, clergy, psychiatrists, sociologists, and educators who saw the tremendous need of persons to deal constructively with the fact of their approaching and inevitable death and how that fact related to their self-understanding and their sense of meaning and significance in life. Daniel Levitan, in his analysis of the phenomenon of death education identifies Herman Feifel's *The Meaning of Death* (McGraw-Hill, 1959) as the early publication which legitimized the study of courses in public schools, colleges, and professional schools of America. The establishment of a professional journal concerning the issues of death and dying, *Omega*,[17] the beginning of serious research concerning the results of death education courses,[18] and the seminal work of Dr. Elizabeth Kubler-Ross[19] and a host of others[20] added up to a genuine breakthrough in American society. The understanding of death and dying was seen as crucial to meaningful living. The taboo of death was beginning to be broken. Critiques of our implied values in our funerals in America awakened us slowly but surely to our tendencies to deny death and to prevent persons from preparing for death. It also became evident that the Christian community had allowed the funeral to become a cultural ritual rather than a sacramental celebration of the "rite of passage" from life through death to a new dimension of life.

Religious thinkers and leaders quickly became a part of the network of those who were doing creative work concerning death and dying. Issues dealt with included the approaches to affirmation of life in the midst of the process of dying, the ethical dimensions of the continuation or termination of life made possible by advanced technology, and the development of constructive religious education of children, youth, and adults concerning the meaning of death. Also, considerable work started to take place concerning the stages of development of persons in respect to their perception of the nature of death.

Death Education and Developmental Issues

While Erikson and Fowler recognized the importance of human finitude in all of their work there was little attention given to the way persons at different stages of human or faith development viewed death. Marie Nagy's early work on the stages of development in respect to death are still informative even though they have been criticized in the light of later research. Nagy identified three stages of development for children. Stage I (until about age five), the child focuses upon the fact of separation between the living and the dead. The dead are described as in a coffin or in a state of sleep, or less alive but not entirely devoid of sensation and functioning. Death is not permanent or inevitable. Stage II (five years to nine years), the child can begin to see that death is final but the lucky or clever child can avoid it. Some children saw death as a person who visits certain unlucky people. Later research did not find the person motif as much. Stage III (nine or ten years and beyond), death is seen as inevitable and universal. Everyone dies, including the child and the child's loved ones.[21] Critiques of Nagy imply that young children need to be able to talk about death much more freely and that young children who have faced death in a fight against leukemia, for instance, are able to describe their condition and the likelihood of their death as well or better than older children with much less experience with the steps in dying and less knowledge of the deaths of other children who were their peers in the hospital. Robert Kastenbaum presents a fine contemporary developmental picture in his study in Herman Feifel's *New Meanings of Death.*[22]

Employing the clues that we can get from such developmental studies we should plan religious education about death and dying for all ages. Perhaps, however, we should start with adults who are more conscious of their own impending and inevitable experiences of dying and death. They, in turn, can be most helpfully involved in their religious education of other persons—from children to older adults. Such education can be undertaken in natural and genuine ways as persons experience the death of loved ones, the severe illness or death of children, youth, or adults in the community. Parents can prepare themselves in informal groups or in course settings to understand contemporary interpretations of death and dying, the normal stages persons go through in understanding death, the stages in the dying process, ways to help persons deal constructively with the death of others and be more prepared for their own affirmation of life during and beyond death. Middle adults in our society are protected from death in that many of their parents are living much longer. We can seemingly develop an immunity to death. Then, some friend dies of cancer or a heart attack. We are unprepared and shocked.

Study Faith Journeys of those Facing Death

Some of the best religious education concerning death can come from the faith journeys of those in our midst who are facing or have faced death prematurely. Herbert Conley, an Episcopal worker-priest who was dean of the Episcopal Cathedral in Honolulu, Hawaii, tells his story of facing death from colon and liver cancer at age fifty-one. His story is one which is informed by accurate medical knowledge but especially by his Christian experience and faith. In *Living and Dying Gracefully* he tells about his inner struggles, his tendency to give in to self-pity, and his pilgrimage toward fullness of life each day as he journeyed toward his death. Knowing that he could live only a few months he decided to write about his faith journey in the midst of dying. A few weeks before his death he looked back in thanksgiving to God, his family, friends and parishoners, saying, "So much has been accomplished, experienced, enjoyed. In some ways, it has been better than all the other years put together. I was also able to put down exactly what I felt I needed to do to have peace of mind at the time of death."[23] Individuals or groups can be led to identify with persons such as Herbert Conley by agreeing with Peter Kreeft when he says that his book is written by a terminally ill person—in that all of us have to face the fact that we are in the process of dying. Kreeft's book, *Love Is Stronger Than Death*, is far from a sentimental discussion of eternal life. He sees death as a stranger, an enemy, a mother, and a lover. In the process of discussing these images a group of adults can deepen their understanding of their own human struggle as well as the Christian meaning of death. Kreeft's mother image fits in well with our emphasis on the funeral as a sacrament of life beyond death. He says that life is a series of little births and little deaths. "Birth and death as such always imply and contain each other; . . . just as our birth is the beginning of our dying . . . so also our death is the beginning of our being born. Death is our mother."[24]

Rich Curricular Resources Are Available for All Ages

In full dialogue with secular death education, religious education has deepened the exploration of the meaning of death. A plethora of rich resources can be found in the literature of most denominations, in their curricular units, books, audio and video tapes. For instance, in the United Methodist Periodical Index for the years 1975 to 1980 there are 115 curricular units or articles cited on death and dying. These units are available for parents, children, youth, adults, and older adults. There are special units on death which can be used spontaneously to help children deal with the death of one of their parents or friends. There are suggestions to help parents and children deal constructively with the issues of death.[25] There are units for youth which help them deal with their own views of death and dying but also the complexity of the issues in our technological society.[26] A similar situation exists in the literature of most denominational or faith groups.

Books that deal creatively with religious education concerning death and dying are Randolph Crump Miller's *Live Until You Die*,[27] with a fine chapter on "children and death," and Linda Vogel's *Helping A Child Understand Death*.[28] One of the most engaging books to use in the religious education of youth is one by our colleague Joanmarie Smith and her co-author Regina Coll. This book, *Death and Dying: A Night Between Two Days*, is imaginatively written with excellent theological, psychological, and sociological grounding. It is broad in its analysis, including consideration of death in other cultures and religions. Still, it is very personal in its appeal to youth to shape their own lives in relation to their view of death.[29]

What is so greatly needed in the religious education of the faith community are existentially engaging *studies of life and death which are biblically and theologically profound*. Fortunately, the literature is increasingly rich. Louis Evely's *In the Face of Death*, translated from the French, captures the secret Christ taught and lived; namely that the life of love and faith is "of itself eternal. . . . We will not surmise or conjecture the existence of a beyond after death but establish in ourselves the presence of a hereafter from this life on. It is our present life which admits of a hereafter, from its appearances, from its mysterious dimension to be indefinitely explored, from the mystery of faith, of hope and of love which convinces us that our reality does not exhaust itself in this present biological existence."[30]

An excellent study of biblical understandings of death to be used primarily with adults is Lloyd R. Bailey's *Biblical Perspectives on Death*. The book opens up the many different images and understandings of death and life beyond death in the Old and New Testaments and also the intertestimental period. The book also focuses on the ramifications of these varying biblical views for decisions regarding bioethics, the care of the dying, the matter of the fear of death, and appropriate liturgical responses.[31]

Education for Ministries with the Dying and their Families

Another approach to death and dying is to educate persons for ministries with those who are dying. Such ministering teams can visit the families of those facing death, be trained to help them deal meaningfully with their anxieties and grief, assist them in building support communities and aiding them in planning for renewal in their own lives after the death of a loved one. The best persons on these teams are often those who have experienced the death of a spouse, child, or close family member and who themselves found new life. Some of the richest communication about life and its fullness have been reported by pastors who have recruited and developed such caring persons. A part of such ministry has often been to support or create a hospice program for the terminally ill. Again, those who have been prepared for this unique ministry have had their own faith deepened and their sense of life's eternal meaning extended.[32]

Dealing with Ethical Issues

Finally, some of the most exciting religious education can take place around the issues of the extension of life or the termination of life made possible by technological breakthroughs. The theological and ethical issues which emerge today in this arena are complex and challenge our previous definitions of life and death. Again, much of the literature is wide-ranging and responsible. Several of the books, written by nurses, physicians, and ethicists, deal not only with the new decisions forced upon us by technological advances but also about our theological and cultural biases concerning death. A book by a medical school professor, for instance, has a fine study of the funeral throughout history.[33] A sound book by a nursing professor has a good history of the perception we have had about death and dying from primitive societies to the present.[34] Such studies by persons beyond the community of theologians or ethicists is revelatory of the depth of the discussions being conducted. The resources written by responsible theologians, Christian ethicists, and ministering persons (pastors, chaplains, counselors, lay professionals) are also significant and in tune with the state of the art in science and technology.[35]

What is needed in the religious education of persons concerning death and dying is the development, not only of sensitive persons who can affirm and celebrate life in relation to the reality of death, but also of ethical norms by which to influence the direction of science and technology and the kind of research on life and death undertaken. One of the most promising educational ventures in this respect has been inaugurated at the Ohio State University in cooperation with the theological schools in central Ohio and the professional associations of medicine, law, nursing, education, social work, ministry, psychology, and allied medicine in the state of Ohio. One of the authors has worked since 1974 with the Commission on Interprofessional Education and Practice, an agency which sponsors credit courses and continuing education of practitioners in ethics, values, and clinical cooperation. The courses or events are taught by faculty from all the above professional schools plus outside national resource persons. Students and practitioners form interprofessional learning teams in the courses or continuing education conferences. Issues of death and dying, the ethics of terminating life or intervening in the birth process through genetic screening, counseling, or engineering are studied with a view to helping professional persons learn how to think and work interprofessionally. Also, the learners seek to find norms which will help them to come to responsible ethical decisions about such issues as euthanasia or natural death, the caring of the dying, living wills, definitions of life and death, organ transplantation, artificial organs and the quality of life made possible, and a host of other ethical issues. The program has been evaluated as very effective and much needed. One of the goals is to strengthen the helping professions so that together they will be able to influence the public policies of the future rather than merely react to what science and technology have already done.[36]

Such a cooperative venture among professional persons may provide a model for communication and cooperation among lay persons who are seeking to find standards which are religiously defensible for their own ethical decisions about life and death in our complex society.

Liturgy

The ministry of healing is gradually recovering its place in the regular worship of Christian people. It has always existed, sometimes on the fringes of accepted liturgy and often outside of what was recognized as "church," but now it is common for churches to devote part of their regular worship to prayer for the sick, sometimes with anointing or laying on of hands, and to hold special services improvised by presiders. There is also a growing body of printed liturgy, with suggestions for use, available.

The *Book of Common Prayer* of the Episcopal Church contains a service for *Ministration to the Sick*. It is a service which is intended to be private but could be public and contains three sections: 1. Ministry of the Word. 2. Laying on of Hands and Anointing. 3. Holy Communion. There are many choices in the liturgy and much of it is optional—

the use of oil, for instance, or the eucharist. The first section of the service, the presentation of the Word, also contains confession and forgiveness. This is an important option in many liturgies of healing, which needs to be handled with care. Much of our human malaise is surely related to real guilt, and nothing is more important for our mental and physical health than for this to be expressed and forgiven. Opportunity for this exchange often needs to be provided in services of healing. Most Christians will want to do this in a way that does not foster the idea that all illness is a consequence of human sin. "Why me?" "What did I do wrong?" are common questions naturally raised by the sick. Some people need to be helped to see the connection between their sin and their sickness. Many other people need the reassurance that their sickness is not God's punishment for their evil action. So the use of the element of reconciliation within a liturgy of healing should be a matter of some careful consideration.

The Episcopalian service contains a prayer for the blessing of oil and two possible formulas to use in the laying on of hands and one to use for anointing. The prayer that blesses oil is at the same time a plea for healing:

O Lord, holy Father, giver of health and salvation: Send your Holy Spirit to sanctify this oil; that, as your holy apostles anointed many that were sick and healed them, so may those who in faith and repentance receive this holy unction be made whole; through Jesus Christ our Lord, who lives and reigns with you and the Holy Spirit, one God, for ever and ever. Amen.[37]

In this service, as in many others, laying on of hands is a definite part of the service and anointing is provided for but in such a way that its omission is not a problem. The holy communion is likewise an option. It is one which should frequently be chosen. Indeed a good case can be made for thinking of the eucharist as our primary liturgy of healing and reconciliation. Are not the bread and wine of the supper signs to us exactly of transformation, of our selves and world created new? Do we have a better symbol of wholeness—of spirit and body, and of our healthy relation to others who are members of this body? The eucharist is probably the primary sign to us of the healing of the world and of its intended wholeness in God. Indeed, because of its multiple meanings, the eucharist is a possible accompaniment of every other sacrament.

In ministry to the sick the eucharist will frequently occur in small groups or even privately as one takes the sacrament to homes and into hospital rooms. Sometimes pastors simply share the elements with the sick. This is absolutely necessary in some situations of extreme sickness. It may even occur that a person may wish to receive the communion, but not be able to eat either bread or wine. In this case the rules of most denominations allow that the elements may be presented to the lips and the sacrament considered valid, even though the elements are not eaten.

In most small settings of the eucharist for the sick in homes or hospitals it is appropriate to provide the full context of the normal service although in radically abbreviated form. The knowledgeable pastor can improvise such a service, with forethought, and perhaps, do it best in this setting working without a fixed text. A workable outline might be:

SCRIPTURE: The length of the lesson should fit the situation. In some cases of dire illness, it might be as short as a single sentence

INTERPRETATION: Perhaps only a few words relating the wider meaning of the text

INTERCESSION: This should include a prayer for the sick person, perhaps with laying on of hands and anointing

THANKSGIVING: A brief prayer over the bread and wine. It should include: thanksgiving; recollection of Christ, probably with reference to the upper room; the prayer for the blessing of the Holy Spirit

THE LORD'S PRAYER: With all joining

COMMUNION

Such a simple service could encompass only a very few minutes. The situation must dictate the extent and length of the liturgy.

There is, in the Episcopalian ritual, in addition to the service referred to above in the *BCP,* "A Public Service of Healing" included in their *Book of Occasional Services.*[38] It is similar in form to the service in the *BCP,* but instead of a time of confession and forgiveness it contains a litany of healing which many may find helpful. It begins with a bidding which asks for the audible naming of those for whom the prayers are made,

Let us name before God those for whom we offer our prayers. (and then continues)
God the Father, your will for all people is health and salvation;
We praise you and thank you, O Lord.

God the Son, you came that we might have life, and might have it more abundantly;
We praise you and thank you, O Lord.
God the Holy Spirit, you make our bodies the temple of your presence;
We praise and thank you, O Lord.
Holy Trinity, one God, in you we live and move and have our being;
We praise and thank you, O Lord.
Lord, grant your healing grace to all who are sick, injured, or disabled, that they may be made whole;
Hear us, O Lord of life.
Grant to all who seek your guidance, and to all who are lonely, anxious, or despondent, a knowledge of your will and an awareness of your presence;
Hear us, O Lord of life.
Mend broken relationships, and restore those in emotional distress to soundness of mind and serenity of spirit;
Hear us, O Lord of life.
Bless physicians, nurses, and all others who minister to the suffering, granting them wisdom and skill, sympathy and patience;
Hear us, O Lord of life.
Grant to the dying peace and holy death, and uphold by the grace and consolation of your Holy Spirit those who are bereaved;
Hear us, O Lord of life.
Restore to wholeness whatever is broken by human sin, in our lives, in our nation and in the world;
Hear us, O Lord of life.
You are the Lord who does wonders;
You have declared your power among the peoples.
With you, O Lord, is the well of life;
And in your light we see light.
Hear us, O Lord of life;
Heal us, and make us whole.[39]

The litany is followed by a period of silent prayer. The rubrics of the service allow for considerable flexibility. At the conclusion of the service those who wish may come forward and receive the laying on of hands and anointing if it is employed. Three textual formulas to accompany this action are suggested. The first and longest reads:

[Name], I lay my hands upon you [and anoint you with oil] in the name of the Father, and of the Son, and of the Holy Spirit, beseeching our Lord Jesus Christ to sustain you with his presence, to drive away all sickness of body and spirit, and to give you that victory of life and peace which will enable you to serve him both now and evermore.[40]

In this action, the pastor should speak and move slowly and deliberately, taking time with each person and letting the hands rest upon each person for a significant amount of time, perhaps for some brief period in silence before speaking. If oil is used it should be administered making the sign of the cross on the forehead with the thumb. If because of pain or injury this is not feasible, another part of the body may be anointed. The traditional oil used is olive oil. It penetrates the skin easily.

The Lutheran *Book of Occasional Services* also contains private and public services for the sick including the gestures of laying on of hands and anointing. The liturgies are similar to those in the *BCP* and, in the Lutheran *Commentary on the Occasional Services*, are analyzed in detail and compared with the *BCP*, Catholic rites, and the Orthodox unction service.[41]

There is a brief service for healing in *Blessings for God's People*, by Thomas C. Simons.[42] It contains a call to worship, word service, intercession and blessing prayer which is, in fact, a prayer for healing. There is a special blessing included for a sick child.

Another type of healing service which one encounters, sometimes on retreats, concerns not so much physical hurt as it does spiritual and psychological hurt. This is called different things, the most common title is "the healing of memories." This is usually a guided meditation in the Loyolan manner, in which a leader suggests themes for contemplation which encompass the life cycle and give opportunity to face hurtful crises memories and to find healing for them. A model for such a service is published, titled, *Prayer Service for the Healing of Memories*, by Benno G. Kornely.[43] The format presented can be adapted to suit many different approaches and circumstances. It is a communal service and concludes with the laying on of hands.

Rites with the Dying

A clear distinction is now being made between the service of unction with the sick and the rite with the dying. In Catholic practice, the rite with the dying includes *viaticum* (literally: something for the journey) which is the last eucharist, as well as prayers which are for "the commendation of the dying." The prayers of this liturgy entrust the person to God and say, "Go forth, faithful Christian." A litany of intercession elaborates the petition, "Free your servant, Lord."[44]

The *BCP* contains an order for "Ministration at the Time of Death." It contains a particularly beautiful "litany at the time of death," and prayers for a vigil.[45] The Lutheran *Book of Occasional Services* contains a service for the "commendation of the dying" which is an edition of the service in the *BCP* with special features, the most remarkable of which is a prayer for "when a life-support system is withdrawn."[46] The *Book of Occasional Services* also contains a liturgy for "comforting the bereaved."

The Funeral

None of the constructive work of liturgists in recent years has been better done than the creation of revised funeral rites and the commentaries which have accompanied them.[47] Especially helpful for Protestants in the free church tradition is the United Methodist supplemental worship resource number seven, *A Service of Death and Resurrection,* which is a small textbook, written by Paul W. Hoon, on the liturgy and the pastoral ministry of the funeral. It includes a liturgy and a wide range of options for different kinds of situations.

In some places funeral services in churches, even for faithful Christians, are becoming rare. This is a situation which desperately needs to be reversed. A church building does not have a higher density of holiness than a funeral parlor, but it is the place where the deceased and neighbors and friends have regularly come together to praise God and to pray. To this place we should return for the funeral sacrament, again together to praise God for life and love and to pray for our friend and for ourselves.

No theme is more relevant to the situation of the funeral of a Christian than what is called the Paschal mystery, the *passover* from bondage and death to freedom and life which is God's gift of salvation. Our primary celebration of this gift is the eucharist, the festival of Christ, the resurrected one, and Christian faith's *new* passover. So the sacrament of bread and wine is especially appropriate for the funeral service of committed Christians. Nothing is more eloquent than our participation together in this rite with the remembrance of suffering and death and yet the celebration of the triumph of love and life. New funeral liturgies of the major denominations all make provision for the eucharist as a possibility within the funeral.

Conclusion

We recognize that the suggestion that unction become three sacraments is anything but the norm. We hope that our rationale for this proposal will stimulate serious dialogue and further study. Again, the direction of the ecumenical discussions concerning unction is really quite revolutionary, not only because of the focus on healing, preparation for death, and the funeral, but because of the nature of sacramentality implied in these changes.

Notes

1. Cf. J. D. Crichton, *Christian Celebration: The Sacraments* (London: Goeffrey Chapman, 1973).

2. James F. White, *Sacraments As God's Self-Giving* (Nashville: Abingdon Press, 1983), p. 90.

3. Charles W. Gusmer, "Liturgical Traditions of Christian Illness: Rites of the Sick," in *The Sacraments*, ed. Michael J. Taylor (New York: Alba House, 1981), p. 225.

4. White, *Sacraments As God's Self-Giving*, p. 89.

5. James F. White, *Christian Worship in Transition* (Nashville: Abingdon Press, 1976), p. 56.

6. Dale Hindmarsh and John Campbell, *Learning Resources for the Sacrament of Unction*. Unpublished research paper. Methodist Theological School in Ohio, 1973.

7. Dionisco Borobio, "The 'Four Sacraments' of Popular Religiosity," in *Liturgy and Human Passage*, ed. David Power and Luis Maldonado (New York: Seabury Press, 1979), p. 89.

8. Charles W. Gusmer, *The Ministry of Healing in the Church of England: An Ecumenical Liturgical Study* (Great Awakening, England: Mayhew-McCrimmon, 1974); Phillip Potter, "Healing and Salvation," *The Ecumenical Review* 33, 1 (January 1981), p. 330.

9. Robert B. Reeves, "Healing and Salvation: A Clinical View and Implications of Recent Studies in Healing Time After Retinal Detachment Surgery," in *Healing and Religious Faith*, ed. Claude A. Fazier, M.D. (Philadelphia: United Church Press, 1974), pp. 94-104.

10. Herbert Benson, *The Relaxation Response* (New York: Morrow, 1975).

11. William Stringfellow, *A Second Birthday* (Garden City, N. Y.: Doubleday 1970).

12. Emily Gardiner Neal, *The Healing Ministry: A Personal Journal* (New York: Crosswood, 1982).

13. Peter S. Ford, *The Healing Trinity: Prescription for Body, Mind, and Spirit,* (New York: Harper & Row, 1971).

14. Paul A. Feider, *Arise and Walk: The Christian Search for Meaning in Suffering* (Notre Dame, Ind.: Fides/Claretian, 1980), p. 85.

15. George Leach, *Hope For Healing* (New York: Paulist Press, n. d.).

16. James K. Wagner, *Blessed to Be a Blessing* (Nashville: The Upper Room, 1980), p. 94.

17. *Omega:* An International Journal for the Psychological Study of Dying, Death, Bereavement, Suicide and other Lethal Behaviors, ed. Richard Kalish (1970).

18. H. Feidel and A. B. Branscomb, "Who's Afraid of Death," *Journal of Abnormal Psychology* 81 (1973), pp. 282-288.

19. Elizabeth Kubler-Ross, *On Death and Dying* (New York: Macmillan, 1969).

20. E. Sneidmann, *Death: Current Perspectives* (Palo Alto, Calif.: Mayfield, 1976). R. Kastenbaum, and R. Aisenberg, *The Psychology of Death* (New York: Springer, 1972); R. Liftorn, *Death in Life: Survivors of Hiroshima* (New York: Vintage Press, 1967).

21. Marie Nagy, "The Child's View of Death," in *The Meaning of Death*, ed. H. Feifel (New York: McGraw-Hill, 1959), pp. 79-98.

22. Robert Kastenbaum, "Death and Development Through the Life Cycle," in *New Meanings of Death*, ed. Herman Feifel (New York: McGraw-Hill, 1977), pp. 18-44.

23. Herbert N. Conley, *Living and Dying Gracefully* (New York: Paulist Press, 1979), p. 40.

24. Peter J. Kreeft, *Love Is Stronger Than Death* (New York: Harper & Row, 1979), p. 64.

25. D. B. Glass, "Parents and Children Learn About Death," *Church School* (May, 1979).

26. R. D. Rowan, "Death and Dying: Ways to Help Youth Learn About It," *Youth Leader* (Summer, 1980).

27. Randolph Crump Miller, *Live Until You Die* (Philadelphia: United Church Press, 1973).

28. Linda J. Vogel, *Helping A Child Understand Death* (Philadelphia: Fortress, 1975).

29, Regina Coll and Joanmarie Smith, *Death and Dying: A Night Between Two Days,* Journey in Faith Series (New York: Sadlier, 1981).

30. Louis Evely, *In the Face of Death*, trans. Camille Serafini (New York: Seabury Press, 1979), p. 57.

31. Lloyd R. Bailey, *Biblical Perspectives on Death* (Philadelphia: Fortress, 1979).

32. See Sandol Stoddard, *The Hospice Movement* (New York: Stein and Day, 1978); Michael Hamilton, and Helen Reid, eds., *A Hospice Handbook: A New Way to Care for the Dying* (Grand Rapids, Mich.: Eerdmans, 1980).

33. Richard G. Benton, *Death and Dying: Principles and Practices in Patient Care* (New York: Van Nostrand Reinhold, 1978).

34. Benito C. Mortocchio, *Living While Dying* (Bowie, Md.: R. J. Brady Co., 1982).

35. Tom L. Beauchamp, and Seymour Perlin, *Ethical Issues in Death and Dying* (Englewood Cliffs, N. J., Prentice-Hall, 1978); Thomas C. Oden, *Should Treatment Be Terminated?* (New York: Harper & Row, 1976); Kenneth Vaux, *Will to Live, Will to Die: Ethics and Search for a Good Death* (Minneapolis: Augsburg Publishing House, 1978), Robert M. Veatch, *Death, Dying and the Biological Revolution: Our Lost Quest for Responsibility* (New Haven: Yale University Press, 1976).

36. Robert L. Browning, "Interprofessional Education and Practice in Ohio: A Critique," in *Education for Ministry: Theology, Preparedness, Praxis*, ed. Gaylord B. Noyce. Report of biennial meeting of the Association for Professional Education for Ministry (Toronto: Trinity College, 1978).

37. *Book of Common Prayer*, p. 455.

38. *Book of Occasional Services,* (New York: The Church Hymnal Corp., 1979), p. 147ff.

39. Ibid., p. 148f.

40. Ibid., p. 151.

41. Philip H. Pfatteicher, *Commentary on the Occasional Services* (Philadelphia: Fortress, 1983).

42. Thomas C. Simons, *Blessings for God's People* (Notre Dame, Ind.: Ave Maria Press, 1983), p. 84f.

43. Benno G. Kornely, *Prayer Service for the Healing of Memories* (Chicago: Loyola University Press, 1981).

44. *The Rites*, Vol. I, p. 608ff.

45. *Book of Common Prayer*, p. 462ff.

46. *Book of Occasional Services*, p. 103ff.

47. Cf. *BCP* and *Commentary on the American Prayer Book; LBW* and *Manual on Liturgies; The Rites*, Vol. I; and Richard Rutherford, *The Death of a Christian: The Rite of Funerals; A Service of Death and Resurrection* (Nashville: Abingdon Press, 1979).

Chapter 16

The Question of New Sacraments and the Sacrament of Footwashing

What Are They?

The logic of our model of sacrament opens the question of the number and character of the particular rites which we might designate as sacraments in the church. Indeed it challenges the assumption that there should be a fixed number or even a definite designation of what is a sacrament. In spite of this "opening" our study has concerned itself with the historic rituals which have been called sacraments. This is testimony to the value we place on the tradition. And all of us must begin with our several traditions.

For most Protestants, baptism and the eucharist are the only sacraments, although many Protestants have some ambivalence about the subject. Witness, for instance the strange footnote in *The Celebration of the Gospel*, a general study on worship written by three Methodists: "Though the Methodist Church recognizes only two *sacraments,* it may be said that the ordinances of confirmation, ordination, marriage, and burial are taken with that devout seriousness that causes them to be sacramental in tone and effect."[1] This sentence, and many others like it that one can read in various places, serves to put the reader on notice that the word "sacrament" draws an, at best, indistinguishable boundary line. The favorite words among Christians to denote those events which are *like* sacraments are *ordinances* or *sacramentals.* The former a common Protestant term and the latter a common Catholic one.

As we have said earlier, the number of sacraments is not a significant question. The significant questions are, what symbols have power to speak to us about the kingdom of God and in what kind of liturgical events may these symbols be embodied? The range of symbols available to us may be much smaller than it used to be, but symbols still have great power in our lives. As Tad Guzie put it: "We use symbols like stones and wedding rings, totems and flags and emblems, precisely because they *work* where logic as a sermon does not. Symbols, not discourses or discussions, do the most effective job of bringing into our awareness the realities of loving and being alive, living and struggling and dying together."[2]

We have come to understand that the symbol in sacraments is not necessarily a corporeal element, like bread or water. There was debate about this in the Middle Ages. The symbol, as we have seen, can be something seemingly abstract, like commitment. But when two people stand together in the church making promises, formally, before God—as the fact of the liturgy manifests—and before us as witnesses, then the commitment becomes a visible symbol and, indeed, in its embodiment, a very tangible thing. The action is a powerful symbol. What symbol/actions can be paradigms of the kingdom of God for us?

It is important, first, to recognize that the fact that this question can be asked seriously today among so many Christians is itself a promising sign. It says to us that we are really ceasing to have that kind of mechanistic understanding of sacraments which knows exactly what the holy events are and how to call down the grace of God into our human situation. The right words said by the right person in the right way. . . and behold! When we break into the system of the sacred seven or the two we force ourselves to get beyond the automatic reductionism that makes sacrament into magic and to consider sacrament seriously in relation to its evolution in history, its origins in scripture and in primary formulations of the faith. When we do this we are liberating sacrament from bonds of our several histories and freeing it to speak to us and involve us in the mystery of the kingdom. This means, strange to say, that we are freeing Christ to transcend our definitions and come to us, not as the ratification of structures we have created to receive him, but as God's *mysterion*, of which we are servants, not possessors and gatekeepers.

It is, secondly, important to recognize that sacrament is always a communal, kairos event. To root the understanding of sacrament in the serious hearing of the word of Jesus, "To you has been given the *mysterion* of the kingdom of God" (Mk. 4:11), is to say that the action is corporate (it is given to all) and that it is of ultimate significance in the lives of those who are involved (the *mysterion* is not an abstract puzzle; it is God coming into human experience: *your* human experience).

In his beautiful little book, *The Book of Sacramental Basics,* Tad Guzie provides an intriguing definition of sacrament:

A sacrament
is a festive action
in which Christians
assemble to celebrate
their lived experience
and to call to heart
their common story.
The action is a symbol
of God's care for us
in Christ.
Enacting the symbol
brings us closer
to one another
in the church
to the Lord
who is there
for us.[3]

For Guzie, the difference between what he calls "raw" and "lived" experience is exactly *significance.* It is, in New Testament terms, the quality of human time as *kairos*—experience as meaning. Sacraments emerge in the church out of our experience of the time of God's kingdom. Unlike the *chronos,* the moving after-each-otherness, *kairos* is a moment we can recover and reenter. We can make of it a festival of meaning, and to it we can return for rediscovery and renewal. As a sacrament of the church this experience involves us personally, but as Guzie's definition indicates, it is a personal involvement in a *common* story.

Christopher Kiesling, in an article entitled "Paradigms of Sacramentality,"[4] takes a different approach to a very similar conclusion. He suggests four criteria whereby we might recognize certain events as sacraments, that is, "paradigms of the sacramentality of all created agents and activities."[5] His first criterion is that a sacrament be an *explicit* expression of God's self-giving and its human consequences. The action of God and the human response must be clear. The second is that a sacrament as paradigm ought to be "an explicit phenomenon of *personalized* grace."[6] God's self-giving is to you and to me. The third is that this explicit and personalized gift be celebrated by us at some *climactic moment.* Sacrament as paradigm is about God's continuous self-giving, but celebrated by us at a climactic moment when our lives have reached a certain high point "when some significant gesture as sacrament becomes appropriate."[7] His fourth criterion is that a sacrament be *public*, recognized by the community as paradigmatic. God's gifts are not restricted to public events and sacraments. Reconciliation, for instance, may take place involving only two persons, but as a sacrament, reconciliation is a family event (even when it involves only two persons), recognized as such by partner Christians and is a paradigm for us all of the kingdom of God as forgiveness and renewal.

Kiesling's criteria are based upon the historical sacraments which have emerged in the life of the church, but they do not limit the possibilities to these. His criteria serve well to denote sacrament as paradigm and to help us as we consider what new event might be a sacrament, but there is at least one point at which they break down. It is hard to consider the eucharist as something always happening at a "climactic moment" in life. This criterion, while helpful, is not universally applicable to the sacraments.

James F. White in *Sacraments As God's Self-Giving* distinguishes between what he calls *dominical* (baptism and eucharist), *apostolic* (reconciliation, healing, and ordination), and *natural* (marriage and burial) sacraments.[8] There are, we think, some distortions in this logic. It is really too literalistic about the distinction between dominical and apostolic. Are not ordination, reconciliation, and healing really founded upon the dominical word ("Follow me,") and action (forgiving and healing)? And the category *natural* sacraments does not do anything to establish a logic of sacramentality. It is just a heading under which one can group whatever is not obviously dominical or apostolic.

Our own criteria for calling a liturgical event a sacrament are those we have presented in chapter 2:

1. A sacrament is a gift of Christ. It is personal and relational. It is the *mysterion* of the kingdom of God given to us.
2. A sacrament is *us*, the receivers of God's gift. It is family, uniquely social.
3. A sacrament is transcendent. Because God's gift in Christ is in the world for the world, every presentation of the *mysterion* is the recognition or appearance of a blessing which we in the family of Christ do not possess or control but cherish and witness to as "servants . . . and stewards" (1 Cor. 4:1).

A sacrament is this realization about *mysterion* translated into *sacramentum:* a specific gesture of commitment; a paradigm-event of affirmation and experience (involving us intellectually and physically) which dramatizes God's explicit gifts to us as individuals and as a people, particularly at climactic moments in our lives.

What the particular sacraments are is a question which needs to be reopened. Tad Guzie rightly reminds us:

> The Middle Ages liked to point out the fittingness of the number seven, because seven symbolizes completeness. This is a bit of theological "fat" which does not interest us very much in a lean age when we have so much difficulty getting in touch with even our most basic symbols.[9]

There is no logical reason, no scriptural reason, and, unless one looks with the most partisan and doctrinaire eye, no good traditional reason why there should be seven or two or any particular number of sacraments. Tad Guzie's dynamic definition of sacraments makes good sense. It is obviously traditional, based upon the sacraments which in fact emerged in the life of the church, and yet it is not arbitrary and etched in stone; there can be adjustment and development.

And we can count on adjustment and development. We may also note as an axiom that we—theologians, administrators, etc.—can never really control this adjustment and development. The question of what communal event will be pictorialization and dramatization of the kingdom of God for the family of Jesus is settled, in part, in a charismatic way. Symbols can atrophy and die; new symbols may emerge. Such matters are not the rational decisions of leaders and planners. We may organize and execute, but not create. The word which leaders and planners may legitimately substitute for *create* is *experiment*. We try to establish criteria and encourage the growing edge which is experiment, while we keep ourselves open to the moving Spirit which will in fact guide us in the evolution of sacrament.

Joseph Martos in *Doors to the Sacred*, realizes this, discussing what he calls the "flowering of novel sacramental customs," and concludes,

> It could almost be said that during the modern period the seven ecclesiastical sacraments became a central part of Catholic doctrine but a marginal part of Catholic religious life.[10]

He recognizes some unofficial "new sacraments" of the charismatic prayer meetings, glossolalia, baptism in the Spirit, and the sacramental dimensions of movements like Cursillo, marriage encounter, focolare, and spiritual retreats.

Martos, and many others, are aware that so-called "sacramentals" or "devotions" like the "Way of the Cross" or the Rosary may be more spiritually powerful in the lives of Christians than the official sacraments. Why would we not be better served if the idea of sacrament, instead of being official and legal, were more a matter of Spirit power and the reality of God's *mysterion* among us as we in fact experience it. For many centuries Christians knew of sacrament without needing fixed definitions. As with God's own time (kingdom) we may not need to know what sacrament is; it may be enough to know what sacrament is like as we experience the *mysterion* given to us in moving, dramatic sign-actions where our participation is our understanding.

Footwashing

A logical place to begin in the "expansion" of the idea of sacrament is with the introduction of Jesus' ministry of footwashing. This is going to strike many as the last thing but logical. It is outside the tradition of many Christians, and it presents serious practical problems; just how do we go about washing feet publicly and what do we do about pantyhose? There may be formidable objections. There are also compelling arguments for the introduction of this "sacrament." It is, in the first place, a sign/action which is scriptural and belongs as a sacrament according to common canons, especially the conservative Protestant ones, of what constitutes a sacrament. It is a definite sign; it is "dominical," that is, it is instituted by Christ; and it is a symbol established by the Lord with a definite injunction that it should be continued: "If I then, your Lord and teacher, have washed your feet, you also ought to wash one another's feet. For I have given you an example, that you also should do as I have done to you" (Jn. 13:14-15). There is no question but that footwashing qualifies as a dominical sacrament, especially when one takes into account that it stands in the Gospel of John exactly at the place where one expects the eucharist.

A second, and more persuasive, argument in favor of footwashing as a common sacrament in the church is its eloquence as a symbol of the servant ministry of the disciples of Jesus. It is archaic; it is inconvenient; it is probably an embarrassment, but it is unambiguous in its significance. Jesus, our master, shows us exactly what it means to be a servant. "I say to you a servant is not greater than his master; nor is he who is sent greater than he who sent him" (Jn. 13:16). This is the final word about "status" in the kingdom of God. Footwashing, is the eloquent sign of this word. Is there a truth about the kingdom we need more to hear? Is there a sign more expressive?

It is true that the washing of feet is not the natural human activity today that it was in the Holy Land during the time of Jesus. As a ritual in church it is definitely an odd activity. But it works, and speaks clearly. One supposes that it won't, but carefully planned and prepared it can be a moving experience. What is necessary is: 1. A good exposition of John 13:1-20. The liturgy will work if people become participants in this powerfully moving scene. Notice that Jesus' servant ministry here is related to our need for reconciliation; it is a cleansing (Jn. 13:8-11). 2. Careful preparation of the congregation. Everyone needs to know what will happen and how; women who expect to participate should wear stockings or socks that are easily removable. People need to be assured that what is intended is, in fact, possible. 3. The service must be exactly worked out to avoid awkwardness, as much as possible, and let the symbol speak.

The fact is, of course, that there is an irreducible awkwardness in a service of footwashing. No one is going to remove footwear and have feet washed by another, or in turn wash another's feet without some awkwardness. Much of the power of the liturgy depends upon the radical break with ususal experience which this symbol entails. As one whose feet are to be cleansed or as the washer of feet, a person is abruptly thrust into a strange new relationship. What takes place is starkly graphic about what it means to be served and to serve.

Some Christian denominations, like the Church of the Brethren, celebrate footwashing as a dominical sacrament, usually combining footwashing, a fellowship meal, and eucharist in what is together called the love feast. With the Brethren, the footwashing is the first stage of the love feast. Basins with warm water are provided, with towels, as well as water and towels for washing hands at the end of the ceremony. The service takes place in a hall or suitable room where "at the proper time designated persons at each table gird themselves with a towel and wash the feet of the person beside them. Then the one whose feet have been washed shall proceed in like manner to wash the feet of the next person and so on until all have participated. It is traditional for men and women to be separated during the footwashing service, although this is not a universal practice. If the salutation of the holy kiss is used in the service, it is usually shared at the time of feetwashing. The use of instrumental music or congregational singing during the feetwashing helps to maintain an attitude of devotion and reverence."[11]

One option in liturgy is to follow this Brethren model of footwashing, where all participate. Obviously, to participate as members of a congregation one at a time would take a long time in many churches. The Brethren model is a group pattern where the persons at one table wash one another's feet. Other means might be used to establish groups. Certain "leaders" might scatter among the people to establish groups, having first perhaps had their feet washed by the pastor. In a small congregation only the presider might wash feet. Our experience of this sacrament, though, leads us to conclude that group models where everyone participates as servant and served are the most helpful. They involve us all as family in this strange sign and, in our participation, convert the sign into symbol, an unambiguous parable of life in the kingdom of God.

Maundy Thursday

Footwashing might take place whenever it seems useful, but there is a point in the church year where it has a traditional, if lately uncommon, place. Maundy Thursday is known as the memorial of the upper room, but the "maundy" is a reference rather to the scene of footwashing at the end of the thirteenth chapter of the Gospel of John which contains the account. "A new commandment I give to you." The new commandment is love." Since John 13 early becomes the fixed lesson for Holy Thursday it became known as *dies mandate,* the day of the commandment, and hence, Maundy Thursday. Footwashing has had a visible place on this day because the bishop of Rome washes the feet of some humble person on this day as a sign of his, and the whole church's stewardship.

Many of the new liturgies make provision for a service of footwashing as part of the observance of Maundy Thursday. The Lutheran order, for instance, places the "washing of feet" directly after the lessons and before the holy communion.[12] Their *Manual on the Liturgy* contains specific instructions for the action.[13] A group of persons, often twelve and sometimes the church council, represents the congregation. They are selected beforehand so that they are prepared to remove their footwear. A pitcher of water, basin, and towel are placed in some prominent place with a large towel for the pastor. Before the representatives are brought forward the minister explains the significance of the action (if not done in the sermon), connecting it to Christian charity and service. The people then come forward, sit on chairs near the altar and remove their footwear, while the minister removes any special vestments (cape, chasuble, stole, surplice) and puts on an apron or large towel. The minister then washes the feet of everyone in the group, pouring water over their feet into the basin and drying their feet with the towel. Nothing is said during the ceremony, but it is suggested that hymn 126 in the *LBW* be sung:

Where charity and love prevail, There God is found;
Brought here together by Christ's love, By love we thus are bound.

Other hymns are also suggested, and the injunction is set forth that washing is the presiding minister's responsibility and no other's.

Somewhat similar suggestions are made in the commentary on the alternate United Methodist liturgy for Maundy Thursday found in *From Ashes to Fire.*[14] The idea of representatives is presented, but so is the suggestion that "mutual footwashing among minister(s) and lay persons would be more symbolic of servanthood." The idea of washing in small groups is proposed, with a basin, sponge, and towel provided for each group. The same text for singing is suggested here as in the Lutheran manual, only in the United Methodist book the text is a nonmetrical translation of *Ubi Caritas,* the Latin original of this Holy Thursday hymn. This is an excellent text for the footwashing sacrament and can be found in various translations and musical settings.[15]

Another resource where footwashing is discussed and liturgical suggestions made is *Ritual in a New Day* (Abingdon, 1976), pp. 24-36.

In the *Book of Common Prayer* (1979) footwashing is indicated as an option for Maundy Thursday and an invitation/address is provided in *The Book of Occasional Services* (The Church Hymnal Corporation, 1979), p. 91. Directions are not provided for the service in this volume or in the *Commentary on the American Prayer Book,* but the invitation speaks of the participants as those "who have been appointed representatives of the congregation."

We mentioned the recommendation of the traditional *ubi caritas* as a suitable hymn to be sung during footwashing. A new song for this sacrament is the simple and lovely song from Ghana making its way into many new hymnals.

Refrain: Jesu, Jesu, fill us with your love,
show us how to serve the neighbors we have
from you.

Verses 1: Kneels at the feet of his friends
silently washes their feet,
Master who acts as a slave to them.

2: Neighbors are rich and poor,
neighbors are black and white,
neighbors are near and far away.

3: These are the ones we should serve,
these are the ones we should love,
all are neighbors to us and you.

4: Loving puts us on our knees,
serving as though we are slaves,
this is the way we should live with you.

5: Kneel at the feet of our friends
silently washing their feet,
this is the way we should live with you.[16]

It is self-evident that the powerful emphasis on servanthood in the sacrament of footwashing is, in itself, a way of acting out a radical concern for all of God's family. It is a modeling of empathy for others, a modeling which has symbolic significance, not only for adults who are growing in faith, but also for children who intuitively sense the value of helping someone in need.

A religious education for servanthood starts in early childhood through the rituals of mutuality in the family and through identification with parents and other adults who are risking rejection by serving others who are forgotten or neglected. The most penetrating religious education takes place as persons are involved directly in attempting to meet concrete needs of those open to being helped. The concreteness of human concerns in the situations of hunger or prejudice raises specific questions about the basic purpose and meaning of life. These questions, then, can be explored biblically and theologically in an effort to deepen the Christian motivation to serve. Discussions about ways to serve with integrity are sharpened as those serving seek to live out their best understandings of how to meet the needs. Then, those being helped respond to those seeking to help. This feedback gets to be more and more honest as the relationships grow in trust. As those being helped gain strength they are educated to serve others in need. Too much religious education about servanthood is reading about, studying about, and discussing areas of human need but not getting involved in any specific effort to be in servanthood. Children and youth can identify with religious education for Christian servanthood much better when they are working together with their parents or other intergenerational groups in concrete forms of caring. The acting out of such self-giving love is strengthened by the action parables of footwashing and the eucharist. Feelings of fear, anxiety, warmth, and love are experienced and shared as they risk washing the feet of those with whom they are serving or risk receiving the gift of footwashing or receiving the elements from others.

As people grow in faith they will see just how difficult it is to be channels of Christ's love and justice to those who do not trust us or who are our avowed enemies. Efforts to serve those who do not trust us or who do not want to have anything to do with us are continued only if our vision of the kingdom of God is strong and our faith deep enough to free us to act.

There could be other candidates for sacramental designation. We have already indicated that preaching the word can be seen as a sacrament, a pointing to and making visible that which is true about life now and eternally. In relation to the development of faith at the different stages of life certain more established sacraments such as the eucharist, baptism, confirmation, or baptismal renewal may be celebrated as means of pointing to and participating in the grace of God in the very fabric of life itself. We have maintained, however, that other sacramental celebrations such as ordination or consecration, reconciliation, marriage, and sacraments related to healing, death and the funeral, as well as the forgotten sacrament, footwashing, have profound significance for those seeking to mature in faith. The fact that the potentiality of sacramental life is being explored genuinely by Catholics, Orthodox, and Protestants alike augers well for the future. It is revolutionary in its promise for the advent of the kingdom of God in our lives.

Notes

1. H. Grady Hardin, Joseph D. Quillian, James F. White, *The Celebration of the Gospel* (Nashville: Abingdon Press, 1964), p. 110.

2. Tad Guzie, *The Book of Sacramental Basics* (New York: Paulist Press, 1981), p. 48.

3. Ibid., p. 53.

4. Christopher Kiesling, "Paradigms of Sacramentality," *Worship* 44 (1970), pp. 422-432.

5. Ibid., p. 422.

6. Ibid., p. 430.

7. Ibid.

8. James F. White, *Sacraments As God's Self-Giving* (Nashville, Abingdon Press, 1983), pp. 70-92.

9. Guzie, *The Book of Sacramental Basics,* p. 69f.

10. Joseph Martos, *Doors to the Sacred* (New York: Doubleday, 1981), p. 127.

11. *Pastor's Manual,* Church of the Brethren (Elgin, Ill.: The Brethren Press, 1978) p. 33f.

12. *Lutheran Book of Worship* (Minister's Desk Edition), p. 138.

13. Philip H. Pfatteicher and Carlos R. Messerli, *Manual on the Liturgy* (Minneapolis: Augsburg, 1979), p. 318f.

14. *From Ashes to Fire* (Nashville: Abingdon Press, 1979), p. 120ff.

15. Cf. Hymn 276 in *New Catholic Hymnal* (New York: St. Martin's Press, 1971); n. 71 in *Biblical Hymns and Psalms* by Lucien Deiss (Cincinnati: World Library Publishers, 1970). And one can consult the Latin in plainsong setting: n. 60 in ICEL Resource Collection (Chicago: G.I.A. Publishing, Inc., 1981).

An excellent project for a local church is the *creation* of antophonal music for the text provided in *From Ashes to Fire,* p. 121f.

16. *Supplement to the Book of Hymns* (Nashville: United Methodist Publishing House, 1982), n. 914.

Index of Biblical Citations

Index